Contents

Activity Finder

No Gym? No Problem!

Physical Activities for Tight Spaces

Charmain Sutherland

Human Kinetics

Library of Congress Cataloging-in-Publication Data

Sutherland, Charmain, 1966-
    No gym? no problem! : physical activities for tight spaces / Charmain Sutherland.
        p. cm.
    Includes bibliographical references.
    ISBN 0-7360-5770-6 (soft cover)
    1. Physical education and training--Study and teaching.   I. Title.
    GV363.S878 2006
    613.7'1--dc22
                                2005016085

ISBN-10: 0-7360-5770-6
ISBN-13: 978-0-7360-5770-7

The Web addresses cited in this text were current as of July 2005, unless otherwise noted.

Acquisitions Editor: Bonnie Pettifor; **Developmental Editor:** Ray Vallese; **Assistant Editor:** Derek Campbell; **Copyeditor:** Bob Replinger; **Proofreader:** Jim Burns; **Permission Manager:** Carly Breeding; **Graphic Designer:** Fred Starbird; **Graphic Artist:** Kathleen Boudreau-Fuoss; **Photo Manager:** Sarah Ritz; **Cover Designer:** Keith Blomberg; **Photographer (cover):** Charmain Sutherland; **Photographer (interior):** © Human Kinetics. Photos on pages 1, 2, 5, 7, 13, 37, 119, 239, and 248 courtesy of Charmain Sutherland; photo of sport stacking cups on page 187 provided courtesy of Speed Stacks Inc., www.speedstacks.com; **Art Manager:** Kelly Hendren; **Illustrator:** Mic Greenberg; **Printer:** Sheridan Books

Printed in the United States of America   10   9   8   7   6   5   4

Human Kinetics
Web site: www.HumanKinetics.com

United States: Human Kinetics, P.O. Box 5076, Champaign, IL 61825-5076
800-747-4457
e-mail: humank@hkusa.com

Canada: Human Kinetics, 475 Devonshire Road, Unit 100, Windsor, ON N8Y 2L5
800-465-7301 (in Canada only)
e-mail: info@hkcanada.com

Europe: Human Kinetics, 107 Bradford Road, Stanningley
Leeds LS28 6AT, United Kingdom
+44 (0) 113 255 5665
e-mail: hk@hkeurope.com

Australia: Human Kinetics, 57A Price Avenue, Lower Mitcham, South Australia 5062
08 8372 0999
e-mail: info@hkaustralia.com

New Zealand: Human Kinetics, Division of Sports Distributors NZ Ltd.
P.O. Box 300 226 Albany, North Shore City, Auckland
0064 9 448 1207
e-mail: info@humankinetics.co.nz

Preface

Don't let another interruption snag your unit plans. Deliver great instruction and activities every day regardless of storms, unforeseen events, and lack of facilities. If the mail can get through every day, so can you! You have an important message to deliver!

Physical activity providers—physical educators, recreation leaders, classroom teachers, and parents—who strive to create purposeful activities and lessons have their plans upset every now and then. If you don't have a gym, you know what I'm talking about—you have no large space available for indoor activity. If you do have a gym, at times it will be unavailable because it is needed for other purposes like science fairs, graduations, assemblies, shows, award ceremonies, concerts, school pictures, and other events that require a large space.

The lack of a large indoor space need not ruin your plans. Instead, you have an opportunity to use the tools of the trade.

A vital teaching tool is flexibility. Surprises and events will arise every year. In some years you will have more surprises and obstacles than you do in others. If you bend a little, you can pull off a great lesson or activity, with lots of action, without having to rearrange your whole yearly plan.

Another teaching tool is this book. Keep it handy on your desk so that you can quickly look up an activity to use when unscheduled events intervene. Find the area that you are working on in the book, and you are set. The book provides a complete lesson plan and activity, with everything that a professional needs. Having this book is like having a spare tire when yours has gone flat. Your plans have been blown out, but you will keep rolling and get to your destination.

Enjoy the journey that physical education and activity take you through. Keep your tools handy and be prepared for, not devastated by, obstacles that you will encounter. Hurdle the obstacles with your flexibility and determination.

Introduction

"Yes, I can do that . . . And I can do that . . . Sure, I'd love to do that too," she answered to each question the principal threw her way, with the enthusiasm of a child receiving the toy that she had been dreaming of. Proud of herself for nailing the interview and securing the number-one job in the whole world, she shook the principal's hand and accepted the job. As the principal and new PE teacher walk side by side down the school hallways, the principal points out the spots of interest—the fields, computer lab, library, staff bathrooms, music room, art room, and lounge. The principal then stops, smiles, and asks the newest staff member if she has any questions.

"Uhm, the school looks great, I can't wait! Now, can we check out the gym? The gymnasium?" the anxious instructor politely asks. She is envisioning kids dribbling and shooting baskets and an equipment room full of fabulous physical education equipment, with an office equipped with a computer, a phone, and maybe even a bathroom–shower combination if she is lucky.

As if the new teacher has just said a curse word, the principal turns to her quickly and folds her arms. "Gym?" she asks. "We don't have a gym. I thought you realized that." The PE teacher is at a loss for words. A thousand thoughts are swirling around in her head. "That won't be a problem for you, will it?" the principal asks.

"No gym?" the PE teacher asks. Thinking quickly, she says brightly, "No problem!"

I'm Lost

Oh, my! What's a "gym" teacher to do without a gym? No time for self-pity. Stop dwelling on what you don't have and find yourself! You weren't trained to be a "gym" teacher; you were trained to teach physical education. "Gym teacher" is an old-fashioned term that some people still use to describe the physical educator, and people may use the word "gym" to describe physical education. I have been in some schools in which the teachers call physical education "gym," even when the school had no gymnasium. If you were trained to be a physical education teacher, then this bump in the road won't lead you too far off course. You are not in the land of the lost, but in the land of opportunity.

Physical education teachers have had 4 years of learning how to teach physical skills to students, by practicing themselves. They likely learned in an ideal place, learning tennis on a tennis court and basketball on a basketball court. So although training took place where college students could learn in ideal conditions, teaching K through 8 students may not always occur in ideal situations. For example, in the first 4 years of my teaching career I taught my middle school students the striking skills of tennis in the school parking lot and the dribbling skills in basketball in the old church, surrounded by wall-to-wall glass windows and asbestos in the ceiling. I taught physical education five days a week for a 55-minute block to sixth, seventh, and eighth graders, without a gym. I taught elementary students for 7 years without a gym and loved it!

Small spaces don't prevent activity—they invite physical activity leaders to become creative, innovative, and resourceful.

You will not only find your way but also become more creative, innovative, and resourceful! Without doubt, a gym is a wonderful classroom for teaching physical education and activities. But don't doubt the possibilities and opportunities that you have to teach great physical education lessons and activities, regardless of your facilities. The options are endless. This book is a road map that will help you with the struggle of limited space. Once you catch on, you will explore places beyond the border of any map, and you will not believe the things that you can put together. Overcoming obstacles and adversity can bring out the best in people. The lack of a normal, or ideal, situation at first forces you, and later invites you, to become more creative. This circumstance seems to keep you on your toes, not allowing you to take anything for granted. Staying fresh is vital to staying professional!

You haven't received a death sentence—you have just been rewarded with opportunity. Being gym-deprived or space-challenged just means that you'll have to squeeze your activity plans into a smaller room, like a classroom. The world of physical activity is yours to bring to all students or participants in your class or program. Sure, the classroom is small, and yes, it has windows, desks, and probably some breakables. But you have 30 to 45 minutes to make physical activity happen and matter to the children whom you are leading. So, face the reality and follow the activities in this book. Your students and participants will be active, learn, and enjoy physical activity.

When it is your time to teach, consider it show time. You have a captive audience. Children take pleasure in few things more than they do activity, fun, and enjoying themselves. So, teach from the moment you walk in the classroom until the moment you walk out. Make your show as worthwhile and beneficial as you possibly can! Your show could be the only action that the child has all day, or even all week. If they have PE only once a week, then this opportunity must be as grand and dynamic as possible.

Gypsy Gym Teacher

A parent has arrived at the school to visit the PE teacher, and checks in with the secretary in the front office. The office staff, normally, can quickly steer visitors to their destination. But when you don't have a gym, suddenly you are the gypsy gym teacher.

Where can you be found? Not in a gym, and not on the fields. The PE teacher roams around all day long, from class to class, creating temporary homes for a half hour or so, and then gathers everything into a cart or bag and looks for the next place to call home.

PE a la Carte

The sounds of a rolling cart on a poor-weather day must mean that the PE teacher is on the way. With roll book, balls, and cones in tow, the PE teacher wheels around the school, physically educating children a half hour at a time.

Tricks of the trade and PE essentials should always be aboard the PE-mobile. On board the cart, or whatever you are traveling with, keep the following items:

- First aid supplies—gloves, CPR mask, adhesive bandages, gauze
- Class rolls
- A set of beanbags (for the many games that you can play with a beanbag)
- A ream of paper (paper games are endless)
- A few Nerf balls
- A couple of small cones and **polyspots** (rubber spots that are flat like a pancake to mark places on the floor)
- A CD player and an upbeat CD
- An emergency back-up classroom plan (your favorite from this book) that you can turn to

Equip your cart with these items and you will be prepared if a rainstorm or emergency pops up. You will also use many of these items with lessons and activities included in this book. Have cart, will travel. Have preparation, will succeed.

PE in a Bag

Sometimes the PE teacher roams the school with a sack on his or her back. Although the teacher may look like Santa, he or she doesn't walk around with toys for students to play with. Santa carries tools to learn with.

The equipment bags should contain the PE essentials, just as the PE cart does. Sometimes carts are not effective. Maneuvering up and down staircases and hills with a cart can be difficult, so sometimes the bag comes into play. The bag is handy but more strenuous to carry. So find your ace in the hole—an activity sure to keep students active and safe—and always keep it handy for the spur-of-the-moment situation.

We don't want to simply fill the equipment bag with toys to play with, just to pass the time. Fill it with equipment to make every second an opportunity for learning.

Look What I Can Do in Here

Just because you don't have a gym doesn't mean you can't use a ball. You just need to be professional, use good judgment, and be able to foresee problems. Your students can safely do the following activities in the classroom:

- Throwing and catching
- Striking and volleying
- Dribbling and kicking
- Rhythms and dance
- Educational gymnastics
- Movement education
- Games
- Fitness

Of course, we won't try to score a field goal by kicking a real football in a classroom or use all our throwing power in army dodgeball, but we can do endless activities in a confined space. Just keep a few important key factors in mind:

- You have a ceiling, so avoid high throws.
- You have windows, and they can break.
- Furniture can injure people if they run into it. Beware of corners, edges, and attractive nuisances.
- You are a visitor in the room; mind your p's and q's.
- Ask before using or moving personal items in the room.
- Be sure to replace anything that you moved.
- Avoid full range-of-motion swinging with long-handled implements.
- Be courteous when listening to music; it's a blast to blare music but remember that the classes next to you need to concentrate on their subjects.

Safety is always number one! Don't forget that for a second. Remember that each classroom or space will be different, so take into consideration what you are working with at your facility. Use the classroom setup diagrams when possible but realize that each classroom teacher or room is set up for the needs of someone else. None of the rooms will be exactly

Kids can be active, learn skills, and have fun even in small spaces like classrooms.

alike. If you see a safety hazard, fix it or avoid it. Your responsibility is to be a reasonably prudent teacher or leader, not a negligent one.

If you are confined to a classroom, remember that you are a guest. But you need some freedom to move around, so it would be valuable to discuss the issue of classroom PE and activity time at the beginning of the school year with your teachers and principal.

Don't Waste Another Day

Let's face it. We know how important our subject is and how crucial it is in the lives of the children we lead and teach. So, can we afford to lose even one class or time period? Not a chance!

Physical education and activity is important for many reasons. We know that without our health, nothing else matters. If we aren't healthy, then we can't do anything to our potential—not reading, not math, not any subject. A report from the surgeon general (U.S. Department of Health and Human Services, 1996) listed the important health benefits of physical activity during childhood, which include maintaining healthy bones, muscles, and joints; controlling weight; and reducing feelings of depression and anxiety. Later in a person's life, physical activity will help reduce the risk of developing heart disease, diabetes, high blood pressure, and colon cancer. According to the report, meaningful lessons and activities taught in physical education can make a real difference in a person's well-being, success, and longevity.

Unfortunately, not all educators see the value of physical education, so it is imperative that we prove these facts by providing excellent opportunities for children to be active. If you are in the classroom, you have an extremely important audience member, the classroom teacher, who can become either your advocate for physical education or your opponent.

All it takes is for that teacher to see how much children learned from you in one activity session. Succeed at that and you've left a lasting impression.

If the lesson was worthwhile, if the kids learned something, and if they were active and enjoyed the activity, you have won a huge battle. If your lesson was inactive and if the students played just a little bit without purpose, then that teacher won't recognize that the time was worthwhile. Well, the teacher may recognize one thing—that the physical education lesson was a break. But that is not how we want to use our time. If the teacher sees physical education only as a break from important activities, then our professional future is bleak. It's never too late to educate others and promote our subject, so if you have a "stuck in the classroom" day, demonstrate our importance by doing one of the activities or lessons in this book.

NASPE Standards and Guidelines

As Elvis would have said, "A little less talk and a lot more action." The National Association for Sport and Physical Education (2004) suggests that children aged 5 to 12 years old need at least 60 minutes of physical activity per day. Robert Pangrazi and Chuck Corbin, professors in the field of physical education and authors of physical education texts, have provided good physical activity research and ideas regarding physical activity and children's need for it. At our AAHPERD convention in 2004, Corbin and Pangrazi presented the need for activity to a standing-room-only crowd. How active are the children in your program? Providing them physical education at school will help them to reach that minimum goal. Recess also helps, but some children are inactive at recess time. So physical educators, recreational leaders, classroom teachers, and active parents must come to the rescue! You can help all children develop healthy habits and increase their activity level.

NASPE (National Association for Sport and Physical Education) recommends the 60-minute minimum and has developed six **National Standards for Physical Education** that physical educators should follow to provide worthwhile physical education and activity:

- Standard 1—demonstrates competency in motor skills and movement patterns needed to perform a variety of physical activities
- Standard 2—demonstrates understanding of movement concepts, principles, strategies, and tactics as they apply to the learning and performance of physical activities
- Standard 3—participates regularly in physical activity
- Standard 4—achieves and maintains a health-enhancing level of physical fitness
- Standard 5—exhibits responsible personal and social behavior that respects self and others in physical activity settings
- Standard 6—values physical activity for health, enjoyment, challenge, self-expression, or social interaction

Reprinted from *Moving Into the Future: National Standards for Physical Education,* 2nd Edition (2004), with permission from the National Association for Sport and Physical Education (NASPE), 1900 Association Drive, Reston, VA 20191-1599.

The ideas and lessons provided have been created with the NASPE standards as the base of the structure. The activities were designed to keep as many students involved as possible, actively and safely, in a classroom environment. These lessons will also help your school meet the requirements of the **No Child Left Behind Law (Public Law 107-110),** which was designed to close the achievement gap with accountability, flexibility, and choice so that no child is left behind. The lessons have been tested by teachers in schools that have economically challenged and disadvantaged students as well as by teachers in schools with advantaged students. We must ensure that no students get left behind physically!

When you encounter weather-impaired days, you can still teach using the standards. Under the detailed portion of the activities in this book, you will find the number of the standard that is covered.

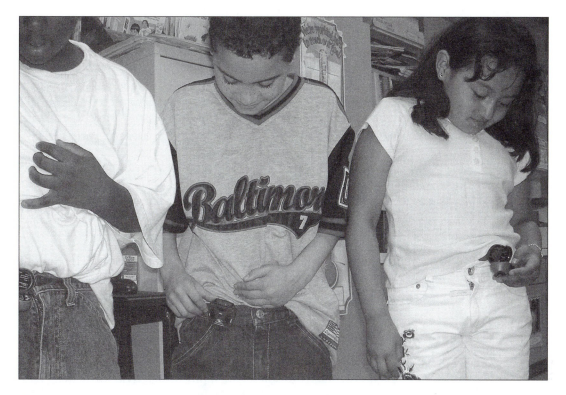

Physical activity can be measured and achieved in small spaces, too.

Health- and Skill-Related Fitness

"Come on, only 499 laps to go!" the PE teacher might be saying if he or she tried to assess students in the mile run in a small classroom. Can you even imagine that scene?

Fortunately, there are many ways to improve and maintain **cardiovascular endurance** and strength in the classroom. But it will take some common sense to ensure that participants will benefit in our programs. If it happens to rain on a planned testing day, don't waste it. Either train some more in a fun and varied activity or test another item that requires less space. Testing of the upper body, flexibility, and **abdominals** can easily take place in a classroom too.

Many school systems or recreation programs have their own physical fitness assessment program. If yours does not, you could try the **President's Challenge** program, **Fitnessgram,** or **Physical Best** program.

In the classroom, you will have no trouble covering the skill-related fitness components. Speed, agility, power, balance, reaction time, and force can all be adjusted using creative methods that deliver the same message with a different design. You'll find running, agility, throwing, catching, striking, tumbling, balancing, volleying, dribbling, and dance activities throughout the lessons. If you are familiar with George Graham, a professor and author in the field of physical education who writes books about pedagogy, teaching physical education, and his style of teaching physical skills, adapting to his ideas will be easy.

Throw out that idea about being stuck in the classroom and use a new phrase, "No problem. It's action-in-the-classroom time."

Genesis of This Book

In Virginia Beach City Public Schools, students have PE every day for 45 minutes, which is fantastic. All the schools have excellent gyms, too. But having six PE classes of 25 students each, each with a PE teacher, in a small elementary school gym doesn't seem feasible to some principals and educators. Some teachers could not handle such large groups involved in activity, and some principals worried about the safety of having 150 active students in one place. So PE teachers had to teach in the classroom. The concern with that approach was that thought and planning would be required to teach a worthwhile lesson in a classroom.

Because of a dangerous public safety issue in the Washington, DC, area in the fall of 2002, students were not permitted to go outside for PE, recess, or after-school activities for about 3 weeks straight. Circumstances such as the following may force us to keep our students inside to ensure their safety:

- Weather
  - Rain
  - Flooding
  - Cold and windchill
  - Snow
  - Excessive heat
- Safety concerns
  - Alerts (dangerous activity in the neighborhood near your school)
  - Unique occurrences (invasion by cicada or other insects, animals on grounds, maintenance concerns)

To those students around the Virginia, Washington, DC, and Maryland areas, 3 weeks was an eternity. Meanwhile, many teachers, staff, physical activity providers, and parents were also beside themselves, suffering with the "I don't know what to do inside these four walls" blues. The struggle only worsened that year, with an incredibly snowy winter and wet spring. I knew then that these activity professionals and leaders needed some help.

I didn't react right away, but another situation arose the next fall. I was working as the project director on a terrific physical activity research project at the University of Maryland called the Be Active Kids project, designed by Dr. Catherine D. Ennis, when I discovered even more opportunities. I witnessed that most PE teachers were teaching without gyms and they had not yet tapped into the possibilities. After seeing the PE teachers' obstacles, it became obvious to the curriculum-writing team that we needed to design dynamic lessons that could be used in a gym or other large space and modified for a classroom. We could not afford to lose a single day of activity during the project, so we made sure that each day allowed for a worthwhile, modified, active lesson.

Classroom teachers who teach PE, as well as other educators and leaders, needed a plan for teaching in the classroom. This need is what drove me to want to help physical educators, recreation leaders, classroom teachers, and parents.

Organization of the Book

This book contains ideas and plans organized into categories and skill themes. The activities are safe and involve participants and students actively most of the time. Students are also involved cognitively. They learn something and appreciate their experience. Active, hands-on time is maximized, even in a minimized space.

The recreation leader or parent who does not need a complete lesson plan can simply open the book, find a skill or activity to do, read the description, and get started. Reading the detailed section of the activity is not necessary.

Warm-Ups

The first category is the warm-up. Several quick warm-ups have proved to be favorites among students when PE must be held in the classroom. Teachers or leaders can use these warm-ups anytime, in any of the lessons described later in the book, but most lessons have a suggested warm-up that fits the lesson. Consult chapter 2 to find full instructions for every warm-up. Simple-to-follow warm-ups include the following information:

- **Activity level.** How active will the students be? Will they all be involved?
- **Intensity.** How intensely will the students be working?
  - High—very active, increased heart rate most of the time
  - Medium—active, increased heart rate some of the time
  - Low—little or no increase in heart rate
- **Standards.** Which NASPE standards does the lesson address?
- **Skills.** What physical skills will the students learn, improve, or maintain?
  - Movement—spatial awareness, **locomotor** patterns, effort, relationships
  - Fitness—cardiovascular strength and endurance, strength, flexibility, agility
  - Throwing and catching—throwing and catching objects
  - Dribbling with hands, feet, or implements—dribbling balls with hands, with hockey sticks, with feet
  - Striking and volleying—striking with implements or hands, keeping an object in the air
  - Gymnastics—tumbling, transferring weight, jumping and landing, balancing
  - Rhythms—dance and activities involving a rhythmic pattern
  - Kicking—kicking a ball, punting a ball
- **Equipment.** What equipment will you need? Considerations have been made knowing that you will be transporting this equipment from room to room and will continue with a lesson after the warm-up. Of course, you will have desks and chairs available in the classrooms where you teach the lessons, so the list of equipment contains only those items that you need to take with you to the room.
- **Organization.** How do you conduct this warm-up?
- **Setup.** What will the room look like?

Basic Action Plan

The second category is the basic action plan. The plan is devised for those who want to run a lesson on the fly and be able to make a quick choice of a skill area that they want to work on. They simply read a description of how to run the activity and go. The basic action plan includes the following:

- **Skill theme.**
- **Skills.** What the lesson focuses on.
- **Activity level.** How active will the students be? Will they all be involved?
- **Intensity.** How intensely will the students be working?
  - High—very active, increased heart rate most of the time
  - Medium—active, increased heart rate some of the time
  - Low—little or no increase in heart rate
- **Standards.** Which NASPE standards does the lesson address?
- **Invitation.** How you will introduce the activity and create excitement.
- **Equipment.** Recommended equipment for use in the classroom. This is the equipment that you will be transporting from room to room. Of course, desks and chairs will be available in the classroom where you teach the lesson.

- **Description.** An explanation of how to participate in the activity. How will the participants be grouped? What will they do? How will it happen?
- **Setup.** Suggestions for classroom setups. Where do the desks go? You will find room diagrams for many activities.

Detailed Lesson Plan

After the basic action plan, a detailed lesson plan follows for physical educators who must include objectives, standards of learning, closure, and specific criteria and details that a professional provides in a lesson plan, including the following:

- **Objectives.** What do you want the students to know and be able to do when they leave your class?
- **Warm-up.** A brief activity to warm up the muscles, increase the heart rate, and prepare the body for more action.
- **Cues and concepts.** Cues are phrases that you can offer to students to help them remember sequences, patterns, and important information about skill development. You may want to repeat these cues several times throughout the lesson. The concepts are ideas about physical activity and health that you can cover with your students.
- **Assessment.** Rubrics that suggest a method for checking understanding, skill development, and effort. The rubrics can measure the cognitive, psychomotor, and affective learning of your students.
  - 3 is the highest mark.
  - 0 is the lowest mark.
- **Safety.** What could make the activity safer and decrease the chance for injuries? Being courteous and polite is another important factor in maintaining a safe classroom environment.
- **Tips and variations.** Ways to make your lesson sparkle or make it easier for the students to grasp. Ideas that should help teachers and students be more successful. Suggestions to enrich the lesson. Modifications for older or younger students.
- **Conclusion and links to real life.** Closure, relating what was just taught and learned back to the objective. Connecting the activity to our real lives and describing how the activity enhances our lives.
- **Try at home.** Homework is provided here. Send your students away with something to relate to or do at home. Try to involve families and relationships that a child is involved in.

The activities include the following:

- **Skill themes.**
- **Game shows, reality shows, and special events get physical.** Reality TV and popular game shows come alive. Using the general idea of the TV show, add action and exercise to make a great physical activity. These activities include special events that involve many skill themes and links to sports.
- **Board games aren't boring.** Instead of just sitting around a board and eating chips, players move physically around the board to play board games.

Cool-Downs

Closing the lesson, decreasing heart rates, and cooling down the muscles from activity are the focus. Preparing participants to settle down for their next teacher or task is important.

Consult chapter 11 to find full instructions for every cool-down. Simple-to-follow cool-downs include the following information:

- **Activity level.** How active will the students be? Will they all be involved?
- **Intensity.** How intensely will the students be working?
  - High—very active, increased heart rate most of the time
  - Medium—active, increased heart rate some of the time
  - Low—little or no increase in heart rate
- **Standards.** Which NASPE standards does the lesson address?
- **Skills.** What physical skills will the students learn, improve, or maintain?
  - Movement—spatial awareness, locomotor patterns, effort, relationships
  - Fitness—cardiovascular strength and endurance, strength, flexibility, agility
  - Throwing and catching—throwing and catching objects
  - Dribbling with hands, feet, or implements—dribbling balls with hands, with hockey sticks, with feet
  - Striking and volleying—striking with implements or hands, keeping an object in the air
  - Gymnastics—tumbling, transferring weight, jumping and landing, balancing
  - Rhythms—dance and activities involving a rhythmic pattern
  - Kicking—kicking a ball, punting a ball
- **Equipment.** What equipment will you need? Of course, you will have desks and chairs available in the classrooms where you teach the lessons, so the list of equipment contains only those items that you need to take with you to the room.
- **Organization.** How do you conduct this cool-down?
- **Setup.** What will the room look like?

Physical activity can thrive in the classroom or a small room. Just choose the skill or idea that you want to work on. Then break it down into what part of the skill you want to focus on. Finally, pick the activity that fits your needs. You will no longer have to ruin your yearly plan because of interruptions, inclement weather, or unusual events. If you don't have a gym, now you don't have any worries either. No gym? No problem!

Warm-Ups and Games

When you were younger you probably went to PE class hoping that you would play your favorite activity that day. I know that I eagerly awaited the time when the teacher orally confirmed the activity that we would do for the day. My classmates would burst into "Hoorays" and "Yeahs" if the activity was something that we really loved to do. Here are some activities that generated a few "Hoorays" and "Yeahs."

To start the lesson, warm up the muscles, and get the students interested in the lesson, begin with a warm-up. A warm-up prepares the body for safe activity and should link in some way to the content of the lesson.

- - - Can You Guess, Judge? - - -

Activity Level	**Intensity**	**Standards**	**Skills**
Everyone is involved.	Low to medium	① ④	**Locomotor** patterns, exercise

Equipment

None

Organization

- Divide participants into groups of four.
- One person sits in a judge's chair, with his or her back to the jury, while the jury, the other three people in the group, do a certain locomotor pattern (jumping, walking, skipping, hopping, leaping, sliding, crawling, or other pattern) around a set of desks.
- One of the jurors is selected to say, "Can you guess, Judge?" This person should disguise his or her voice. All jury members must keep moving.
- The judge has 10 seconds to guess who was talking. If the judge is correct, he or she does 20 jumping jacks for joy and sits back down. If the judge is incorrect, the one who fooled him or her becomes the judge.

Setup

None

- - - Demo Show - - -

Activity Level	Intensity	Standards	Skills
Each person moves for approximately 30 seconds, rests, and then repeats.	Medium	② ⑤	Fitness, agility, reaction time

Equipment

None

Organization

All students should watch a properly executed push-up, crunch or curl-up, and jumping jack. One partner performs the exercises twice, and the other reviews the action to help his or her partner learn the correct form. The partners then switch roles.

Setup

None

- - - Do, Re, Me, Fa, So, La, Te, Do - - -

Activity Level	Intensity	Standards	Skills
Everyone participates at all times.	Medium to high	② ④ ⑤ ⑥	Fitness, strength, endurance

Equipment

None

Organization

With imagination and uninhibited freedom, students perform while singing the scale (do, re, me, fa, so, la, te, do) to the following exercises. If they can sing the scale from low to high and then from high to low, they will have even more fun. Students perform the following actions:

- Arm circles forward, then backward
- Heel raises
- Twists, with bent knees
- Push-ups
- Vertical jumps

Setup

None

--- Exercard Battle ---

Activity Level	Intensity	Standards	Skills
Everyone moves vigorously every 15 seconds.	Medium	① ⑤	Fitness, locomotor patterns

Equipment

- Three decks of cards
- Chart of exercises (a poster-size chart or a copy of the chart for students to use at their seats)

Organization

- Each participant is given five cards, face down.
- Participants work in pairs to play Exercard Battle.
- Each person turns a card face up. The person with the highest card wins a chance to exercise and takes the opponent's card. You should post the exercises on the board or a poster or provide a sheet for players to use at their seats.
- Players then turn the second card and repeat the process until someone runs out of cards.
- Once a player runs out of cards, the game is over.
- Reshuffle and play again.

Setup

None

No Gym?

If this card wins . . .	. . . do this exercise.
2	Jog around the room once
3	Jump around the room once
4	Hop around the room once
5	Skip around the room once
6	20 jumping jacks
7	20 arm circles each way
8	10 push-ups
9	20 crunches
10	Gallop around the room twice
Jack	30 jumping jacks
Queen	30 arm circles each way
King	25 curl-ups
Ace	Winner's choice

No Problem!

- - - Exerdice 100 - - -

Activity Level	Intensity	Standards	Skills
Everyone moves vigorously every 15 seconds.	Medium	① ⑤	Fitness, locomotor patterns

Equipment

- One piece of paper, one pair of dice, and one pencil per pair
- Exercise grid on board

Organization

- Players get into pairs. Each pair of players has a pair of dice and a piece of paper and pencil between them.

Name	Name
Roll 1	Roll 1
Roll 2	Roll 2
Roll 3	Roll 3
Roll 4	Roll 4
Roll 5	Roll 5
Roll 6	Roll 6
Roll 7	Roll 7
Roll 8	Roll 8
Roll 9	Roll 9
Roll 10	Roll 10
Total	Total

- Players take turns rolling the dice. Whatever the dice add up to on the roll is the exercise that the roller must perform. The numbers correspond to an exercise. You should post the exercises on the board or poster.

2	3	4	5
Heel raises (20)	Push-ups (10)	Crunches (20)	Arm circles (20 each way)
6	7	8	9
Skip around the room twice	Jumping jacks (20)	Crab walk around the room	Hop backward across the room
10	11	12	
Jog in place (15 seconds)	Dance in place (15 seconds)	Double sixes– your choice!	

- ⑤ If a person performs the exercise properly, he or she earns the point total shown by the dice.
- ⑤ After each roll, the player adds up his or her total and keeps track of it. The first person to reach 100 points wins.

Setup

None

--- Find the Leader ---

Activity Level	Intensity	Standards	Skills
Everyone moves at all times, except one person.	Low to high	① ⑤	Fitness

Equipment

None

Organization

- ⑤ Choose one person to be the guesser, who must leave the room for a few seconds.
- ⑤ Choose one person to be the leader, who will lead the group in an exercise or movement for 15 seconds and then must change the exercise every 15 seconds thereafter.

The guesser has 10 seconds to guess who the leader is. Allow the guesser three guesses. If the guesser guesses the correct leader, then he or she continues to be the guesser. If the guesser guesses incorrectly, then the leader becomes the next guesser. The participants follow the same procedure: The guesser goes out. The leader is chosen. The leader leads the group in movement. The guesser returns while the leader and the group are already engaged in moving. The guesser tries to guess the leader.

- The tricky part is for the group to follow the leader and catch the exercise changes without giving away the leader's identity.
- Give the participants some examples of exercises that they can do so that they perform smooth transitions.

Setup

None

--- Fit Tic-Tac-Toe ---

Activity Level	Intensity	Standards	Skills
Everyone moves vigorously every 15 seconds.	Medium	①	Fitness

Equipment

- One piece of paper and one pencil per pair
- Exercise grid on board

Organization

1. Players get into pairs. One player will be X's, and the other will be O's.
2. The pairs play a game of Fit Tic-Tac-Toe, using their own paper and looking at the board or prewritten poster for exercise directions.

Skip around the room twice	30 jumping jacks	10 push-ups
Jog in place for 15 seconds	Stretch hamstrings and quadriceps (thighs) for 15 seconds	20 crunches
Jump around the room twice	Do 15 squat thrusts	30 arm circles each way

3. One person goes at a time, placing his or her symbol on the grid and then performing the exercise in an attempt to get three symbols in a row. The person who does so wins the round.

4. Once a round is finished, play again. Winners go last.

Setup

None

--- Flexapalooza ---

Activity Level	Intensity	Standards	Skills
Everyone moves at all times.	Low	④ ⑤	Fitness, flexibility, creativity

Equipment

An option is to use slow, relaxing music such as "Kokomo" by the Beach Boys or reggae songs by Bob Marley. You'll need a CD player.

Organization

- Each person is invited to show off his or her flexibility at this show.
- Participants are welcomed to the front of the room to display their 10-second flexing act while the audience follows them. Then another act comes to the stage.
- Try suggesting which body parts to stretch if the participants get stuck. Encourage safe creativity. If students fall or are not balanced, consider the stretch unsafe.

Setup

The leader is on center stage, at the front of the class, while the other students are in the middle of the room, with room to stretch.

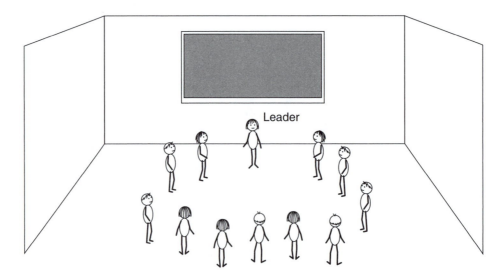

Leader

--- Fruit Basket Upset ---

Activity Level	**Intensity**	**Standards**	**Skills**
Movement occurs at least every 30 seconds.	Low with medium bursts	①	Strategy, teamwork, reaction time

Equipment

None

Organization

- Divide the students into four groups and group the desk or chairs together. Name each group a fruit. For example, name one group Apples.
- Call the names of two groups. Only those two groups switch places. For example, call, "Apples and Oranges, switch." The object is for the group to work together and quickly change spots with another group, on signal, and sit in the other group's seats. Each group called tries to sit in the others' seats before the other group can all be seated.
- Groups should use strategy to help the whole team be seated. The activity is a group effort, not a one-on-one effort.
- The group that is completely seated first scores a point.

Setup

Group chairs and desks into four groups.

- - - Hand Jive - - -

Activity Level	Intensity	Standards	Skills
Everyone moves all the time.	Medium to high	① ⑥	Fitness, rhythms and dance

Equipment

CD player and hand-jive, cool jerk, or fast 1950s or 1960s music

Organization

Have participants work on their own and perform the following sequence:

- Hit both hands on thighs twice.
- Clap twice.
- Make the motions of being safe on the baseball field, twice.
- Repeat the safe motion, with the opposite hand on top this time.
- Make two fists, right hand on top, and hit the left fist with the bottom of the right fist twice.
- Repeat the fist knocking, with the left hand on top.
- Make the hitchhike motion, taking the right thumb over the right shoulder twice.
- Make the hitchhike motion, taking the left thumb over the left shoulder twice.
- Repeat the sequence.

Setup

None

- - - Jacks and Jills Move Cube - - -

Activity Level	Intensity	Standards	Skills
Everyone is involved.	High	① ④	Exercise

Equipment

Five or six move cubes. Any size is fine, as long as the students can read them. The larger they are, the more fun they are to roll.

Organization

- Divide into groups of four people. Each group gets its own cube.
- The cube can be a box or can be made out of paper.
- Each side has one of the following exercises:
  - Full jacks (full jumping jacks)
  - Half jacks (arms raised only to shoulder height)
  - Four-count jacks (1—legs together, arms down; 2—legs apart, arms out, shoulder height; 3—legs together, arms straight up high; 4—legs apart, arms out, shoulder height, back to position 1)

- Jumping jills (straddle legs forward, right foot forward, left foot behind; arms out in front, one arm up and one arm down; alternate arms shifting up and down, and different legs moving forward and back)
- Jacks and jills (alternate one jack and then one jill)
- Jacks of choice (the students choose their favorite exercise from the cube)

☙ The first person in the group tosses the move cube, and the group performs four repetitions of the exercise that is shown on the side of the cube that is facing up when it lands. The second person tosses the cube, and the group performs three repetitions. The third roll allows for two repetitions, and the fourth roll allows for one repetition.

☙ You could adjust the number of repetitions to fit time, intensity, and the number of students in the group.

Setup

None

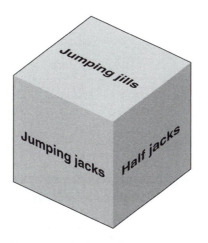

--- Lucky Four Corners ---

Activity Level	Intensity	Standards	Skills
Everyone is moving for 5 to 10 minutes.	Medium	①	Movement, locomotor patterns

Equipment

CD player and an upbeat musical CD or whistle

Organization

☙ Number the corners in the room (1, 2, 3, 4).

☙ Each person stands in one corner of his or her choice.

☙ On the whistle or when the music begins, students perform a designated locomotor movement around the room for 30 seconds and then find a corner that they feel will be lucky for them. They stand still for 5 seconds.

☙ You, as the teacher or leader, whistle or stop the music and call out a number. The participants lucky enough to be in that corner do 20 jumping jacks for joy and score one point.

ⓒ The object for participants is to try their luck at each corner, attempt to do the specific locomotor pattern around the room each time, and rack up points by choosing the lucky corner.

Setup

Arrange the room as shown in the following diagram.

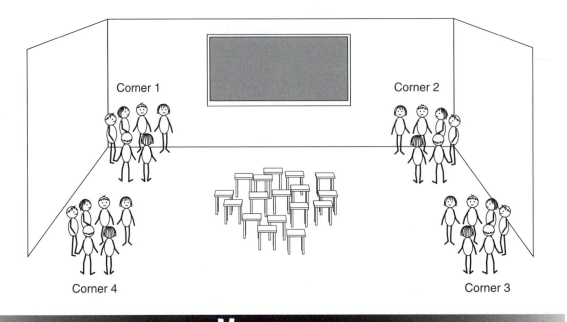

- - - Macarena - - -

Activity Level	**Intensity**	**Standards**	**Skills**
Everyone moves all the time.	Medium to high	① ⑥	Fitness, rhythms and dance

Equipment

CD player and "Macarena," found on *Jock Jams 2* or by Los Del Mar

Organization

Have participants work on their own and perform the following sequence:

ⓒ Extend right hand out face down.

ⓒ Extend left hand out face down.

ⓒ Extend right hand out face up.

ⓒ Extend left hand out face up.

ⓒ Touch right hand to left shoulder.

ⓒ Touch left hand to right shoulder.

ⓒ Place right hand behind right side of head.

ⓒ Place left hand behind left side of head.

ⓒ Touch right hand to left hip.

ⓒ Touch left hand to right hip.

ⓒ Touch right hand to right back side.

ⓒ Touch left hand to left back side.

- Roll hips around three times and then jump.
- Turn a quarter turn to the right.
- Repeat the sequence.

Setup

None

--- Over, On, and Beside ---

Activity Level	Intensity	Standards	Skills
Everyone participates at all times.	Medium to high	① ② ⑤ ⑥	Fitness, strength, endurance, reaction time

Equipment

One ball per person

Organization

Students place the ball on the floor and will move their feet somewhere in relation to the ball, according to your instructions.

- Right
- Left
- Straddle
- Over
- Over
- Over
- Repeat for 2 to 3 minutes, varying the order of instructions and speed

Setup

None

--- Over, On, and Beside With Sticks ---

Activity Level	Intensity	Standards	Skills
Everyone participates at all times.	Medium	① ② ⑤ ⑥	Fitness, striking, reaction time

Equipment

One beanbag per person, one hockey stick per person

Organization

Students place the beanbag on the ground and place their stick somewhere in relation to the beanbag, according to your instructions. After the students grasp the idea, have them speed up.

- On top
- Right
- Left

- Across
- Inside
- Across
- Inside
- On top
- Repeat for 2 to 3 minutes

Setup

None

--- Physical Musical Chairs ---

Activity Level	Intensity	Standards	Skills
Everyone moves at all times.	Medium	①	Fitness, locomotor patterns

Equipment

Polyspots for the participants (two fewer than the number of people that you have), CD player, CD

Organization

- Place polyspots in two rows in the middle of the room, as if making a row of chairs facing one way and the others facing the other way (like in musical chairs). Participants move using various locomotor patterns, which you designate, around the spots, when the music starts.
- When the music stops, participants must quickly go to a spot and then jump up and down on it.
- If a person does not make it to a spot, he or she does not get to jump. The person must try harder next time to get the chance to jump. Players are never eliminated though.

Setup

Set up two anchor chairs that the students must go around. The other chairs should be against the wall.

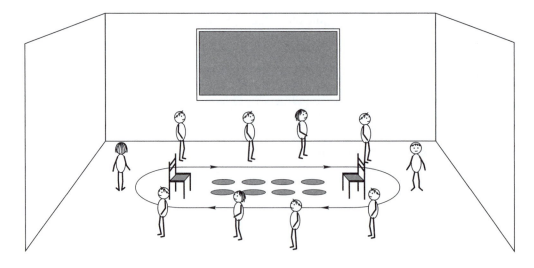

- - - Push-Up Wave - - -

Activity Level	Intensity	Standards	Skills
Everyone participates at all times.	Medium to high	② ④ ⑤ ⑥	Fitness, strength, endurance, reaction time

Equipment

None

Organization

- ☞ Have the students arrange themselves in a circular or square formation with the abdomen, legs, toes, and palms on the floor. On your signal, the student nearest you rises into a push-up position. Then the next person does the same, followed by the next and the next. When the last person rises into position and the sequence of movement, the wave, gets back to the beginning, the students return to the floor in sequence, one by one. Repeat several times.
- ☞ After several times around, have the group perform the wave in the opposite direction.
- ☞ Have fun by adjusting the speed.

Setup

None

- - - Quick Feet - - -

Activity Level	Intensity	Standards	Skills
Everyone moves all the time.	High	① ② ⑤ ⑥	Fitness, agility, reaction time

Equipment

Tennis ball or other small ball

Organization

All participants stand facing you. Take a ball in your hand and ask the participants to follow it. They move their feet quickly to the right, left, and right as they slide left, forward, backward, and right, according to the direction in which you move the ball. You control the ball by raising it above your head and moving it in the direction that you want them to go.

Setup

None

- - - Rock, Paper, Scissors—Action - - -

Activity Level	Intensity	Standards	Skills
Everyone moves at all times.	Low to high	① ⑤	Fitness

Equipment

None

Organization

- Partners start facing each other and gently hit their fists into their other open palm three times, saying, "One, two, three." After the third hit, each partner says, "Show!" and displays one of these hand signals:
  - Rock (closed fist)—smashes scissors
  - Paper (hand open, palm down)—covers rock
  - Scissors (index and middle fingers out while the other fingers form a fist)—cuts paper
- If a person wins he or she does the exercise posted on the board. The exercise bank could include push-ups, jumping jacks, jumping jills, running in place for a certain number of seconds, hopping on one foot, arm circles, twists, crunches, and hurdle stretches. Participants must pay attention to the board because the teacher or leader will change the exercise every 30 seconds.
- The exercise intensity builds as the game goes on. Each time a person wins, he or she keeps track of the wins and does that number of exercises. For example, if Mia wins 10 times and the exercise on the board is jumping jacks, she does 10 jumping jacks.

Setup

None

- - - Run and Scream - - -

Activity Level	Intensity	Standards	Skills
Everyone moves all the time.	High	① ④ ⑥	Fitness, **cardiovascular endurance**

Equipment

None

Organization

- Participants practice improving their lung capacity by running until they run out of breath.
- Each person, on a signal, runs in place as he or she lets out a scream. The person runs in place until the scream ends, when the runner needs to take a breath.
- Require a 15-second rest and then give the signal to run and scream again.

Setup

Advise neighboring classes that you will be doing a quick warm-up that involves screaming.

--- Shoot on the Floor and Scoot After Four ---

Activity Level	Intensity	Standards	Skills
Everyone participates at all times.	Medium to high	① ② ⑤ ⑥	Fitness, strength, endurance, reaction time

Equipment

One ball per pair

Organization

- Students find a partner and receive a ball.
- Lying flat on the floor, one partner uses good shooting technique and shoots toward the other partner, who is standing at the side of the shooter's head to catch the shot. After four shots, the partners exchange roles.

Setup

None

--- Simon Says, "Action" ---

Activity Level	Intensity	Standards	Skills
Everyone moves at all times.	Low to high	① ⑤ ⑥	Fitness

Equipment

None

Organization

- Divide the participants into four groups. Each group works in a corner of the room.
- As in the game Simon Says, one person is Simon and the others follow along, doing whatever Simon says to do. When Simon says, "Simon says," the other players must perform the action. If Simon doesn't say, "Simon says," then the players should not do the action.
- If someone does something without the proper signaling, he or she gains a letter, A. If the person is tricked again, he or she earns a C. This pattern continues until the person has spelled out the word *Action.*
- Switch Simons after someone has spelled out *Action* or after 2 minutes.

Setup

None

- - - Step and Scream - - -

Activity Level	Intensity	Standards	Skills
Everyone moves all the time.	High	① ⑥	Fitness, cardiovascular endurance, technology

Equipment

Pedometers

Organization

- Participants practice improving their lung capacity by running or jogging until they run out of breath. The challenge is to see how many steps they can take with one breath.
- Each person needs a pedometer.
- Each person, on a signal, runs in place as he or she lets out a scream. The person runs in place until the scream stops, when the runner needs to take a new breath.
- At this time, the participants look at their pedometers and see how many steps they took during the scream.
- Require a 15-second rest, ask participants to reset their pedometers, and then give the signal to step and scream again.

Setup

Advise neighboring classes that you will be doing a quick warm-up that involves screaming.

- - - Thumb Jack Wrestling - - -

Activity Level	Intensity	Standards	Skills
Everyone moves at all times.	High	① ⑤ ⑥	Fitness

Equipment

None

Organization

- Partners start facing each other and interlock right fingers, with the thumbs free to move on top.
- Partners do jumping-jack legs, in unison (apart, together, apart, together).
- With their thumbs, they try to take down the partner's thumb by placing theirs on top. If successful, they win the round and do 10 complete victory jumping jacks.
- Have participants switch to the left hand and repeat.

Setup

None

--- Warm-Up Bingo ---

Activity Level	Intensity	Standards	Skills
Movement should occur approximately every 10 seconds.	Low to high	①	Fitness

Equipment

One Warm-Up Bingo card per person; 16 spot markers; 20 numbers (for you to call out); a cup, hat, or bag for the numbers

Organization

- Everyone needs a Warm-Up Bingo card and 16 cut-up pieces of paper or objects to place on top of their spots.
- You can use the cards on these pages, or you can have the participants choose numbers 1 through 20 and write 16 of them randomly on the blank Warm-Up Bingo cards.
- You draw a number from a cup or hat (numbers 1 through 20) or call out a number. The participants put a marker on the number that you call. The object is to get four numbers called in a row (across, diagonal, or down). That arrangement is a Warm-Up Bingo.
- With each match, participants perform an exercise, which you designate, in the amount that was called. So, if a 6 is called, and the exercise is push-ups, they do 6 push-ups.
- When someone gets Warm-Up Bingo, he or she skips three victory laps around the room. If the room setup does not allow for laps, create a path that the students can follow without hitting desks, chairs, or objects.

Setup

None

Warm-Up Bingo

1	3	5	7
15	13	11	9
2	4	6	8
20	12	14	10

Warm-Up Bingo

1	3	5	20
15	18	11	9
2	4	19	8
16	12	14	17

From *No Gym? No Problem! Physical Activities for Tight Spaces* by Charmain Sutherland, 2006, Champaign, IL: Human Kinetics.

Warm-Up Bingo

16	3	14	7
15	13	12	9
2	19	6	8
20	1	5	10

Warm-Up Bingo

10	3	5	17
15	19	11	13
4	2	5	8
7	12	14	1

From *No Gym? No Problem! Physical Activities for Tight Spaces* by Charmain Sutherland, 2006, Champaign, IL: Human Kinetics.

Warm-Up Bingo

15	13	5	7
1	3	19	17
20	14	6	18
2	12	4	10

Warm-Up Bingo

From *No Gym? No Problem! Physical Activities for Tight Spaces* by Charmain Sutherland, 2006, Champaign, IL: Human Kinetics.

- - - Watch the Shoes - - -

Activity Level	Intensity	Standards	Skills
Everyone moves at all times.	High	① ⑤	Fitness, reaction time

Equipment

None

Organization

- Partners start facing each other and hold the other's forearms.
- The object is to watch their shoes and quickly move their feet out of the way of the opponent. At the same time, each person wants to tap the top of the shoe of the opponent.
- Keep score of each successful tap of the shoes. When someone reaches 10 taps, the pair stops.
- Change partners every 30 seconds.

Setup

None

Fitness

Long gone are the boring laps and calisthenics that physical activity providers once used to work on fitness. Now we can adapt principles of creating enthusiasm and desire for participants to enjoy fitness even inside a small space like the classroom. The following activities focus on **muscular strength, muscular endurance, cardiovascular endurance,** and flexibility. They also reach into technology, sports, science, and current trends in fitness.

- - - Push-Up Power - - -

Fitness—strength

Skills	Activity Level	Intensity	Standards
Fitness, health-related fitness, upper-body strength, endurance, speed, reaction time	Everyone is actively involved.	High to medium	① ② ④ ⑤

Invitation

"How strong are your arms? Strong enough to hold up your whole body? Could you play hockey by using only your arms? Can you do a dance while doing a push-up? Let's see how strong your **biceps** and arm muscles are by doing some activities that will stress the upper-body muscles."

Equipment

- 13 beanbags of one color and 13 beanbags of another color
- CD player and CD of Macarena music

Description

Participants work in pairs at first. They do the Macarena push-ups individually.

Push-Up Hockey

- Partners face each other in push-up position, 3 feet (1 meter) apart, with their arms shoulder-width apart.
- Partners hold themselves up with one arm while pushing a beanbag back and forth with the other, attempting to slide it through hands of the opponent, to score a goal.

Push-Up Steal the Beanbag

- Partners begin in the same position as they did in Push-Up Hockey, with a beanbag in the middle of the two players.
- Say, "Ready, set, go." On "Go," the students attempt to react fast and reach for the beanbag first.
- Increase the difficulty by calling out which hand the students must use to grab with, forcing them to react and think before moving.

Push-Up Dancing

Participants perform the Macarena dance with one arm and hand, as the other arm and hand stabilize the body. Participants should attempt to hold up their body weight as long as possible with one hand, but they may put their other hand down when needed. Encourage them to go further and further each time.

- Palm down twice.
- Palm up twice.

- Left shoulder tap.
- Right shoulder tap.
- Tap head twice.
- Tap left hip.
- Tap right hip.
- Tap right rear.
- Tap left rear.
- Shake hips from right to left, log roll, and get back up on both arms and into push-up position.
- Repeat with the other arm this time.
- Repeat.

Push and Give

One partner sits with legs crossed, facing a partner with hands out and palms up. Partner 2 is in push-up position, waiting for the partner to call the actions. The red and blue beanbags are between the partners, about 6 inches (15 centimeters) from each partner. Partner 1 calls the following commands to partner 2:

- Right hand blue (places blue beanbag in partner's right hand).
- Left hand blue (places blue beanbag in partner's left hand).
- Beanbag up (places blue beanbag in the air).
- Beanbag down (places blue beanbag down on the ground).
- Right hand red (places red beanbag in partner's right hand).
- Left hand red (places red beanbag in partner's left hand).

Partner 2 counts how many beanbags he or she can transfer from the ground to the partner's hands without falling onto the knees or floor. Partner 1 sits with arms out. Partner 2 places one beanbag at a time into the hands of partner 1.

- Left beanbag up.
- Right beanbag up.
- Left beanbag to the floor.
- Right beanbag to the floor.
- Repeat until the knee or body hits the floor, or the push-up form is lost.
- Switch once the knee or body hits the floor.

Setup

Look first; rearrange if necessary; put it back together.

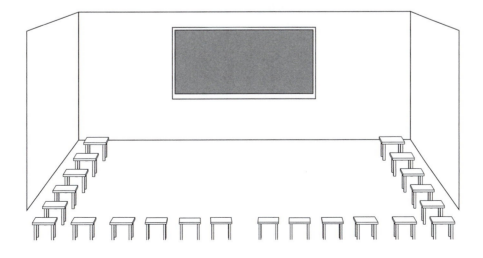

Break It Down in Detail

Lesson plans and in-depth information follow.

Objectives

- ⬭ Students explore their upper-body strength in activities that focus on upper-body strength, endurance, reaction time, and reaction speed.
- ⬭ Students become aware of the upper-body muscles.

Warm-Up

Push-Up Wave

Cues and Concepts

Carry out the activities using the following cues:

- ⬭ Upper-body strength—your muscles above your waist are working hard.
- ⬭ Shaky is OK—if your arms are shaky, you are working your muscles. They will be OK.

Include the following concepts:

- ⬭ Discuss the muscles being worked and direct the students to point to those muscles (biceps, **triceps, deltoid**).
- ⬭ Discuss reaction time. How fast can the brain tell the deltoid to move to grab the beanbag?
- ⬭ Discuss what the other muscles in the other arm are doing, that is, stabilizing the body.
- ⬭ Ask students how long their muscles can work without letting the body down. The time that they can work represents their upper-body endurance.
- ⬭ Have students count how many beanbags they can give before they are exhausted in the Push and Give.
- ⬭ Can they endure arm dancing, in push-up position, throughout the whole song?

Assessment

Rubric

3 = Endured throughout all push-up and arm activities

2 = Attempted all activities and felt the upper body work; stopped at times

1 = Attempted to stay in push-up position but couldn't; went to knee push-ups

0 = Could not or did not perform activities using upper-body strength

Safety

Each student should be at least 2 feet (60 centimeters) away from other sets of partners. Students must show proper form.

Tips and Variations

- ⬭ Show a push-up with proper body position. Show poor push-ups as well so that students can help their partners maintain proper alignment. If a student has a disability or weight issue, permit a modification such as knee push-ups.
- ⬭ To allow students to feel successful, permit those who try to do push-ups but can't support themselves to do modified push-ups, with the knees on the ground instead of the toes.

Conclusion and Links to Real Life

"How does your upper body feel? What muscles did you work today? What did it mean if your muscles were shaking? We have to work at being strong, but staying strong can be fun."

Try at Home

"Ask your family and friends to do an upper-body challenge with you at home. Can they support themselves?"

--- Flexology ---
Fitness—flexibility

Skills	Activity Level	Intensity	Standards
Moving through a full range of motion, stretching, warming up, increasing flexibility for more agile joints	Everyone is active the entire time.	Medium and low	① ② ③ ④ ⑤

Invitation

"Have you ever tried to stretch a cold piece of silly putty? It doesn't stretch very well, does it? In fact, instead of stretching it breaks in half. But what if I made my muscles warm, by warming up the silly putty? Yes, the silly putty stretches waaaay out, and it doesn't break as easily. (Warm up the putty and show the difference). This is what our muscles and joints are like. Let's find out more about becoming as flexible as a piece of putty."

Equipment

- One egg of silly putty or Play-Doh or clay for each student
- Music—fast for the 20 seconds going around the desks, slow music for performing the action for 15 seconds
- One Flexology sheet per pair

Description

Everyone has an egg of silly putty, which represents a cold muscle and joint. At first, you lead them in an exploration. Then they work with partners.
The leader or teacher prompts the activity as follows:

- Pull your putty.
- We can quickly pull the putty apart because it is cold.
- Working with a partner, we squeeze and warm up the putty in our hands as we skip, jump, hop, gallop, and slide around the desks for 20 seconds.
- After 20 seconds we use the Flexology guides to mold and shape the silly putty into a shape on the sheet.
- Notice how much easier the putty is to bend and stretch after it is warm. Your muscles and joints work the same way.
- After 15 seconds perform the action represented by the symbol on your Flexology sheet that your partner has designed for you. Hold that position for 15 seconds.
- Then we will repeat the process.

Setup

Look first; rearrange if necessary; put it back together when finished. If you can pull a desk, chair, or table away so that students have enough space to jump around it without bumping into others, that arrangement will work.

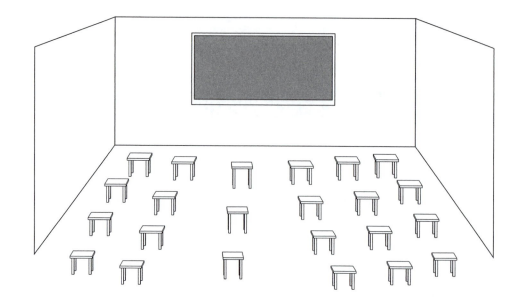

Break It Down in Detail

Lesson plans and in-depth information follow.

Objectives

- ❦ Students increase their flexibility by warming up their muscles and joints through exercise.
- ❦ Students improve the range of motion in their joints by stretching and exercising.
- ❦ Students perform **static stretches** for at least 15 seconds.

Warm-Up

Flexapalooza

Cues and Concepts

Carry out the activities using the following cues:

- ❦ Hold the stretch—stay in the position without bouncing for 15 seconds.
- ❦ Use the full range of motion—move the joint through its full capability of movement.

Cover the following concepts:

- ❦ Have students stretch the following muscles:
  - Legs—**hamstrings, quadriceps, gastrocnemius**
  - **Gluteus maximus**
  - **Abdominals**
  - Arms—biceps, triceps, deltoids
  - **Trapezius**
  - **Latissimus dorsi**
- ❦ Explain the need for static stretching. Static stretching is a still, nonbouncing stretch. Have students stretch for at least 15 seconds.
- ❦ Explain how stretching will help the body avoid injuries and move more smoothly.

Flexology

- Move around the desk for 20 seconds; warm the putty in your hands.

- Form one of the shapes below out of your putty.

- Perform the stretch that corresponds to the shape created by your partner. Hold the stretch for 15 seconds.

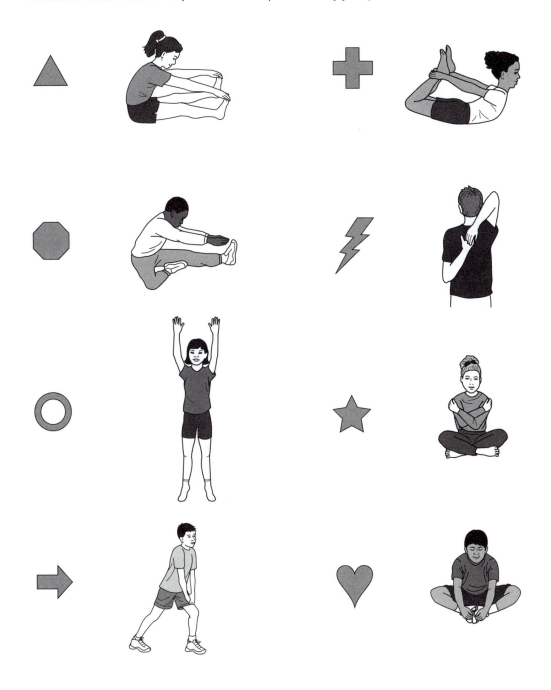

From No Gym? No Problem! Physical Activities for Tight Spaces by Charmain Sutherland, 2006, Champaign, IL: Human Kinetics.

Assessment

Rubric

3 = Attempted all stretches safely; held static stretches for at least 15 seconds

2 = Attempted all stretches safely; held stretches for almost 15 seconds

1 = Performed stretches but not properly or safely; did not hold stretch

0 = Did not attempt to do stretches properly; did not try to hold stretch

Safety

Students should hold stretches still without bouncing. Sometimes students try to bounce or try to imitate unsafe stretches that they might have seen a coach do. Beware of the old-school stretches that can do more harm than good.

Tips and Variations

- A piece of gum or a rubber band is another fantastic visual that can help students see a warmed-up muscle. The students will have fun trying to chew the gum too. Students will break gum that is cold. Then they will chew it and warm it up with their mouths. They will realize what a warmed-up, flexible muscle can do. If you have permission from the principal and patience, try the gum experiment. A word to the wise: Have students spit out their gum after the experiment.

- If students can't perform the stretch properly, give them encouragement and secondary goals. They should attempt to improve flexibility regardless of whether they can reach the target. Each attempt to stretch should increase their flexibility.

Conclusion and Links to Real Life

"What a fun way to discover how our muscles stretch. You don't want to grow older and fall apart, or not be able to bend without breaking, right? This is why we must stretch our muscles and joints. We should stretch every day."

Try at Home

"Design a workout that stretches your muscles and joints from head to toe. Do your stretches each day, maybe as you watch TV or right before breakfast. Invite your family to join your stretching routine."

--- Curl-Up Hockey and Steal the Puck ---

Fitness—strength, abs

Skills	Activity Level	Intensity	Standards
Fitness, strength of abdominal muscles, quick reflexes	Everyone is active at all times.	Medium to high	② ③ ④ ⑤ ⑥

Invitation

"Do you get bored sometimes by doing crunches, sit-ups, curls-ups, or other exercises that you need to do to keep strong abdominal muscles? This activity will work on your abs, but not your boredom."

Equipment

One object (beanbag, puck) or piece of paper per pair

Description

Participants need only an object and powerful abs for this activity.

Curl-Up Hockey

- Participants are in curl-up position, feet to feet, 12 inches (30 centimeters) apart, with a beanbag, piece of paper, or puck centered 6 inches (15 centimeters) from each player's foot.
- Players start by lying back on the floor.
- On your signal, they quickly curl up and either strike the puck with their hands or block it with their hands.
- If the puck goes between the opponent's feet, a goal is scored.
- Play restarts in the center after each goal.

Curl Up and Steal the Puck

- The activity is the same as the previous one, except that players only need to curl up and steal the object before the opponent does.
- Have students rotate after two trials so that they challenge a different person each time.
- Put two groups together after several attempts have passed. One pair holds the feet of the other pair so that they can have leverage to come up after the abdominals have started to get tired. The feet holders sit on the outside of the players performing the curl-ups, holding a foot from each player.

Setup

Look first; rearrange if necessary; put it back together. Little or no rearranging is necessary. Participants only need room to curl up and down.

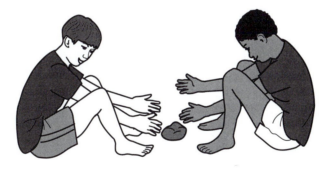

Break It Down in Detail

Lesson plans and in-depth information follow.

Objectives

- Students strengthen their abdominal muscles by participating in fun activities.
- Students improve abdominal strength through fun competition.
- Students appreciate others' capabilities through challenging activities.

Warm-Up

Run and Scream

Cues and Concepts

Carry out the activities using the following cues:

- ☞ Use your core—use the strong muscles of the abdomen to help you get up.
- ☞ Use only the abs—use the ab muscles; don't cheat by using your elbows or rolling to your side.

Include the following concepts:

- ☞ Our abdominals must be strong to do all the work that the body is faced with.
- ☞ If your stomach muscles are sore, it is OK. A little soreness means that you were working those muscles.
- ☞ The more you work a muscle, the stronger it gets.
- ☞ Don't give up if you feel a little discomfort; some soreness is normal. The soreness means that your muscles are getting stronger.
- ☞ Try to do crunches, curls, or steals when you are watching TV or each evening just before you go to bed.
- ☞ If you struggled to get your body up, don't feel bad or give up. Keep doing these exercises and you will soon get stronger.
- ☞ Your form will start to get sloppy after a few trials, so we will add another set of partners to hold your feet so that you can regain your form.

Assessment

Rubric

3 = Participated with best effort

2 = Attempted with best effort most of the time

1 = Attempted but didn't try with best effort

0 = Did not participate with effort

Safety

Protect the back by bending the knees and keeping the feet on the floor.

Tips and Variations

- ☞ Discuss all the ways that our abdominal muscles work (getting up in the morning, lifting a leg up to put a sock on). Invite the students to try these actions to realize how important our abdominal muscles are and how we need them to be strong.
- ☞ Pre-K through grade 2—start with the groups in pairs to create more opportunities for students to do curl-ups with better form.
- ☞ Grades 3 through 8—make the students cross their arms as they come up to isolate the abs.

Conclusion and Links to Real Life

"What muscles can you really feel right now? The abdominals! If you worked hard throughout this class, then you will realize how often you use your stomach muscles, because you will feel a slight discomfort when you are using your abs. You will notice it because you have overloaded the muscle with work, and therefore the muscle will send you signals of slight soreness each time you use it."

Try at Home

"Try to make abdominal exercises like the ones we did today part of your and your family's routine. Challenge them to a steal the puck competition."

--- And the Beat Goes On ---

Fitness—cardiovascular strength

Skills	Activity Level	Intensity	Standards
Cardiovascular awareness, increasing heart rate	Everyone is involved; half are involved in Ups and Downs game.	Low to medium to high	② ③ ④ ⑤ ⑥

Invitation

"Something inside us keeps us living. It's like our engine and battery. It's our heart. Let's experiment with what our heart is about."

Equipment

20 cones

Description

Invite participants to feel their heartbeats. Take the participants through a brief journey of the body at work.

- "Find your heart; it is on the left side of your chest."
- "Feel your heart beat."
- "Find your pulse. You can find it in your neck, the carotid artery, or in your wrist, the radial artery."
- "Count the beats for 6 seconds when I say, 'Go' (grades 3 and up); place a 0 at the end of that number." (Students in lower grades should just feel it beating slowly.)
- "This is your starting pulse rate."
- "Let's see what happens when we move."
- "Walk in place, moderately, for 30 seconds."
- "Stop, check your heart rate. Ready, find your pulse. Count." (Have them count for 6 seconds.)
- "Did you have more beats than you did when you started? If so, it is because your legs were pumping blood and oxygen through your heart."
- "Now, let's play a quick game of Ups and Downs." (Place 10 cones on their sides and 10 cones standing upright. The object is for an Up team to set up all the cones and for the Down team to knock down all the cones with their hands.)
  - Half of the class watch for 1 minute, while the other half play the game.
  - After 1 minute, allow the Ups to switch with the Downs. After 1 more minute, allow the group watching a chance to play. Then switch again, allowing the Ups and Downs to switch jobs.
  - After each 1-minute trial, have students check their pulses.
- "Feel your heart rate now."

Setup

Look first; rearrange if necessary; put it back together. Place 10 cones down and 10 cones up for the game.

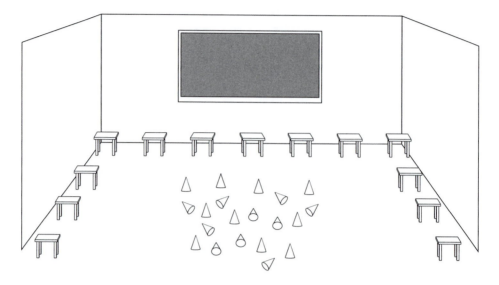

Break It Down in Detail

Lesson plans and in-depth information follow.

Objectives

- ☙ Students realize where the heart is located.
- ☙ Students locate places on the body to feel a heart rate.
- ☙ Students realize ways to increase their heart rate.
- ☙ Students check their pulse and calculate their heart rate (grades 3 through 8).
- ☙ Students participate in exercises of various intensity levels and relate the intensity to physiological effects.

Warm-Up

Skip the formal warm-up so that students can feel a resting heart rate.

Cues and Concepts

Carry out the activities using the following cues:

- ☙ Find your pulse—find your heart, carotid pulse, or radial pulse.
- ☙ Count—count the beats of the pulse in a 6-second period.

Include the following concepts:

- ☙ What happened when you played the Ups and Downs game? Your heart rate increased with activity that was more vigorous.
- ☙ As your heart rate increased you had more beats of your heart.
- ☙ You can increase your beats even more by playing longer or harder.
- ☙ Giving your heart exercise is important. We should try to increase our heart rate every day! We can do fun games to make it happen.
- ☙ What is preactivity heart rate? It is a heart rate that is low, before starting an activity.

Assessment

Rubric

3 = Attempted all tasks with best effort; attempted to find heart rate after each task

2 = Attempted all tasks but didn't try hard with all of them; attempted to find heart rate after each task

1 = Attempted most tasks but didn't try hard with most of them; attempted to find heart rate after each task

0 = Made little or no attempt at the tasks; may or may not have attempted to find heart rate after each task

Safety

Allow only half the class to participate in Ups and Downs so that students don't collide with one another.

Tips and Variations

- Allow a few students to feel your pulse after exercise. The students enjoy involving their teacher in learning. Students who cannot find their pulse may be able to locate it by feeling your pulse.
- If K through 2 students are ready to find their pulse, teach them the locations and reasons that they feel it at the wrist and neck.
- As an extension, describe how you count your pulse with a 10-second count (multiply by 6). Also, perform a 30-second count (multiply by 2). Explain that for efficiency, we use the **6-second pulse check** (grades 3 through 8).

Conclusion and Links to Real Life

"Because you know that increasing your heart rate with exercise is a healthy thing to do, start thinking about what you can do every day. You now know how to check your heart rate to see whether the exercise is high intensity, medium, or low."

Try at Home

"Plan a month's worth of activities that increase the heart rate for you and your family to do each day. The activities can be long or short, but be sure to make them fun!"

- - - Circuit Training - - -

Fitness—cardiovascular, strength, flexibility conditioning

Skills	Activity Level	Intensity	Standards
Cardiovascular endurance, strengthening, stretching	Everyone is involved, actively.	High	① ② ④ ⑤ ⑥

Invitation

"People often work out by doing a cardiovascular activity first and then strength-building activities. There is another option that will condition your body as well as keep your cardiovascular system working throughout the whole workout. Keeping your heart rate up for a longer period has many benefits. One way to do that is by circuit training. Circuit training is a fun way to keep your cardiovascular system working as you are strengthening or stretching."

Equipment

- CD player and CD with upbeat music
- Other equipment, depending on which stations you choose (beanbags if you choose Curl Up and Steal the Puck)

Description

Participants work in a group at a station for 3 minutes. When the participants hear music, they move to the center of the room and follow you in a 2-minute cardiovascular session. After 2 minutes, turn the music off to signal them to move to the next station to their right from where they left off. Doing this sequence of activities will keep their heart rates up for a 25-minute period while they also work on strengthening and stretching. Working at five stations will take approximately 25 minutes. Add more stations if you have longer than 30 minutes to work with.

Ideas for the Cardiovascular Sessions

- Do a knee raise and kick 8 times to the right and then switch to the left.
- Do a front kick and a back kick, and then punch 1, 2, 3. Repeat 16 times.
- Do jumping jacks.
- Jog in place.
- Walk fast in place.
- Hit a speed bag with the arms (imagine hitting a speed bag or small punching bag that springs back quickly after you hit it with your fists as fast as you can).

Ideas for Stations

- Crunches
- Curl Up and Steal the Puck (see page 45). Participants are foot to foot, in curl-up position. On a signal, they curl up quickly and attempt to steal the object (puck or beanbag), which is between the partners' feet.
- Push-Up Hockey (see page 38). Participants are in push-up position. They attempt to push the object (puck or beanbag) through the arms of the partner.
- Push-ups.
- Stretching:
  - Inside hurdle stretch
  - Zipper stretch
  - Sit and reach, or V-sit stretch

Setup

Look first; rearrange if necessary; put it back together.

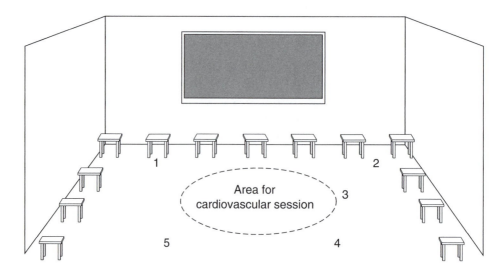

Break It Down in Detail

Lesson plans and in-depth information follow.

Objectives

- Students participate for at least a 25-minute period, keeping their heart rates elevated.
- Students strengthen their bodies by performing strengthening activities at the stations.
- Students increase their flexibility by performing flexibility activities at the stations.
- Students realize the importance for strengthening, stretching, and increasing the heart rate during exercise.

Warm-Up

Thumb Jack Wrestling or Rock, Paper, Scissors—Action

Cues and Concepts

Carry out the activities using the following cue:

- Do your best. When working in fitness stations, you have to work to your own best ability, not anyone else's.

Include the following concepts:

- Our heart rates should increase during exercise to work the heart muscle. We should try to increase our heart rates by exercising every day, if we can. Daily exercise keeps us healthier.
- Stretching our muscles and joints will help our bodies move more freely, with greater range of motion. We should stretch every day.
- Strengthening our bodies helps our muscles, bones, and posture. Being strong will help us do more activities safely and live stronger and longer.

Assessment

Rubric

3 = Participated with best effort

2 = Attempted most tasks with best effort

1 = Attempted all tasks but didn't try hard with all tasks

0 = Did not attempt most tasks

Safety

Students should do flexibility and strengthening activities only according to your direction. Before starting, demonstrate the activities as you go through the descriptions of the tasks for each station. Students must be able to follow your directions and stay on task.

Tips and Variations

- Make the time for the cardio portion fun, yet challenging. We want students to love to come to the center for a cardio workout! Your music should be upbeat and something that the students love to hear.
- If students are dragging to the cardio portion, try to cut down the time.
- If students are dragging out to the stations, give them challenges that are more personal, like standards listed on a poster for the V-sit (sit and reach stretch), push-ups, or curl-ups.

Conclusion and Links to Real Life

"When you all are older, I hope you'll keep doing some kind of training like this one. There are many gyms and workout centers that adults can go to. I hope you will continue to work out, somehow, every day, and always."

Try at Home

"Check out what the adults in your life do to stay fit. Ask to visit their gym. If they don't do anything, show them how they could work out at home."

- - - Cruise the American Border - - -
Fitness—cardiovascular

Skills	Activity Level	Intensity	Standards
Cardiovascular fitness, fitness with technology	Everyone is actively involved.	Medium to high	② ③ ④ ⑤ ⑥

Invitation

"Have you ever wondered what it would be like to walk around America? Let's start stepping around the coast and border of the United States. Using **pedometers,** let's measure how far we would have traveled around the coast and borders of America."

Equipment

- Pedometers
- Cruise the American Border sheet

Description

Participants can do this as a club (in which you invite students to belong to an activity that occurs repeatedly, every month for example), as a warm-up, or as a lesson. Participants walk, jump, and move, according to your directions, to accumulate steps.

- Record participants' step counts and convert into mileage. Record the mileage as amounts that will allow them to visit certain states around the border of America.
- Award a state for each 100 steps that they accumulate.
- Have rest stops every 3 minutes. The participants will have a fellow student initial in the corresponding square the states that they have visited. With younger students, you can verify the states and mileage. Every 3 minutes you can verify half the class with your initials, and you can verify the other half at the next 3-minute rest period. Every 6 minutes you will have verified each participant's state checklist.
- Start in Maryland and work your way down and back around the country until you end up in Delaware. You can make the hike more exciting by providing narration about the states, as in the following example:
  - Normal hike—walk in place.
  - Yikes, avoid the crabs in Maryland—hop quickly from left to right.
  - Climb a mountain in Virginia—lift your knees high.
  - Swim down the banks of North Carolina—swim with the arms as if swimming the crawl, lie on your back and kick your legs up and down.
  - Jump for the peaches in the trees in Georgia—jump.
  - Hopscotch jump in the Florida Keys—hopscotch.
  - Take big gigantic steps around the room in Texas.

Cruise the American Border

1 100 Maryland	**2** 200 Virginia	**3** 300 North Carolina	**4** 400 South Carolina
5 500 Georgia	**6** 600 Florida	**7** 700 Alabama	**8** 800 Mississippi
9 900 Louisiana	**10** 1,000 Texas	**11** 1,100 New Mexico	**12** 1,200 Arizona
13 1,300 California	**14** 1,400 Oregon	**15** 1,500 Washington	**16** 1,600 Idaho
17 1,700 Montana	**18** 1,800 North Dakota	**19** 1,900 Minnesota	**20** 2,000 Wisconsin
21 2,100 Illinois	**22** 2,200 Indiana	**23** 2,300 Michigan	**24** 2,400 Ohio
25 2,500 Pennsylvania	**26** 2,600 New York	**27** 2,700 Vermont	**28** 2,800 New Hampshire
29 2,900 Maine	**30** 3,000 Massachusetts	**31** 3,100 Rhode Island	**32** 3,200 Connecticut
33 3,300 New Jersey	**34** 3,400 Delaware	**Congratulations!** You made it around the border of the United States.	

From *No Gym? No Problem! Physical Activities for Tight Spaces* by Charmain Sutherland, 2006, Champaign, IL: Human Kinetics.

- Mexican jumping beans on the border of New Mexico—jump.
- Arizona—leap over the Grand Canyon.
- Surf in California—jump sideways, as if on a surfboard.
- Run in place fast through Washington—it's a little cold.
- It's windy in Illinois—twirl around.
- Catch a show or a game in New York—imitate your favorite star or sports figure.
- It's chilly in Maine—skip briskly.
- Cruise down the Jersey turnpike—as you are driving speed up or slow down to pass safely through traffic.

⮠ Narrate and change the **locomotor** patterns anytime you want. If you know that several people are approaching a certain state, you may want to perform an action corresponding to that state. You may have to move throughout the room to accommodate students who are ahead or behind the majority.

Setup

Look first; rearrange if necessary; put it back together. No rearranging is necessary.

Break It Down in Detail

Lesson plans and in-depth information follow.

Objectives

⮠ Students keep moving to reach a goal.

⮠ Students realize how far they actually walk while their bodies are in motion.

⮠ Students use technology to measure activity.

⮠ Students use their imagination to exercise so that they can reach a goal.

Warm-Up

Step and Scream

Cues and Concepts

Carry out the activities using the following cues:

⮠ Every moment and movement counts. As long as you are moving, it makes a difference—just see the proof on the pedometer.

⮠ Don't shake it. If you shake the pedometer, you are cheating. I'll take it from you.

Include the following concepts:

⮠ Technology helps us measure activity more accurately.

⮠ Recommendations are to step between 8,000 and 10,000 steps per day to stay healthy.

⮠ The pedometer can help us to see how active we really are.

Links to other subject matter:

⮠ Social studies, history, United States geography

⮠ Math—addition

Assessment

Rubric

3 = Walked as much as possible; eager to walk from state to state

2 = Walked enough to make it through several states

1 = Walked casually but not with a purpose to reach the goal

0 = Walked slowly, without desire to accomplish the task

Safety

Students should stay in their personal space.

Tips and Variations

⮠ The excitement of seeing yourself accomplish a goal is the best. When your students see that they have reached from one state to another, they will feel a great sense of accomplishment. Have them celebrate with a scream or cheer each time they cross the border into a new state.

- ☙ Talk about each state, and if you know some history, share it. You can go into detail about important people associated with the state, what the state is famous for, and how far it is from your home state.

Conclusion and Links to Real Life

"Do you think that you could walk 10,000 steps a day? Try it. Pedometers are available free from many well-known companies and even from some cereal companies. You can buy inexpensive pedometers at Kmart, Wal-Mart, Sports Authority, and most sports stores. It was exciting to see you move from state to state. We can try this again or even travel out of the United States into other countries."

Try at Home

"See how many steps it takes you to walk around your neighborhood. How about around your house? Can you reach 10,000 steps per day?"

- - - Intensity Investigations - - -
Fitness—intensity, fitness awareness

Skills	Activity Level	Intensity	Standards
Cardiovascular endurance, intensity of exercise	Everyone is involved.	Medium to high	② ③ ④ ⑤ ⑥

Invitation

"If you wanted to stay strong and give your heart and body some good exercise, do you know what you would do? If you only had a small amount of time, what exercise would you choose to get your heart rate up? Let's investigate."

Equipment

- ☙ Six pedometers (or participants could count steps or laps walked)
- ☙ Yardsticks, rulers, or a marked measurement to measure the long jump and jump and reach
- ☙ CD player and music (upbeat)
- ☙ Two marked lines, **polyspots,** or cones, placed between 6 feet (2 meters) and 10 feet (3 meters) apart depending on the space available, for the pacer jump

Description

Participants work in groups of four to six. They experience various levels of exercise intensity at each station. At each station they record their heart rate (with a 6-second pulse check) and the physiological effects that they can observe. Play energetic music.

Station 1: Jumping

- ☙ Participants do the jump and reach (reach arm up and mark the height; jump upward and mark the highest spot reached; measure the distance) and the long jump. They try to improve each jump, each time.
- ☙ On the assessment, this would be a moderately intense exercise.

Station 2: Pacer Jump

- Participants jump from one line to the other every 10 seconds (jumping or hopping is OK). Lines are parallel, 6 feet (2 meters) apart. They try to see how many times they can make it from one line to the other before they fail to cross the line in time.
- On the assessment, this would be a vigorous, high-intensity exercise.

Station 3: Stretching and Flexibility

- Participants perform arm and leg stretches. Show or display some of the exercises that participants should do. Explain that they should hold each stretch for 10 to 20 seconds.
- On the assessment, this would be a low-intensity exercise.

Station 4: Step Relay

- Participants put on a pedometer and attempt to walk with a partner in relay form. One partner walks in place, while the other walks to the front of the room, touches the wall, and then comes back and tags the partner's hand so that the partner may walk to the front and repeat the relay. They walk as many steps as they can.
- On the assessment, this station would be moderate-intensity exercise.

Station 5: Strength and Strengthening

- Participants perform 1 minute of curl-ups. They use the **President's Challenge** form: A partner holds the feet, while the person doing the curl-ups bends the knees, places the hands across the chest, curls up so that the elbows hit the thighs, and then returns the shoulders to the floor. They switch after each minute.
- Participants perform as many push-ups as they can in the time remaining, after the 1 minute of curl-ups.
- On the assessment, this would be a moderate-intensity exercise but focused on strength rather than cardiovascular endurance.

Assessment

1. Record your heart rate before we start doing any activity. This is our preactivity heart rate. _____ (feel for 6 seconds and add a 0)
2. Record your heart rate on the assessment sheet and circle whether you think the activity was a high-, moderate-, or low-intensity exercise. Then circle what physiological effects you felt.

Setup

Look first; rearrange if necessary; put it back together.

Break It Down in Detail

Lesson plans and in-depth information follow.

Objectives

- Students distinguish between high-, moderate-, and low-intensity exercises.
- Students connect the physiological effects of exercise to the intensity of the exercise.
- Students collect data from the experiences that will help them make good choices for themselves and their health now and in the future.

Warm-Up

Students should not warm up before answering question #1 on the assessment. After question #1, they should do simple stretches because you don't want to interfere with the heart rate at each of the stations.

Station 1: Jumping

Heart rate: _____

Intensity: High   Medium   Low

Physiological effects: Sweaty   Cold   Shaky   Hot

Station 2: Pacer Jump

6–10 feet

Heart rate: _____

Intensity: High   Medium   Low

Physiological effects: Sweaty   Cold   Shaky   Hot

Station 3: Stretching and Flexibility

Heart rate: _____

Intensity: High   Medium   Low

Physiological effects: Sweaty   Cold   Shaky   Hot

Station 4: Step Relay

Heart rate: _____

Intensity: High   Medium   Low

Physiological effects: Sweaty   Cold   Shaky   Hot

Station 5: Strength and Strengthening

Heart rate: _____

Intensity: High   Medium   Low

Physiological effects: Sweaty   Cold   Shaky   Hot

From *No Gym? No Problem! Physical Activities for Tight Spaces* by Charmain Sutherland, 2006, Champaign, IL: Human Kinetics.

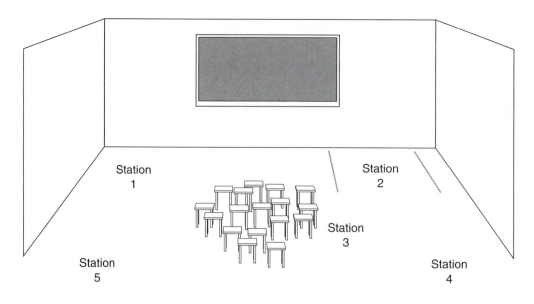

Station 1

Station 2

Station 3

Station 5

Station 4

Cues and Concepts

Carry out the activities using the following cues:

- ⑤ Feel—how you are feeling after exercise is a physiological effect.
- ⑤ Work hard—exercise so that your body is working with great effort.

Include the following concepts:

- ⑤ Intensity is how hard the activity is or how hard it makes you work.
- ⑤ Physiological effects include how you feel (hot, cold, sweaty) and what happens to your body (shaky, sweats). These effects are the benefits of exercising.

Assessment

Rubric

3 = Participated in all stations and tasks with best effort

2 = Participated in all stations; attempted to work hard at most tasks

1 = Participated in all stations; attempted to work hard at some of them

0 = Participated in all or some stations; did not work hard at all of them

Safety

Students must follow your demonstrated examples and stick to the designated tasks.

Tips and Variations

- ⑤ Students should realize that working hard and feeling the physiological effects of exercise is good for them, not bad. A little discomfort is good for the body. Sometimes students think that they are injured or sick, but they must come to understand the real meaning of beneficial physiological effects.
- ⑤ Younger students can display their response to the physiological effects on the assessment by raising their hands.

Conclusion and Links to Real Life

"You will have many opportunities to play and do activities in the future! Some of you will play sports, maybe even be in the Olympics, and some of you may choose to be less active. You have had experiences that will help you choose healthy activities. I hope you will enjoy them and include them in your life."

Try at Home

"Choose a sport or activity. Break down some of the things that you can do to get better at the sport or activity. Think about which ones are high or low intensity. If you would like to play basketball better, you might dribble, play catch, shoot baskets, or run sprints or laps. Running would be the highest intensity."

- - - Jump Start Your Heart - - -
Fitness—cardiovascular endurance

Skills	Activity Level	Intensity	Standards
Cardiovascular endurance	Everyone is involved in counting and running.	High and low	① ② ④

Invitation

"Let's jump right into high gear and find out how strong our heart and cardiovascular system is."

Equipment

- Noise maker—whistle, bell, hand clap, drum, or other item
- Optional—**Fitnessgram** (a physical fitness assessment program), a CD for the proper cadence, or *Physical Education Sound Tracks* by Charles Corbin

Description

Participants work in groups of six or eight. This activity is similar to the **Pacer Test,** the cardiovascular test from the Fitnessgram program. Three or four people jump or hop 6 to 10 feet (2 to 3 meters) from one line to a second line. The same participants stop, stand behind the second line, and wait for the signal to jump or hop back across to the other line. Your signals are 8 seconds apart. Participants try to do this as many times as possible, until they can no longer keep up with the pace of your signals.

- Divide into groups of six to eight. Half jump, while the other half count and record how many times their partners can cross the line in time.
- Depending on your participants' ability to comprehend, they can record the score on the Jump Start Your Heart Chart by checking each successful jump. Alternatively, they can just count each successful jump across in their heads. If possible, use the chart!
- When a jumper can no longer keep up, he or she stops and walks in place next to the person who was counting or scoring for him or her.
- After 25 signals, stop. Allow the partners some time to discuss their scores and switch positions.
- Goals for K through grade 2 could be to make 12 jumps; for grades 3 through 5, 16 jumps; and for grades 6 through 8, 20 jumps.
- Participants keep the Jump Start Your Heart Chart to take home and brag about.
- Keep a record for yourself, so that when you revisit this activity you can show the participants how much they have improved.

Setup

Look first; rearrange if necessary; put it back together.

Jump Start Your Heart Chart

Name:

1	2	3	4	5
6	7	8	9	10
11	12	13	14	15
16	17	18	19	20
21	22	23	24	25

From *No Gym? No Problem! Physical Activities for Tight Spaces* by Charmain Sutherland, 2006, Champaign, IL: Human Kinetics.

Break It Down in Detail

Lesson plans and in-depth information follow.

Objectives

- Students **pace** themselves to endure as long as possible while performing a cardiovascular activity.
- Students jump or hop to work the cardiovascular system.
- Students pace themselves to reach a cardiovascular goal.
- Students follow procedures to assess themselves and others.

Warm-Up

Exercard Battle or Exerdice 100

Cues and Concepts

Carry out the activities using the following cues:
- Pace yourself—move at a speed that will allow you to continue for a long time without wearing out, yet is not too slow.
- Feet together—if you are jumping, your feet must stick together as if they were glued together.
- One leg only—if you are hopping, you must choose one leg to hop on, while the other leg stays out of the way.

Include the following concepts:
- The more you pace, the longer you can keep going.
- Using too much energy too fast will exhaust the muscles.
- Get to the line in time. If you do not make it, you must end the test.
- The more cardiovascular work you do, the stronger your heart and muscles will become.
- Principle of progression: If we increase the number of laps that we do, we will increase our cardiovascular endurance.

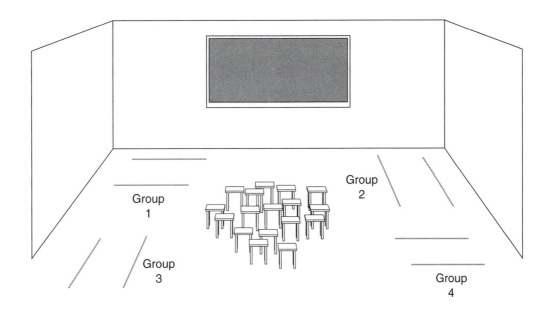

Assessment

Rubric

3 = Participated with best effort; made it past the goal

2 = Participated with best effort; made it to the goal

1 = Participated in jumping; tried to meet the goal

0 = Jumped very little; didn't attempt to meet the goal

Safety

Everyone should respect the space of other jumpers. Partners should stay off to the side, out of the way of the jumpers.

Tips and Variations

- ◉ This activity is much harder than it sounds. A quick exaggerated demonstration from you will give the students the idea that they should attempt to pace themselves.
- ◉ Use any type of locomotor pattern that you like instead of jumping.
- ◉ For grades 5 through 8, permit the students to keep going if they pass 25 signals (if time allows).

Conclusion and Links to Real Life

"You can see how much energy it takes to jump. You found out how to pace yourself so that you can keep jumping for a long time or to meet a goal. Pacing is important in running, working out, playing, and even watching television. We have to plan how we spend our time and how much energy we use or save. Pacing is important throughout our whole life."

Try at Home

"Limit your TV watching and video gaming time to 1 hour today. Figure out how you will pace yourself. Maybe you'll decide which show you really want to watch. You'll also have to talk to the people in your home to figure out who wants to watch or use the TV and when."

--- Noodle and Chair Workout ---
Fitness—flexibility, strength

Skills	Activity Level	Intensity	Standards
Strength training, muscle awareness, flexibility	Everyone is actively involved.	Medium	② ④ ⑥

Invitation

"If we can't get outside and can't use the gym or a big room to move around in, we'll have to use our noodle. That's right! We'll literally use our noodle, not just the noodle we call our brains. We will use the chair and the foam noodle to work our muscles!"

Equipment

- One foam pool noodle per person
- CD player and CD with one slow song for stretching and cooling down and several upbeat songs for the strengthening and cardiovascular exercises

Description

Everyone has a noodle and a chair or chair–desk combination. Participants follow your directions as you call out the muscles and then describe and demonstrate how to work them.

Stretching

- Latissimus dorsi, trapezius, deltoids, **obliques,** biceps, and triceps. This stretch, called the *ray of sunshine,* stretches all those muscles. Participants take the noodle above the head with both hands and keep the arms straight. They lean sideways to the left for 10 seconds and then sideways to the right, stretching the obliques and shoulders.
- Hamstrings, lower back. This stretch, called *foot creepers,* stretches the hamstrings and lower back. Students place the noodle under one foot and hold the ends with their hands. They keep the leg almost straight and slowly try to inch down the noodle toward the foot. They change legs after 20 seconds.

Strengthening

- Deltoids. To do *arm circles,* students hold the arms straight out to the sides. They circle 16 times forward and 16 times backward, using a small 5-inch (12-centimeter) circle. Then they repeat with a larger 10-inch (25-centimeter) circle.
- Trapezius. To do *I don't knows,* students shrug the shoulders up and then down again. They shrug right and then left. Use this exercise intermittently to break up the intense strengthening exercises.
- Abdominals. To do *chair crunches,* participants hold the seat of a chair while sitting in it. They lift both knees up toward the chest, hold for 2 seconds, and let them down.
- Quadriceps and abdominals. To do *seat extensions,* students hold the seat of a chair while sitting in it. With the abdomen pulled in, they keep the legs out straight, parallel to the ground, and hold for 1 minute. They repeat three times.
- Quads, abs, hamstrings. To do *bicycles,* students pedal a bike for 1 minute while holding the seat of the chair and sitting in it.
- Balance. To do the *noodle balance,* participants place the noodle on the floor and put one foot on the noodle. They balance with one knee bent and both arms on the head for 30 seconds and then switch legs.

- Cardiovascular. To do the *noodle jump rope,* students use the noodle as a jump rope.
- Cardiovascular. To do *noodle skiing,* students jump over the noodle while it's on the ground, from left to right, progressing forward to the end. They return by turning around and skiing to the other end of the noodle.
- Cardiovascular. To do *noodle tinikling,* three people work together. Two people hold the ends of their noodles on the floor. They tap them on the floor twice, 1 foot (30 centimeters) apart, and then lift them together and tap twice. The third person attempts to jump in and out of the space between the two noodles. Participants switch places after 1 minute of jumping.
- Flexibility. To do the *limbo,* two people hold the noodle while the third bends backward to go under it. They change positions each time someone gets through.
- Cool-down. To do *no's,* students slowly turn their heads from right to left, as if saying, "No."
- Cool-down. Have students do *ray of sunshine* and *foot creepers.*

Setup

Look first; rearrange if necessary; put it back together when finished. No need for much setup, if any.

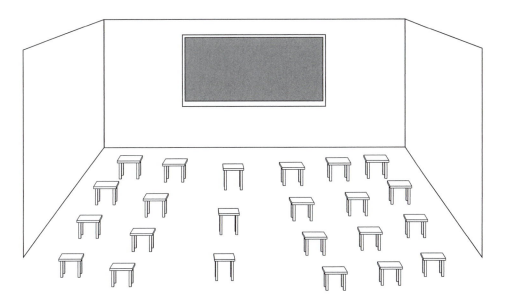

Break It Down in Detail

Lesson plans and in-depth information follow.

Objectives

- Students strengthen muscles by using innovative techniques.
- Students stretch muscles and joints by creative means.
- Students realize fitness possibilities instead of limitations.

Warm-Up

Warm-Up Bingo or Fit Tic-Tac-Toe

Cues and Concepts

Carry out the activities using the following cues:

- Use your own space—it is tempting to poke or strike someone with your noodle, but keep your noodle to yourself.
- Focus on fitness—although working with the noodle is fun, focus on the task that you should be doing.

Include the following concepts:

- Remind students to hold the stretches still and not to bounce.
- Explain the difference between cardiovascular, strengthening, and flexibility exercises.
- Ask students to tell you what fitness exercises are included in the activities.

Assessment

Rubric

3 = Tried all exercises and activities; used the noodle safely

2 = Attempted all exercises or activities; lacked some focus with the noodle

1 = Attempted some exercises or activities; didn't practice safety and spatial awareness

0 = Didn't attempt many exercises or activities; didn't practice safety and spatial awareness

Safety

Students must control the noodles and use them properly. Show students the proper use of noodles.

Tips and Variations

- Playing with noodles is just plain fun. We like them in the pool, and they serve us well in physical education activities. Use the phrase "Use your noodle, don't lose your noodle" to keep kids on track.
- Ask students if they have ideas of how to use noodles for a stretch or exercise. Try their innovative idea with the noodles or chairs.

Conclusion and Links to Real Life

"As you have seen today, we can work on our cardiovascular, strength, and flexibility fitness in many ways. Today we used a pool noodle and chair. We can always find a way to exercise, and if we think about it, we can make it fun too."

Try at Home

"What other unique ways can you think of to work your muscles and cardiovascular system? Think about how we took the noodle out of the pool and created a unique way to work our muscles. After you create a new way to work your muscles, show us after you have practiced it."

- - - Step Club - - -

Fitness—cardiovascular

Skills	Activity Level	Intensity	Standards
Cardiovascular fitness, fitness with technology	Everyone is involved actively.	High to medium	② ③ ④ ⑥

Invitation

"Have you ever thought about how much you really walk, or move your legs? Let's challenge ourselves and find out."

Equipment

- Pedometers
- Awards—beads, certificates, ribbons, tokens

Description

Participants can do this as a club (in which they revisit the activity several times), as a warm-up, or as a lesson. Participants walk and record their progress. You can keep a master record of steps accumulated. Participants aim to accumulate as many steps as possible. They can add to the total throughout the year. Reward students for steps accumulated with small tokens, like beads or certificates, or with some type of recognition, like their names on a wall.

When to Do It

- Do this for a warm-up for 5 minutes, every time you are stuck inside.
- Do this as a club, every week.
- Do this as a monthly activity.

Recognition

- Award beads, certificates, or ribbons for progress
  - Red = 1,500 steps; 0.5 miles (0.8 kilometers)
  - Blue = 3,000 steps; 1 mile (1.6 kilometers)
  - Yellow = 4,500 steps; 1.5 miles (2.4 kilometers)
  - Green = 6,000 steps; 2 miles (3.2 kilometers)
  - Purple = 9,000 steps; 3 miles (4.8 kilometers)
  - Keep the challenges going with increments of one-half mile and mile markers. Award every half-mile and mile achievement.
- Recognize participants in a newsletter, marquee, bulletin board, or school announcements.
- Record participants' step counts as mileage.

Name	Sept.	Oct.	Nov.	Dec.	Jan.	Feb.	Mar.	Apr.	May	Jun.

From *No Gym? No Problem! Physical Activities for Tight Spaces* by Charmain Sutherland, 2006, Champaign, IL: Human Kinetics.

Setup

Look first; rearrange if necessary; put it back together. No rearranging necessary.

Break It Down in Detail

Lesson plans and in-depth information follow.

Objectives

- Students participate in walking activities for health, enjoyment, and challenge.
- Students use technology to measure physical activity more accurately.
- Students choose to participate regularly in walking activities.

Warm-Up

Step and Scream or Find the Leader

Cues and Concepts

Include the following concepts:

- Use technology to measure physical activity. Count the steps to see how far you get.
- Personal best: This is your body and your physical goal. No one matters but you, because you take care of your own goals, challenges, and body.
- If walking becomes boring, create a fun way to reach your goal. Change locomotor patterns, talk to a friend, or use your imagination.

Assessment

Rubric

3 = Participated with best effort, as often as possible

2 = Participated on a regular basis

1 = Did not participate on a regular basis

0 = Did not participate

Student Assessment

- Students monitor their own progress.
- Keep a record of the students' scores.

Safety

Students should be aware of others and immovable objects in the classroom.

Tips and Variations

- Belonging to a club is cool at all ages. Promote the club! Whether you do this activity as a warm-up, class, or club, stress its benefits.
- Increase or decrease the number of steps or landmarks to fit your students' needs. If they need more encouragement, decrease the number of steps required to earn the first award. If the goals are too easy, redesign the number to challenge the students.

Conclusion and Links to Real Life

"How did you do in the club today? Any stepping and moving is better than no moving! What is your goal for next time?"

Try at Home

"Have you ever thought about creating a step club at home? Create one with your friends at home or recess. Maybe your family will be up to the challenge too."

- - - Tae Bo, Pilates, and Yoga - - -

Fitness—cardiovascular, strength, flexibility conditioning

Skills	Activity Level	Intensity	Standards
Cardiovascular endurance, strengthening, stretching	Everyone is active.	High, medium, and low	② ③ ④

Invitation

"Someone will always be discovering a newer, better way to work out. You will often see these advertised on TV. The adults you know may go to a gym to do a workout. They may have videos that they work out with too."

Equipment

- TV, video player or DVD player
- Video or DVD
  - Tae Bo, as presented by Billy Blanks or others
  - Pilates, as presented by Denise Austin or others
  - Yoga, as presented by Denise Austin or others

Description

Participants work individually, following along with a video or with you as the leader. Participants leave you with a much better understanding of current trends in fitness and what each workout will do for their health and fitness.

- Tae Bo—Total-body workout. Cardiovascular, strength training, flexibility. High energy. Kids get excited about working out with Tae Bo because of the kicking and punching.
- Pilates—Working from the core. Strengthening and lengthening muscles.
- Yoga—Strengthening and stretching.

Setup

Look first; rearrange if necessary; put it back together.

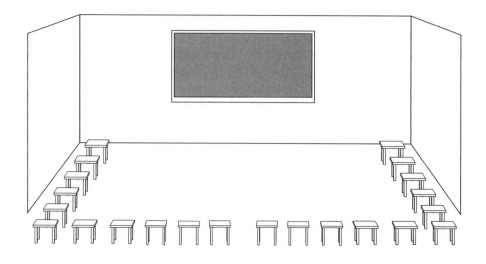

Break It Down in Detail

Lesson plans and in-depth information follow.

Objective

Students participate in high-intensity cardiovascular, stretching, and strengthening workouts.

Warm-Up

Warm-ups are typically included in videos and should take up about 3 minutes of the workout time.

Cues and Concepts

Carry out the activities using the following concepts:

- How intensely are you working? Check your heart rate.
- **Isometric holds and balances,** in which we hold our muscles in a still position for a long time, strengthen the muscles of the body even though we are not lifting weights or moving weight.
- We are strong when our core is strong. Our core is our abdominals and obliques. When we do almost any activity, our abdominals and obliques are involved.
- Ask the students if they know which muscles they are working.

Assessment

Rubric

3 = Participated with best effort

2 = Participated in all exercises

1 = Participated in most exercises

0 = Participated in few or none of the exercises

Safety

Make sure that the students know how to do the moves safely. If you know that your students are not familiar with an exercise, discuss it before performing it.

Tips and Variations

- Whether students are following you as the leader or a video, they will enjoy working out if you keep it interesting. If exercise is boring, students will drop out. Offer variety and keep up with safe trends to maintain interest.
- Ask students to lead the exercises.
- Have sixth through eighth graders come up with an exercise routine involving cardiovascular, flexibility, and strength training.

Conclusion and Links to Real Life

"It's great to watch professionals on the videos perform exercises, but you did everything that the professional did. If you couldn't do it as long, don't worry. It takes a while to train your body to be able to endure, but as you saw, it is possible. You will get stronger and stay healthier if you work your total body."

Try at Home

"Can you find a workout video on TV, at home, or in the video store? If so, check it out and see if you can keep up. If you don't have one, ask an adult family member to do a total-body workout."

- - - Physactinology = Physical Activity + Technology - - -

Fitness—cardiovascular strength

Skills	Activity Level	Intensity	Standards
Cardiovascular awareness, checking pulse and heart rate with technology, using technology to be more accurate	Everyone is involved at all times (physically involved at least every other minute).	Medium, high	② ④ ⑥

Invitation

"Technology can help us stay healthier. Technology makes many things simpler, faster, and more reliable. Look at how computers have enriched and added excitement to our lives. And what would most of us do without television? We can use technology to measure heart rate in a way that is more reliable than measuring it with our fingers. We can use technological instruments to count our steps and help us measure how far and how long we have traveled."

Equipment

- 20 cones
- Pedometers, stopwatches, or other technology equipment

Description

Select an activity such as Guess the Time, Line Tag, or Ups and Downs to experiment with technology. First, try Guess the Time.

Guess the Time

- ☙ Ask participants to run in place fast. Allow them to run for about 20 seconds.
  - Ask them how long they think they ran. Some will say 2 minutes; some will say 1 minute.
  - Ask them to run again for an amount of time that they think is 20 seconds. They can collaborate with someone and have one person timing and one person running. They can compare their timing to that of a stopwatch.

Line Tag

- ☙ Make a course with tape on the floor or with the desks in the room.

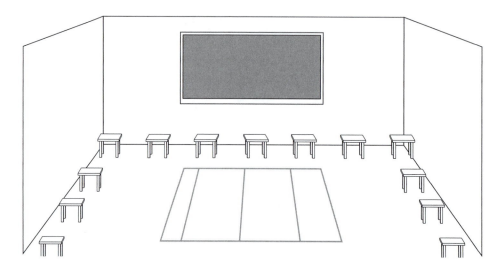

- ☙ Select one person to be "It."
- ☙ "It" is the tagger.
- ☙ If someone is tagged, that person stands on the line where they were tagged.
- ☙ The tagged players may tag anyone that comes near enough to reach.
- ☙ If the tagged player tags someone, they jump up and down in place 10 times.
- ☙ Every time someone is tagged, those previously tagged jump.
- ☙ After the game, ask the participants to tell you how many times they jumped. All will probably say that they don't know.
- ☙ Play again with pedometers. This time they will know how many times they jumped because pedometers will accurately count their movements.
- ☙ Perform these games and allow participants to measure their heart rates with pulse meters, heart rate monitors, or pulse sticks.
  - Pulse meters are worn on the hips like a pedometer.
  - Pulse sticks, which participants hold with their hands to measure their pulse, should be available for students to check in an organized manner (five people go to one pulse stick to check their pulse; they should be in a line to keep it flowing).
  - Students wear heart rate monitors around the chest or wrist.

Ups and Downs

- ☙ Place 10 cones on their sides and 10 cones standing upright. The object is for the Up team to set up all the cones and for the Down team to knock down all the cones.
- ☙ Half of the class watches for 1 minute, while the other half plays the game.
- ☙ After 1 minute, have the Ups switch with the Downs. After 1 minute, allow the group watching a chance to play. Then switch again, allowing the Ups and Downs to switch jobs.

- After each 1-minute trial, check pulses. Use a pulse meter, pulse stick, or the manual method.
- "Feel your heart rate now."
- Have students check the step count before and after the game. Students can try to count the steps and compare their count to the pedometer's count.

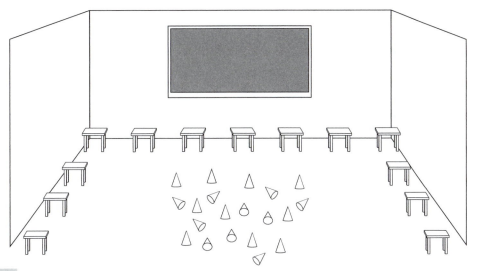

Setup

Look first; rearrange if necessary; put it back together.

- Tape a course or use the desks to make the course.
- Place 10 cones down and 10 cones up for the Ups and Downs game.

Break It Down in Detail

Lesson plans and in-depth information follow.

Objectives

- Students use technology to measure physical activity.
- Students use technology to measure time during physical activity.
- Students use technology to measure heart rate during physical activity.

Warm-Up

Run and Scream or Step and Scream

Cues and Concepts

Carry out the activities using the following cues:

- Check your pulse—check carotid or radial pulse for a 6-second count. Add a 0 to that number to find out how fast the heart is beating for 1 minute.
- Step check—keep the pedometer on and check to see how many steps or jumps you have taken.

Include the following concepts:

- We can measure our physical activity and our heart rate ourselves, but we aren't always as accurate as a machine would be.

- Technology helps us by decreasing the time required to do tasks and by making our data more reliable.
- Can you imagine doing races without a stopwatch? Think about how inconsistent the times would be. People all over the world would suddenly be breaking world records.

Links to other subjects:

- Science—technology
- Math—counting, estimating

Assessment

Rubric

3 = Realized the contribution of technology; worked hard in activities

2 = Realized the contribution of technology; tried all activities

1 = Observed the contribution of technology; participated in some activities

0 = Did not realize the contribution of technology; did not try in most activities

Safety

In Line Tag and Ups and Downs, use the chairs and desks to help with the course, not to hinder it. Make sure that no sharp edges or furniture hazards can potentially injure a student.

Tips and Variations

- Start your class by challenging students to be seated or to stand up within a certain amount of time. As you are looking at a stopwatch and timing the action, students will be eager to please and to see what efficient movers they can be.
- Students in grades 3 and up can handle pedometers and stopwatches. Many K through 2 students can too, but you should make that decision based on your students' prior knowledge and capabilities.
- Your older groups can certainly use heart rate monitors and pulse meters, but if your younger students are ready, get them involved too.

Conclusion and Links to Real Life

"Huddle next to me and focus. How long will it take us to huddle? Ready, go. How long do you think it took us? Well, your guesses are great, but they are guesses. Through our Physactinology lesson today, we realized how we can use technology to help us in physical activity."

Try at Home

"Do the same thing at home that we did in PE class. Here are some ideas for you to use with your family and friends:

- How long will it take us to set the table for dinner?
- Estimate how many steps you can take in 5 minutes, and then do it.
- How fast can you climb the stairs?"

--- It's Up to You ---

Fitness

Skills	Activity Level	Intensity	Standards
Strength training, muscle awareness, flexibility, cardiovascular endurance, being active	Everyone is involved.	Low	② ③ ④

Invitation

"If we want to stay healthy, not get fat, and stay strong, we should try to do activity for at least 60 minutes a day. We don't have PE every day, so what do you guys and girls do on your own to make up the 60 minutes per day? One day you will not have school or a teacher to tell you what to do or to design your activity. Will you be able to design your own workout to stay healthy and meet your activity goal?"

Equipment

- CD and CD player; inspirational music such as *Rocky* ("Eye of the Tiger," by Survivor), "Chariots of Fire" (Vangelis), or the "Olympic Fanfare and Theme" (the last two available on the CD *Summon the Heroes,* by John Williams and the Boston Pops Orchestra)
- Activity calendar

Description

Participants design a month's worth of activity that will help them reach their goals and keep them active for 60 minutes per day.

Ask students to design their goals and activities with the following guidelines in mind:

- Raise your heart rate each day to at least 130 beats per minute.
- Work all areas of the body.
- Try to work the components of fitness into your activities:
  - Cardiovascular endurance, muscular endurance and strength, body composition and nutrition, flexibility
  - Agility, reaction time, speed, balance
- Write a goal statement below the calendar. Read the statement at least once each week to see whether you are on track.
- Perform one jumping jack, one crunch, and one push-up after each completion of the activities for the day.
- Invite another participant to check your activity calendar. He or she should assess the fitness components and evaluate whether the activities are fun and will help you reach your goals.

Setup

Look first; rearrange if necessary; put it back together when finished. No need for any setup.

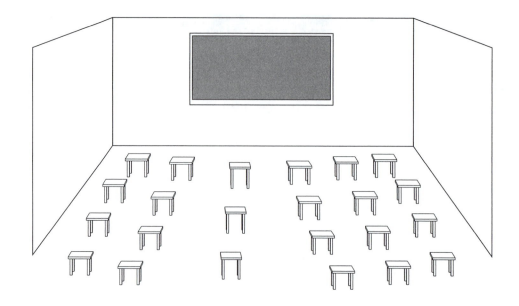

Break It Down in Detail

Lesson plans and in-depth information follow.

Objectives

- ⑤ Students take responsibility for their own fitness and activity level.
- ⑤ Students design a goal and a plan for achieving 60 minutes of activity per day for a month.

Warm-Up

Jacks and Jills Move Cube or Exercard Battle

Cues and Concepts

Carry out the activities using the following cues:

- ⑤ Reach 60 a day—make sure that the activity will last for 60 minutes.
- ⑤ Keep the goal in mind—make your plan with the goal as the reason for everything you do.

Include the following concepts:

- ⑤ Students should consider the excitement level of their plans. They should realize that having fun is what will make them want to keep exercising and stay active. If the activities are not fun for them, they will not have a strong desire to do them.
- ⑤ Use peer assessment. Have students check and critique a fellow student's work.

Assessment

Rubric

3 = Created a calendar based on goals and interesting activities

2 = Created a calendar based on goals and activities

1 = Created a calendar with little attention to goals or interesting activities

0 = Did not finish a calendar

Safety

Check students' activities for safe exercises.

Tips and Variations

- Design your own calendar and show it to the students before they start theirs. Explain why you chose the activities on your calendar. Relate the activities to your goals.
- Younger students can create a calendar as a group, with input from everyone in the class. You write out the calendar. Copy the calendar and distribute it to the students the next time you see them.

Conclusion and Links to Real Life

"You will not always have a teacher or parents that will design and plan activities for you. But now you have the knowledge and tools to be in control of your own fitness."

Try at Home

"Come up with fun activities that you can do over the weekend to equal 60 minutes per day."

Monday	Tuesday	Wednesday	Thursday	Friday	Total time:
Monday	Tuesday	Wednesday	Thursday	Friday	Total time:
Monday	Tuesday	Wednesday	Thursday	Friday	Total time:
Monday	Tuesday	Wednesday	Thursday	Friday	Total time:
My fitness goal is:					

From *No Gym? No Problem! Physical Activities for Tight Spaces* by Charmain Sutherland, 2006, Champaign, IL: Human Kinetics.

Monday	Tuesday	Wednesday	Thursday	Friday
Basketball practice	PE Tag at recess	Ride bike Capture the flag at recess	PE Skating	PE Soccer at recess

From *No Gym? No Problem! Physical Activities for Tight Spaces* by Charmain Sutherland, 2006, Champaign, IL: Human Kinetics.

- - - How Healthy Am I? - - -

Fitness—strength, endurance—assessment

Skills	Activity Level	Intensity	Standards
Upper-body strength, abdominal strength	Active every other minute.	High to low	② ③ ④

Invitation

"Are you strong? Are your muscles strong? Do you think you are healthy? There is only one way to learn how healthy or strong you are. Let's find out."

Equipment

- Fitnessgram, the CD for the proper cadence, or *Physical Fitness Sound Tracks* by Corbin
- Carpet squares or the carpet in a room
- How Healthy Am I? scorecard

Description

Participants test themselves to see how strong they are by performing in a fitness test. Students can use two tests—the President's Challenge physical fitness test or the Fitnessgram test. We will use modifications of both. The participants work with others to find their own level of fitness. Because this activity is intense, use a fun warm-up like Watch the Shoes or Run and Scream.

Participants need a partner, preferably one with abilities similar to their own. They take turns performing and assisting. Hand out a "How Healthy Am I?" scorecard. Students fill this out on their own. The scorecard is theirs to keep and to take home.

Students carry out the fitness test for arm strength and endurance by performing President's Challenge or Fitnessgram push-ups and recording their scores.

- One person is in push-up ready position, with arms straight and body in line (no buttocks in the air or droopy abdomens). The participant must go down to a 90-degree angle and back up. The shoulders must come down so that they are parallel with the elbows. The partner can place his or her hands at the elbow level to ensure that each push-up comes down to the proper angle. Every beat, or every second and a half, participants must do one repetition. If they can no longer keep up and miss twice, they stop and record the score.

- Students perform the fitness tests for abdominal strength and endurance.

    - Perform President's Challenge curl-ups. One person lies on the floor with arms crossed across the chest. The knees are bent, and the feet are flat on the floor, about 12 inches (30 centimeters) from the buttocks. A partner firmly holds the person's feet down. Participants curl up and touch their elbows to their thighs and go back down, at least placing the shoulder blades on the carpet square, as fast as they can, as many times as they can, for 1 minute.

    - Perform Fitnessgram curls. The student lies on the floor with the knees up and feet flat on the floor, about 12 inches (30 centimeters) from the buttocks. Place a strip of thick paper, 3 inches (8 centimeters) wide and 3 feet (90 centimeters) long, under the knees on the floor. The arms are on the floor at the beginning of the strip of paper. The student curls up to the beat, or every second and a half, and reaches to the end of the strip. Then the student lies back down. The student continues until he or she can't keep up and misses the end of the strip twice.

- Fill out the chart according to the student's age. The statistics and standards change frequently, based on national norms. The President's Challenge changes each year.

You can easily find the standards by going online to the President's Council Web site (see "Related Organizations" on page 246). Choose how you want to create your standards and then adjust them as needed. The idea is to create an environment in which students will have an idea of what their fitness level is and will want to improve it.

How Healthy Am I?

Presidential push-ups	Fitnessgram push-ups	Presidential curl-ups	Fitnessgram curls
Check below to see if you match the recommended healthy score for your age.			
ex. 9 years old Boy—15 Girl—14	ex. 9 years old Boy—15 Girl—15	ex. 9 years old Boy—39 Girl—37	ex. 9 years old Boy—34 Girl—35

From *No Gym? No Problem! Physical Activities for Tight Spaces* by Charmain Sutherland, 2006, Champaign, IL: Human Kinetics.

◉ The following are examples, not taken from either publication.
  • For the President's Challenge, participants can try to reach two levels—Presidential, in the top 15%, and National, in the top 50%.
  • In Fitnessgram, participants can see whether their scores fall within a certain **Healthy Fitness Zone.** Check the Fitnessgram Web site for more information.

Setup

Look first; rearrange if necessary; put it back together.

Break It Down in Detail

Lesson plans and in-depth information follow.

Objectives

◉ Students realize and determine their fitness level.
◉ Students measure their fitness level.
◉ Students make choices to maintain or improve their fitness level.

Warm-Up

Run and Scream or Watch the Shoes

Cues and Concepts

Carry out the activities using the following cues:
  ◉ Test yourself—use one of the assessments to see how fit you are.
  ◉ Cross your arms—on the President's Challenge curl-ups, cross your arms across your chest; do not raise them.
Include the following concept:
  ◉ Fitness is for individuals. Individual scores do not matter to anyone but that individual. What is healthy for one person may not be healthy for another. Students should make a plan for what is healthy for them.

Link to math. Students can read the graphs and charts to find a score that meets the average for their age and gender.

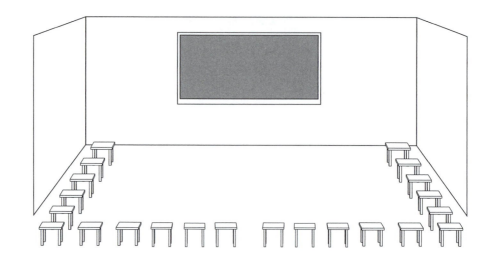

Assessment

Rubric

3 = Participated with best effort

2 = Attempted most tasks with best effort

1 = Attempted all tasks but didn't try hard with all of them

0 = Attempted some tasks but not all of them

Students can use their "How Healthy Am I?" charts as assessments. Allow students to take them home to show their parents.

Safety

Show students the proper techniques for each test and be sure that they follow them.

Tips and Variations

- Pump kids up for fitness. Show them what their goals could be in order to become and stay healthy. One way to do this is to do a test yourself or tell a story of a goal you had in order to stay healthy, and describe what you did to get there.
- Have students participate in the Fitnessgram fitness testing. Use the charts and information provided by Fitnessgram.
- Have students participate in the President's Challenge physical fitness test. Use the charts and information provided by the President's Council.
- Offer incentives for being healthy and setting goals. The President's Council offers awards like patches and certificates. Simple incentives like beads, stickers, and certificates are valuable too.

Conclusion and Links to Real Life

"So, how healthy are you? Could you tell what you need to work on? Where are you strongest and weakest? What is your goal for maintaining or improving your fitness? Now that you know ways of measuring your fitness level, you can maintain it and monitor it yourself."

Try at Home

"Keep your 'How Healthy Am I ?'card handy at home. Do monthly checks to see how you are doing. Make your monthly workout plans according to your body's need for improvement or maintenance."

Movement and Gymnastics

How would I be moving if I placed my right foot down on the ground in front of me and then transferred my weight to the left foot, as it moved alongside and in front of the right? When students can visualize and realize what their bodies are doing in space, and why they are purposely moving this way, they can develop skills that will make them successful in many sports and skill themes. The movement that I was describing was walking. When students can make decisions based on space, relationships, and effort, then they have the building blocks to successful moving. Gymnastics and movement education provide an important link to body awareness and coordination.

--- Classroom Highway ---

Movement—locomotor patterns, directional and spatial awareness

Skills	Activity Level	Intensity	Standards
Spatial awareness, grouping, directional patterns	Everyone is involved actively.	Medium	① ② ⑤ ⑥

Invitation

"Let's head out to the highway! Our classroom has just become a busy highway, full of zooming cars, traffic, and directional signs, and you have a license to drive. The control is all yours! Can you make it through the classroom highway without a crash?"

Equipment

- CD player and CD
- Deck ring or hula hoop for each person

Description

Give each participant a steering wheel (ring, hoop, etc.). On a signal from the music, all drivers start their engines. They respond to your signals and cues. Later they can create maps. Older students can incorporate directions, like east and west, and use keys and mileage in their maps.

Have students decide what color or type of vehicle they are driving.

- Blue, yellow, red, black
- Jeep, Ferrari, motorcycle, Mini

When you call out a vehicle color or type, students respond by performing the appropriate actions. Vary the actions for the different colors and types to get people going in various directions.

- Drive forward.
- Stop.
- Slow—it's rush hour.
- ____ vehicles pass on left (repeat for each vehicle type or color).
- You are home. Reverse and back into a parking space (a desk).

Design a course.

- A beltway (everyone goes around all the desks).
- A town or city (roads go through desks).

____ vehicles get off at certain exits. Participants must do certain actions at each exit.

- Gas—pull off the highway, into a corner, and do 20 push-ups.
- Hungry—go to a McDonald's, but do 40 jumping jacks before returning to the road.
- Rest stop—you need to rest, so lie down and do 30 crunches.
- Flat tire—uh oh, you have to change a tire. Do 30 arm circles, forward, backward, front, and up high.
- Restroom break—jog in place for 1 minute, because there is a line to use the restroom and you really have to go.

Call out these actions.

- Drive through the tunnel—move at a low level, bending your knees to stay low to the ground.
- Drive over a bridge—move at a high level, moving on your toes.
- Bumpy road—jump.

Call out these actions for the different colors and types to get people going in various directions. (Fill in the blanks with the color and type.)

- ⬣ ____ vehicles make a U-turn.
- ⬣ ____ vehicles turn right.
- ⬣ ____ vehicles turn left.
- ⬣ ____ vehicles drive slow (hop).
- ⬣ ____ vehicles drive fast (skip).
- ⬣ ____ vehicles speed (walk briskly weaving in and out of traffic).
- ⬣ ____ vehicles cruise (walk).

Draw directional patterns for certain vehicles to follow on paper: zigzag, curves, circles, straight lines.

Allow the participants to draw maps for each other to follow. Include east, west, south, and north; detours; stop signs; tunnels; waterways.

It's a convoy. On your signal have students do the following (fill in the blanks with the color and type.):

- ⬣ ____ drive forward in a row.
- ⬣ ____ circle behind one another in the roundabout.
- ⬣ ____ drive backward in a row.
- ⬣ ____ weave in and out.

In partners, have one person lead the other by giving directional signals, while the driver has his or her eyes closed. Partners switch after 2 minutes.

- ⬣ Driver should try to avoid collisions.
- ⬣ If a collision occurs, the direction caller gets a warning.
- ⬣ On a second collision, the driver gets a warning.
- ⬣ On a third collision, a ticket is given.
- ⬣ On a fourth collision, the vehicle is totaled, and the driver and caller must sit down and stretch out in their seats.

Setup

Look first; rearrange if necessary; put it back together.

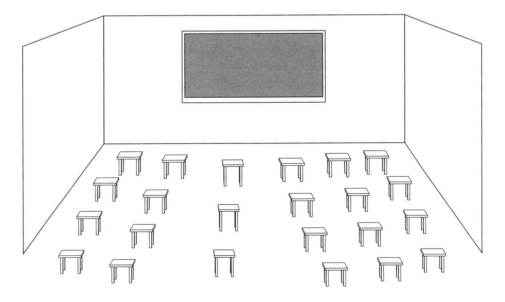

Break It Down in Detail

Lesson plans and in-depth information follow.

Objectives

- Students find clear pathways and design pathways.
- Students work as a team to reach a goal.
- Students use their imaginations as they focus on effort, levels, directions, and spatial awareness.

Warm-Up

Fruit Basket Upset

Cues and Concepts

Carry out activities using the following cues:

- Open spaces—look for open spaces to avoid collisions.
- You are—use your imagination to become the object and act the part.

Include the following concepts:

- Notice the differences in speeds—slow, fast, gradual slowing, quick stops.
- Helping others stay safe is important.
- Foresee potential limitations and possibilities.

Links to social studies: directions, map skills.

Assessment

Rubric

3 = Completed all tasks; maintained safety; helped others move safely and find clear pathways

2 = Completed most tasks; maintained safety

1 = Attempted all tasks but didn't try hard with all of them; maintained safety

0 = Attempted some tasks but not all of them; did not maintain safety

Safety

You must address and control collisions and speed. Establish strict rules and consequences before having students begin movement. Stress defensive driving. Instruct students to look out for each other and anticipate that some drivers may not see others. Stress that students want to avoid the consequences of crashes.

Tips and Variations

- Put on the music and have students start their engines. They begin cruising around the room in their vehicles. They should cruise aloud around their classroom highway, waving or honking to others as they pass on the beltway. Leave the students yearning to move.
- Let your students choose other types of vehicles and situations. A student may choose a sporty red Mini, back out of the driveway, cruise onto the beltway, and suddenly be trapped in stop-and-go rush-hour traffic.

Conclusion and Links to Real Life

"I hope you didn't end up with your car in the shop or in the hospital from lack of spatial awareness. If you were careful in finding your pathways and drove cautiously, varying your speeds and levels, I think that your car and life are safe. This couldn't be more true to life in the real world. Keeping up the cautious defensive actions will pay off in many ways."

Try at Home

"Create a map and see if your friends or family can follow your pathways and obstacles."

- - - Locomotor Shuffle - - -

Movement—locomotor patterns, directional and spatial awareness

Skills	Activity Level	Intensity	Standards
Locomotor movements and patterns	Everyone is active.	Medium to high	① ② ④

Invitation

"Walk around with me. Can you do the locomotor movements and patterns that I do or say?"

Equipment

- CD player and CD
- Chart with key to values on the cards
- Set of cards

Description

You have already invited participants to walk with you around the room. Now challenge them to perform various locomotor patterns while reacting to directional changes and spatial awareness strategies.

Direct the participants as they listen to music and your cues. Stop every 15 seconds. Students must stop on cue. Shuffle the cards:

- Participants go to the center chairs or desks and pick up a card. After picking it up, they put it right back down and move away from the center.

- Participants perform the action on the card. Provide a chart with the actions that correspond to the value on the card.

- For younger students, have the chart available for the participants to see and ask a volunteer to shuffle and pick just one card for the entire class to work with. Everyone does the action on the card.

- Older participants will have more fun doing it themselves, and this approach creates a bigger challenge of spatial awareness. They have to move without running into others!

Setup

Look first; rearrange if necessary; put it back together.

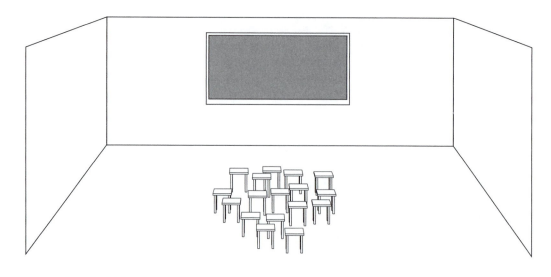

Break It Down in Detail

Lesson plans and in-depth information follow.

Objectives

- Students perform various locomotor movements to the best of their ability.
- Students demonstrate the ability to analyze, evaluate, and improve locomotor movement of themselves and others.
- Students change their speed, direction, and level on demand.
- Students will realize that this is a high-intensity workout, and they can test it by measuring their heart rate.

Warm-Up

Walking around with the teacher

Cues and Concepts

Carry out the activities using the following cues:

- Move with a mission—move using only the action represented by the card.
- Meet the criteria—try to move with correct form by following the criteria, and watch others perform, checking the criteria.
- Stop on signal—control your speed so that you will be able to stop as soon as you hear the signal.

Include the following concepts:

- Instruct students to control their speed according to their ability to maintain proper form of the designated locomotor action.
- Ask students to describe when they would vary their level when traveling in real life.
- Remind them to find clear pathways and adjust speed so that they can move with the others, passing safely when necessary and slowing or moving to the side when necessary.
- Ask students to analyze a partner's locomotor movements, and evaluate and improve the movement.

No Gym?

Card	Action
2	Walk
3	Skip
4	Jump
5	Gallop
6	Hop
7	Slide
8	Leap
9	Tiptoe
10	Your choice
Jack	Same pattern, low intensity
Queen	Same pattern, medium intensity
King	Same pattern, high intensity
Ace	Same pattern, any intensity you want
Clubs	Same pattern, forward
Hearts	Same pattern, backward
Diamonds	Same pattern, sideways
Spades	Same pattern, in place

No Problem!

Assessment

Rubric

3 = Attempted all locomotor actions and movements with proper form; safe and cooperative with others

2 = Attempted all locomotor actions and movements; safe and cooperative with others

1 = Attempted most locomotor actions and movements; was not always safe and cooperative with others

0 = Did not attempt most tasks

Safety

Controlled speeds are essential. Do not permit students to run into the chairs and desks in the middle to pick up cards. Students must move away from the middle once they have seen their cards.

Tips and Variations

- As if you are doing a magic trick, shuffle the cards as you begin class. Doing this will create an "I wonder" effect on your students. They will wonder why you are shuffling the cards, what shuffling cards has to do with PE, and how soon can they become involved!

- Make a criteria checklist of locomotor movements that your older students can use to analyze their movement patterns and those of others:
  - Jump = Keep both feet together.
  - Hop = Use one foot.
  - Leap = Two feet to one foot.

- Skip = Step, hop right; step, hop left.
- Gallop = The left foot stays in front as the right foot slides up to meet it, and then the left foot leaps in front again.
- Slide = The right foot steps to the side and the left foot slides sideways to meet it. The right foot is always in the lead.

Conclusion and Links to Real Life

"We don't move by walking at the same **pace** all the time. We sometimes have to climb or jump over something or slide by in some tight situations, and we have to adjust our speeds and levels to stay safe."

Try at Home

"Shuffle a deck of cards and ask a friend or family member to give you a physical exercise to do. Have them pick a card. You have to do the number of repetitions that they choose for you. Involve them in the exercise too, of course!"

- - - Road Test, Test Drive—Movement Assessment - - -

Movement—locomotor patterns, directional and spatial awareness

Skills	Activity Level	Intensity	Standards
Spatial awareness, locomotor patterns, directional patterns	Everyone is involved.	Medium, low	① ⑤ ⑥

Invitation

"How well can you perform different locomotor patterns and move in different directions? If you were a car, someone would take you out for a road test and see how you perform. Show off your movement skills, as if you were being taken for a test drive."

Equipment

- ☢ CD player and CD
- ☢ Deck rings or hula hoops for each person
- ☢ Road test sheet and pencil for each person

Description

Participants give a road test to a partner. One partner performs, while the other has a checklist and assesses the other's skills. Give each person a test sheet. They take turns giving the test. Be sure to demonstrate each locomotor movement because participants may not remember the proper form. To drive through the tunnel, students move at a low level, bending their knees to stay low to the ground. To cross the bridge, they move at a high level, moving on their toes. To follow the twisty line drawn on the sheet, the participant follows instructions called out by the partner—sharp right turn, smaller left turn, sharp left turn, and so on.

Setup

Look first; rearrange if necessary; put it back together.

Road Test

Directional movements

___ Turn right every five steps

___ Turn left every five steps

___ Follow this pattern

Stopping

___ Able to stop within 2 seconds at slow speed

___ Able to stop within 3 seconds at medium speed

Driving, locomotor tests

___ Skip around the room (alternate forward legs)

___ Hop around the room (one leg)

___ Gallop around the room (same leg forward)

___ Jump around the room (two feet glued together)

___ Slide around the room (move to the side, same lead foot)

Levels

___ Drive through the tunnel (low level)

___ Drive over the bridge (high level)

Test drive

___ Close your eyes and follow the directions of your partner

___ Courteous and cautious

___ Driver was patient and courteous, allowing other drivers to drive safely

___ Driver had no collisions

Score

16 checks = superb driver

13-15 checks = good driver

10-12 checks = okay driver; work on your skills

9 or fewer checks = stay off the road until your skills get sharper

From *No Gym? No Problem! Physical Activities for Tight Spaces* by Charmain Sutherland, 2006, Champaign, IL: Human Kinetics.

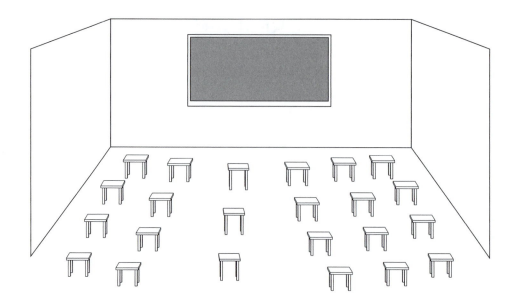

Break It Down in Detail

Lesson plans and in-depth information follow.

Objectives

- Students analyze and evaluate locomotor movements of themselves and others according to set criteria.
- Students display their best physical and cognitive ability.

Warm-Up

Exercard Battle

Cues and Concepts

Carry out the activities using the following cues:

- Give positive feedback—help your test driver become a more skilled mover by offering helpful, positive advice on how to improve his or her movement.
- Stay alive and drive—try your best to follow the criteria and directions; avoid crashes and tickets.

Include the following concepts:

- Evaluating others helps students become more skillful.
- Being courteous, cautious, and helpful is important in both driving and life. Remind students that if they are not courteous, cautious, and helpful, others may not return the favor, and they could find themselves in some crashes and tough situations.

Assessment

Rubric

3 = Scored 16 on the assessment; helpful and positive with testing others

2 = Scored 13 to 15 on the assessment; helpful and positive with testing others

1 = Scored 9 to 12 on the assessment; helpful and positive with testing others

0 = Scored below 9 on the assessment; conducted test for others poorly

Safety

Students should not purposely attempt to crash for fun. Address this issue before beginning the activity.

Tips and Variations

- Amuse your students with stories of poor drivers and how they lack spatial awareness skills. Describe an incident when someone was courteous to you on the road (allowing you to merge over four lanes because you missed a turn; someone giving you directions when you were lost), and how it made you feel.
- Middle school students should get extra credit for displaying polite behavior, because they sometimes lose their manners around this age. Create an opportunity for them to receive more points if they exhibit the behaviors.

Conclusion and Links to Real Life

"Have you ever been driving with someone who slams on the brakes and everything flies toward the front of the car? This person needs to think about spatial awareness, adjusting speed, and being courteous. Try not to forget this as you walk through the halls. Remember to stay on your side and not to crowd or push people. This makes everyone much happier."

Try at Home

"Politely analyze your adult family members the next time you are in the car with them. Use your positive evaluating skills to help them improve."

--- Circus and Cirque Du Soleil ---

Gymnastics—tumbling, balancing, spatial awareness

Skills	Activity Level	Intensity	Standards
Jumping, landing safely, balancing, tumbling	Everyone is involved and active.	Medium	① ⑤ ⑥

Invitation

"It's the greatest show on earth. The circus is in town. No . . . it's in this classroom! Imagine that you are part of the greatest show on earth, and you are in the circus. If you are great at balancing, you may be in Cirque Du Soleil."

Equipment

- Two small mats
- One hula hoop
- 18 scarves and beanbags
- CD player and CD such as *Hooked on Classics* or CDs by the Art of Noise

Description

Participants imagine and act as if they are an act in the circus. As they move to each station, they pretend as if they are in a five-ring circus. Play music such as that by the Art of Noise, *Hooked on Classics,* or soundtracks from a circus.

- Station 1—Jumping through hoops. Imagining that a hula hoop is on fire, participants hold it for each other and attempt to go through it without hitting it. They can adjust the height and angle each round.

● Station 2—Circus animals. As if they were the animals in the circus, participants perform animal movements, such as bear walks, lame dog walks, duck walks, leapfrog, the worm (roll from feet to knees, to thighs, to chest, to hands, and back to feet; use a mat for this one), and seal crawls (hands pull while legs drag on the floor).

● Station 3—Acrobat. Participants tumble and transfer their weight.

- Egg roll (with the body in a ball position, weight goes from back to left side, left arm, and left leg to knees to right side, right arm, and right leg to back)
- Log roll (with the body straight, weight goes from back to left side, left arm, and left leg to belly to right side, right arm, and right leg to back)
- Forward roll
- Backward roll

● Station 4—Clowning around. Students juggle scarves or beanbags.

● Station 5—Cirque Du Soleil. Participants move fluidly in 5-second poses from one balance to another. They should create balances that are challenging and safe. For example, they could move from a balled-up squat position to a one-leg stork stand. They should perform all poses safely and without falling down. Each pose should last 5 seconds.

Setup

Look first; rearrange if necessary; put it back together.

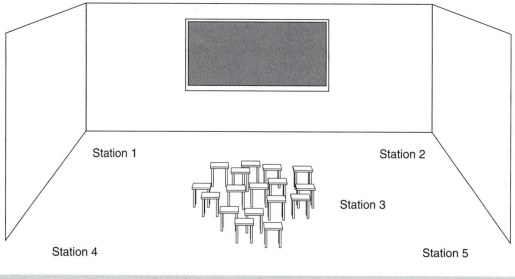

Break It Down in Detail

Lesson plans and in-depth information follow.

Objectives

● Students perform gymnastics and tumbling sequences that combine traveling, transferring weight, balancing, and rolling.

● Students move their bodies in relationship to objects.

● Students vary the effort as they participate.

● Students create movements based on their imagery and their imagination.

● Students safely transfer weight from one part of the body to another.

● Students move smoothly when transitioning from one gymnastic sequence to another.

Warm-Up

Can You Guess, Judge?

Cues and Concepts

Carry out the activity using the following cues:

- Quiet landing—when you jump up, you can explode, but you should come down softly and gently.
- Absorb the landing—when landing, imagine that you are slowly sinking into the floor, like a sponge slowly absorbing water.
- Smooth transitions—flow smoothly and quietly from one balance to another.
- Muscles tight—keep your muscles tight and strong when rolling sideways.
- Round body—when transferring weight in rolling forward or backward, keep your body round, like a ball.
- Chin to chest—when rolling forward or backward, protect the neck and tuck your chin to your chest.

Include the following concept:

- Encourage students to use their imaginations! Tell them that circus performers are so entertaining that each year we pay to see them do tricks and movements that amaze us. They should become circus characters and have fun.

Assessment

Rubric

3 = Participated 100% at all five stations

2 = Participated 100% at most of the stations

1 = Participated safely but not with full effort

0 = Participated minimally or not at all

Safety

Position yourself at the transferring weight (acrobat) station. Remind students to tuck the chin on forward and backward rolls. The hula hoop should not be more than 1 foot (30 centimeters) off the ground. Students should not attempt moves that will cause them or others to fall down.

Tips and Variations

- If you have a clown nose, hair, hat, or shoes, you can set up this class for an awesome show. Use props to make your class feel as if they are really at a circus! Use a megaphone and say, "And now, ladies and gentlemen, we bring you the greatest show on earth." Start your circus music and perhaps begin with some scarf juggling. The stage is set!
- This activity is best suited for students through grade 2.
- You can replace the animal walks with a safe virtual activity (mimicking actions from a video) that would interest older students.

Conclusion and Links to Real Life

"If I had never seen the greatest show on earth before, then I have now! What a great show! I liked the display of the animals walking through the ring of fire, and the tigers jumping through the ring and landing softly. I enjoyed watching you transfer your weight as you tightened your muscles for the sideways rolls and curled like a ball for the forward and backward rolls. The balancing acting was as smooth as the Cirque Du Soleil performers. I'll be looking for you the next time I watch the circus."

Try at Home

"If you get the chance, go to a circus or to see Cirque Du Soleil. Put on a circus act in your neighborhood. You can use the playground for some of your props."

- - - Jump, Bounce, and Balance - - -

Gymnastics—jumping, landing, balancing

Skills	Activity Level	Intensity	Standards
Jumping, landing safely, balancing	Everyone is involved, actively, 90% of the time.	Medium to high	① ⑤ ⑥

Invitation

"Let's jump right into our activity."

Equipment

- Three or four yardsticks
- Paper or board, 4 feet (120 centimeters) long with inches (centimeters) marked along its entire length
- Mat or carpet squares for balancing (optional)
- CD player and CD such as *Jump, Jive an' Wail* by the Brian Setzer Orchestra or *Hooked on Classics* (optional)

Description

Participants practice jumping and landing in stations. Participants also practice balancing activities.

- Station 1—Jumping high, landing softly.
  - Participants jump high, against a board 4 feet (120 centimeters) long with inches (centimeters) marked all along its length. Place the board on the wall approximately 1 1/2 feet (45 centimeters) above the head of the shortest person in the class.
  - Students reach up and see how far they can reach. They measure the distance covered by their jumps (from the highest point reached by standing to the highest point reached by jumping); without the measurement, shorter people would not seem as successful.
  - They should land with their ankles, knees, and hips flexed to absorb their weight so that the landing is soft and quiet.
- Station 2—Broad jump.
  - Participants stand with their feet together and jump out as far as they can.
  - They must land softly and on both feet.
  - Use three yardsticks to measure the distance jumped.
- Station 3—Jump creatively. Participants take turns doing creative jumps, such as twists, turns, straddles, and skater jumps (both legs bend behind the body with heels nearly touching the **gluteus,** and hands touch feet). Alternatively, they can create their own safe jumps.
- Station 4—Jump with a partner.
  - Perform any safe jump with a partner.
  - Perform nonsymmetrical (not the same) and symmetrical (both doing the same) jumps.

€ Station 5—Balance. Participants practice static balances and hold them for 5 seconds

- Stork (on one leg).
- Three bases on the floor (bases are the parts of the body that touch the floor and are used for support).
- One base; no feet allowed.
- In connection with a partner, balance on a certain number of bases.
- In connection with the whole group, balance while being connected to a group on a certain number of bases.
- Participants should do all balances without falling to the ground.

Setup

Look first; rearrange if necessary; put it back together.

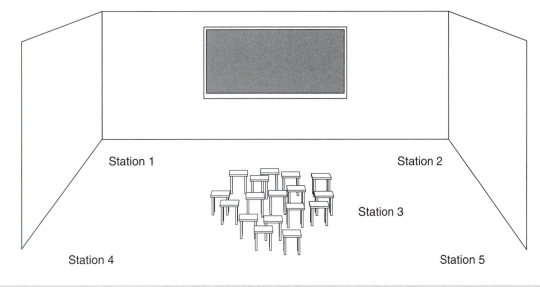

Station 1   Station 2

Station 3

Station 4   Station 5

Break It Down in Detail

Lesson plans and in-depth information follow.

Objectives

€ Students jump and land safely.
€ Students vary the effort with which they jump.
€ Students jump for a height and a distance.
€ Students vary their takeoffs and landings.

Warm-Up

Simon Says, "Action"

Cues and Concepts

Carry out the activity using the following cues:

€ Swing up—swing both arms upward and then lift off with the feet.
€ Swing out front—swing both arms out from back to front and then lift with the feet.
€ Takeoffs—jump with feet on the ground into the air, using both feet or just one foot.
€ Landings—end the jump on your feet, using both feet or just one foot.
€ Creative shapes—create jumps and balances incorporating various shapes.

Include the following concepts:

- ⚙ Relationships could include wide, narrow, round, straight, twisted, turned, over, under, on, off, symmetrical, nonsymmetrical, front, back, around, together, apart, between (all of these relationships were used during the jumps).
- ⚙ Effort could include fast, slow, soft, strong, light, heavy, hard.
- ⚙ Students should land softly with flexed joints to protect themselves from an injury such as a broken bone or a sprained ankle.

Assessment

Rubric

3 = Safely followed jump and balance tasks according to directions; used creativity

2 = Safely followed jump and balance tasks according to directions; used little creativity

1 = Did not safely follow jump and balance directions for every task; lacked creativity

0 = Did not safely participate in jump and balance tasks; unsafe; lacked creativity

Safety

Describe and demonstrate a safe jump and landing. Do not tolerate unsafe jumps or falls.

Tips and Variations

- ⚙ You can probably jump farther and higher than most students under 13 years of age, so when you demonstrate you are creating not only a level of excitement but also a challenge. So, jump to it!
- ⚙ For grades 5 through 8, add the total amount of feet and inches (centimeters) the group has jumped. Compare with others, if you want a competition. (This would be an excellent link to measurement and adding skills in math.)

Conclusion and Links to Real Life

"We jumped right into our lesson, and we jumped in different ways. When would you ever need to jump in real life? How can we jump? Why is it important to land softly? We use our balance every day, just for walking around."

Try at Home

"Reach with your hand to the ceiling, to a spot on the wall. Now, jump up and see how high you can jump. You can measure this from month to month to see how much you are growing and how much stronger and powerful your jumps are becoming. Be sure to have a quiet landing, especially if you are upstairs."

- - - Gymnastics Stations and Assessment - - -

Gymnastics—jumping, tumbling, balancing

Skills	Activity Level	Intensity	Standards
Jumping, landing safely, balancing, tumbling	Everyone is involved actively in three out of four stations.	Medium to low	① ⑤ ⑥

Invitation

"Let's see what we can do with gymnastics and what we know about jumping, landing, tumbling, and balancing."

Equipment

- One or two small mats
- An assessment and a pencil
- CD player and CD
- Four yardsticks for measuring broad jump and jump and reach

Description

Students participate in four stations that will test their skill and knowledge of basic gymnastics and tumbling.

- Station 1—Tumbling, transferring weight (acrobat). Participants tumble and transfer their weight.
  - Egg roll
  - Log roll
  - Forward roll
  - Backward roll
- Station 2—Jumping and landing. Participants demonstrate safe and quiet landings while
  - jumping for distance in the broad jump,
  - jumping for a height (jump and reach with arm), and
  - creatively jumping.
- Station 3—Cirque Du Soleil. Participants move fluidly in 5-second poses from one balance to another. They should create balances that are challenging and safe. For example, from a balled-up squat position they can move to a one-leg stork stand.
  - Each balance must be static for 5 seconds.
  - Participants should do all balances safely and without falling down.
  - Participants can work as a group but only after they have tried individual balances first.
- Station 4—Assessment.
  1. Describe how to perform a forward roll.
  2. Draw how to perform a roll.
  3. When you jump, should you land hard or soft? Ask third through eighth graders to explain why.
  4. Which balance is static?
     a. rocking back and forth
     b. still
     c. bouncing
  5. Have older participants create a routine of sequences that uses jumping, transferring weight, and balancing. Draw and map the details here.

Setup

Look first; rearrange if necessary; put it back together.

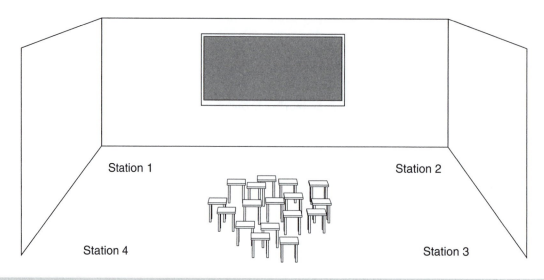

Station 1   Station 2

Station 4   Station 3

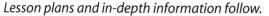

Break It Down in Detail

Lesson plans and in-depth information follow.

Objectives

- Students demonstrate their abilities in gymnastics through various stations.
- Students test their knowledge of gymnastics with a five-item written assessment.

Warm-Up

Find the Leader or Simon Says, "Action"

Cues and Concepts

Make sure that you have covered the concepts before assessing. Give a quick review of cues and concepts from your gymnastics unit.

Assessment

Rubric

3 = Answered and completed all items correctly on the assessment

2 = Answered and completed all items on the assessment, missing no more than two

1 = Completed the assessment but answered more than two incorrectly

0 = Did not complete the assessment or answered all items incorrectly

Safety

On rolls, participants should stay rounded and tuck chin to chest. They should flex and bend ankles, knees, and hips when landing after a jump. Be sure that all desks and sharp objects are away from jumpers' fall zones.

Tips and Variations

- Let your students know how excited you are to find out how much they know about gymnastics. Use your enthusiasm to encourage students to try hard with their responses. Tell them that you can't wait to read over them. Of course, after the assessment, be prompt with feedback and returning the assessment to your students.
- See assessment items. Older students will create a routine on paper, involving sequences, balances, transferring weight, and jumping and landing. They can map out their plan with diagrams and explanations.

Conclusion and Links to Real Life

"This is great! Now I will know what you really understand about gymnastics. Do you really know how to do a roll safely? Do you know how to land safely? I'll find out soon. This assessment will enable us to learn and to try more advanced skills in the future."

Try at Home

"After you get your assessment papers back, show them to your family. Or give them the test first and then show the assessment to your family. Demonstrate the activities that the test covered in front of your family."

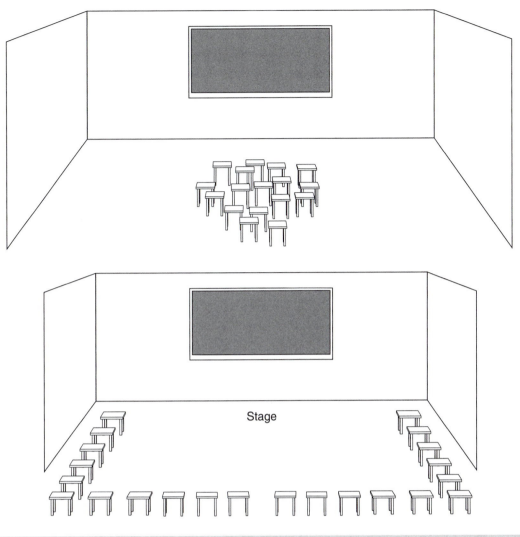

Break It Down in Detail

Lesson plans and in-depth information follow.

Objectives

⑤ Students express themselves through a rhythmic routine that they design, prepare, practice, coordinate, and perform.

⑤ Students attempt to meet five criteria as they cooperate and appreciate rhythmic activities.

⑤ Students make and understand aesthetic judgments in dance.

Warm-Up

Do, Re, Me, Fa, So, La, Te, Do

Cues and Concepts

Carry out the activities using the following cues:

⑤ Let your body talk—dance so that we can see your expression.

⑤ Be yourself—let your dancing show how individual you are. Own it—make your dance your own and be proud of it.

Include the following concepts:

- Students attempt to meet the criteria by forming groups or deciding to work alone. Students enjoy giving their group a name!

- Allow students time to prepare and create. Depending on many times per week you have physical education class, you could allow one day or several days for them to prepare. Explain that no one will be eliminated but that all will attempt to be the best that they can be.

- Show time! Introduce each act with enthusiasm and let the students perform for you and their classmates. Expect and allow for applause. Afterward, discuss with the class the rhythmic value that you observed. For example, say, "Tom's group displayed dancing coordination, teamwork, and dribbling skills by performing their routine to 'Who Let the Dogs Out.' Great job!"

Assessment

Rubric

3 = All five criteria achieved

2 = Four out of five criteria achieved

1 = At least two out of five criteria achieved

0 = Little or no attempt to meet criteria

Use the criteria from the description.

Safety

Describe and show the dimensions of the stage before practice. Explain limitations caused by desks and unique furniture or setups in the classroom.

Tips and Variations

- Create enthusiasm—to get the fire started, show a clip from MTV, BET, VH1, or a reality TV show that demonstrates rhythm.

- Demand appropriate behavior for school activities.

- Students love to see themselves on TV. Show the video afterward.

- Make it special. Create a banner: Classroom Superstars 2006; or Rhythms 2006.

- If someone is shy or lacks confidence to perform in front of others, allow the person to prepare in class and participate as a supportive audience member, but permit him or her to perform without the peer audience.

- At lunch or during your planning time, ask the student to show you his or her rhythmic routine for 2 minutes.

Conclusion and Links to Real Life

"Each time you hear or watch a reality show in which people are displaying their talents, you can now feel the passion that they do. You have put on your show and know the skills and effort involved in performing a rhythm in front of others."

Try at Home

"Have a Family or Neighborhood Superstars at your house. See if you can achieve the criteria with your own competition."

- - - Club Dance - - -

Rhythms—dancing, expression

Skills	**Activity Level**	**Intensity**	**Standards**
Dancing, moving to various music to express oneself	Everyone is actively involved.	Medium to high	① ⑤ ⑥

Invitation

"It's your debut in the spotlight. Imagine that MTV or VH1 has come to visit and that they want to check out the rhythm in this place. We will move as if the camera is going to broadcast our production to the entire world. So express yourself and dance for the camera."

Equipment

CD player and CD

Description

Students participate individually, expressing themselves by moving to a rhythm. The music should change each time you visit a new set or club. If time allows, set up a camera and a TV together so that the dancers can be seen as they dance.

- Start out at American Bandstand with a current pop song and let everyone perform freestyle. Students will need at least one song to calm down after they see themselves on TV. Do a line dance like the cha-cha slide that everyone can do, because the singer explains exactly what to do during the song.

- Go to Club MTV, play a song, and see if each person can come up with a unique rhythm.

- Then head out to VH1 and play a different song during which participants try to work with another person or group to choreograph a video.

- Finally, visit Soul Train.

  - Make two lines that face each other.

  - The two people at the back of the line dance on through the middle of the soul train line until they reach the front. Then they join the sides and slide down each time a person comes down the line. Eventually, they will be at the back and will go through the line again.

  - The dancers on the side do a subtler dance and clap for those going down the line.

Setup

Look first; rearrange if necessary; put it back together.

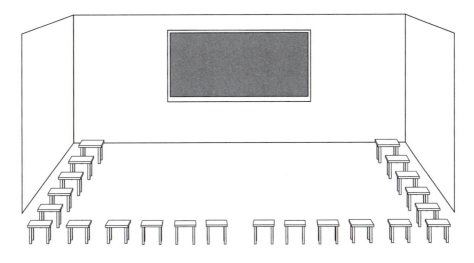

Break It Down in Detail

Lesson plans and in-depth information follow.

Objectives

- Students experience dance through their own creative expressions.
- Students appreciate others' expressions and interpretations through dancing.

Warm-Up

Macarena. Play the Macarena song from the *Jock Jams 2* CD.

Cues and Concepts

Carry out the activity using the following cue:
- Feel the beat—move to timing of the beats and rhythm.

Include the following concept:
- Encourage students to interpret their emotions through dance: happiness, sadness, joy, anger.

Assessment

Rubric

3 = Danced with enthusiasm to every rhythm; appreciated others' interpretations

2 = Danced to every rhythm; appreciated others' interpretations

1 = Danced with hesitation to most rhythms; appreciated others' interpretations

0 = Did not dance to most rhythms; did not appreciate others' interpretations

Safety

Keep your dance floor clear of desks and chairs; discuss your boundaries.

Tips and Variations

- Immediately strut your stuff and invite students to dance. Show them your joy and excitement for dancing! This invitation says, "Let's enjoy moving, through dancing."
- Encourage inhibited students to dance, even if they only do the side–step together (step to the left with the left foot; bring the right foot over to meet the left; step to the right with the right foot; bring the left foot over to meet the right; repeat).
- Students could also exercise to the music, if they can't quite feel the rhythm.

Conclusion and Links to Real Life

"Do you realize that some people are so serious about expressing themselves through dance that they dance so that they can communicate? You've heard of the rain dance—that's an example. What about the dances that football players do when they score a touchdown? That's an example of showing emotion, like joy, through dance."

Try at Home

"Act out your emotions through dance. See if your family can figure out what you are trying to say."

--- Dance Through the Decades ---

Rhythms—dancing

Skills	**Activity Level**	**Intensity**	**Standards**
Dancing, dance moves that were popular throughout various decades	Everyone is active.	Medium	① ⑤ ⑥

Invitation

"Disco Fever swept the world in the 1970s. Other dance crazes were popular in other decades. Let's look at the dances that were popular in the last few decades."

Equipment

CD player and CD. Suggested music: "Cha-Cha Slide" by Mr. C, the Cha-Cha Slide Man; *Like Mike* soundtrack featuring Lil' Bow Wow; "Macarena" by Los Del Mar from the *Jock Jams 2* CD; *Jock Rock 1* and *Jock Rock 2* CDs; *Saturday Night Fever* soundtrack; "Rock It" by Herbie Hancock; songs by The Romantics, The Go-Gos, Billy Idol, C+C Music Factory, and MC Hammer.

Description

Students participate as a group, following your directions.

Dances From the 1960s

- ⌘ Pony
  - Put right leg out front and step.
  - Step back on left; step on right; step on left.
  - Put left leg out front and step.
  - Step back on right; step on left; step on right.
  - Repeat.
  - This is a rocking forward and back motion.
  - Songs to use—"Mony Mony," "Louie Louie," "Wooly Bully."
- ⌘ Swim
  - Legs do the pony.
  - Arms act out the motions of swimming (crawl, breaststroke, backstroke, dive).

Dances From the 1970s

- ⌘ Disco Fever
  - Legs may side step or grapevine (step to the left side with left foot; cross the left foot with the right foot; step to the left side with the left foot; step to the left with the right foot; and then repeat to the right side) to four or eight counts.
- ⌘ On any chorus of any disco song, do the following:
  - Roll hands in front of the stomach; right arm and hand roll toward the body while left arm and hand roll away (as if they are tumbling over each other in a chase). Roll twice.
  - Freeze with legs apart, right arm up to the sky and index finger pointing upward, left arm down, and index finger pointed downward.
  - Music to use—most songs from the *Saturday Night Fever* soundtrack, Bee Gees, KC and the Sunshine band.

Dances From the 1970s and 1980s

- The Robot
  - Rigid movements that even the "no rhythm" person can look good doing.
  - Students pretend that they are robots, using poses and stiff movements.
  - Music to use: Herbie Hancock, Zapp, Gap Band, KC and the Sunshine Band.

Dances From the 1980s

- Break dancing
  - Dancing on the ground with spins and pops.
  - The Worm—rock from toes to knees, thighs to stomach, to chest to hands, back to toes, and repeat, moving the body forward.
  - Music to use: Herbie Hancock or any dance song with a beat.

- The Wop
  - Jumping up and down with the legs.
  - Right and left arms bend at the elbows and move to right. On a beat, snap fingers and bring the forearms close to the body. Then both arms loop around away from the body to the left and snap.
  - Repeat jumps and arms.
  - Music to use: Romantics, Go-Gos, Billy Idol.

Dances From the 1990s

- Running Man
  - Step left foot to front; right foot is back.
  - Slide left foot to center; right knee is bent and foot is off the ground.
  - Step right foot to front; left foot is back.
  - Slide right foot to center; left knee is bent and foot is off the ground.
  - Repeat.
  - Music to use: "Gonna Make You Sweat" by C+C Music Factory, MC Hammer, and most fast songs.

- Macarena: The steps to Macarena are presented in chapter 2 (see page 24).

Dances From the 2000s

- Harlem Shake
  - Jerky shoulder movements with quick, random poses.
  - Occasionally pretend to brush something off the shoulder with two strokes of the fingers pushing the imaginary object away.
  - Music to use: Lil' Bow Wow in *Like Mike* soundtrack, rap, hip-hop music.

- Cha-Cha Slide
  - This dance must be done with the "Cha-Cha Slide" by Mr. C, the Cha-Cha Slide Man, because the singer makes the calls.
  - The calls are extremely simple, consisting of slides and jumps at a **pace** that everyone can keep up with.

Setup

Look first; rearrange if necessary; put it back together.

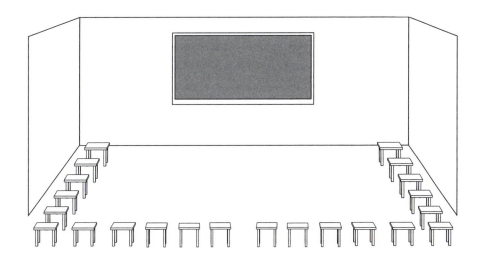

Break It Down in Detail

Lesson plans and in-depth information follow.

Objectives

- Students demonstrate an understanding of dances throughout our recent history.
- Students perform various movements and sequences that express ideas and typify dances throughout various decades.

Warm-Up

Watch the Shoes

Cues and Concepts

Carry out the activities using the following cue:

- Follow—simply watch and copy the moves that I do.

Include the following concepts:

- Explain that following others can make someone a great dancer.
- If people didn't copy the dance moves of others, none of these dances would have caught on.
- People usually dance at weddings. Dance is a way that people celebrate.

Assessment

Rubric

3 = Attempted all dances with enthusiasm

2 = Attempted all dances

1 = Attempted most dances

0 = Did not attempt most or any dances

Safety

Be sure to designate your boundaries. Students should stay in their personal space.

Tips and Variations

- Break out your high school moves for a few seconds. The students will laugh, but they will be talking about it and imitating your moves later!
- Use the "Hokey Pokey" or "If You're Happy and You Know It" with younger students.

Conclusion and Links to Real Life

"You danced through the decades today. If you could go back in time, you would be involved in some of those dances. What do you think this decade will be remembered for? Will any current dances go down in history?"

Try at Home

"Ask your parents and grandparents to show you some dances that they did as teenagers. Maybe you have learned one that they know. Dance together. Then show them a current dance."

- - - Rhythmic Freeze Dance - - -

Rhythms—dancing, creative movement

Skills	Activity Level	Intensity	Standards
Dancing, rhythmically moving to a beat or music	Everyone is active 90% of the time.	Medium	① ⑤ ⑥

Invitation

"You must dance or create a rhythm using sticks, basketballs, or scarves to move to a song, beat, or rhythm. Suddenly, you will be frozen in time and must stop everything."

Equipment

- CD player and CD (music such as that in the *Jock Jams* series; music in a variety of genres so that students gain experience with diverse types of music and rhythms)
- Lummi sticks
- Basketballs
- Scarves

Description

Students participate individually, moving to a rhythm. When the music or beat stops, they must freeze like statues.

- Participants can try to be the most frozen person, by being as still as possible.
- The teacher or leader can record points for the person who is the most frozen each time.
- Require participants to move both their arms and their legs during the moving session.

Setup

Look first; rearrange if necessary; put it back together.

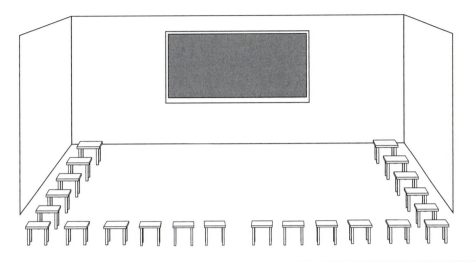

Break It Down in Detail

Lesson plans and in-depth information follow.

Objectives

- Students use creative movements and rhythms with manipulation objects to express themselves.
- Students use perceptual skills as they perform in response to music, dance, signals, and rhythm.

Warm-Up

Hand Jive

Cues and Concepts

Carry out the activities using the following cues:

- Show your feelings—as you dance and move, express how you are feeling through the use of your rhythm implement.
- Stop on signal—stop immediately when you hear the signal to stop.

Include the following concepts:

- Use objects to demonstrate how students can use rhythmic movements and expression safely and with purpose.
- Explain that many dances are designed with expressions to communicate what the dancer wants others to know: siren sounds to alert people; strong beats to indicate more passion; flowing movements to suggest that everything is peaceful; abrupt, rigid movements to show that not all is peaceful; fast beats to suggest anxiety or excitement.

Assessment

Rubric

3 = Created rhythms that were unique; responded to signals promptly

2 = Created some rhythms; followed others; responded to signals promptly

1 = Followed others' rhythms; responded to signals

0 = Did not follow or create a rhythm; did not respond to signals

Safety

Participants should handle manipulation objects as they were intended. Give a brief overview of the dos and don'ts when handling equipment.

Tips and Variations

- Clap your hands lightly and slowly for 10 seconds. Then clap your hands forcefully and rapidly for 10 seconds. Ask the students to distinguish one set from the other. Ask which time they were tired or bored and which time they were excited.
- Have students use their hands and feet if you do not have enough manipulation objects. Show how this works by pretending that you have a manipulation object in your hands and hit and move your hands accordingly. Show how the feet can move and flow to the rhythmic beats too.

Conclusion and Links to Real Life

"Recognizing signals and responding to them is important in school, in sports, and in life. Signals take many forms. You can even receive signals through dancing. We can use our bodies to make and respond to signals."

Try at Home

"With some friends in the neighborhood, create rhythms and dances. You could put on a show, like the production of *Stomp* or *Bring on the Noise, Bring in the Funk,* which are dynamic shows from the theatre that ooze energy and rhythm. They use various items that you might find at home to make noises and create rhythms."

- - - Tinikling - - -

Rhythms—rhythmic movement

Skills	Activity Level	Intensity	Standards
Moving to a rhythm, timing, moving equipment or manipulation objects to a rhythmic beat	Everyone can be involved at once.	Medium	① ⑤ ⑥

Invitation

"In a dance called tinikling, you bang big, long sticks on the ground while someone jumps in and out of them. Dancers can vary rhythms and style of dance as they move in and out of the sticks."

Equipment

- CD player and CD from the *Sun Splashin'* series, *Survivor: The Official Soundtrack to the Hit CBS TV Series,* or *Songs You Know by Heart* by Jimmy Buffet.
- 12 tinikling sticks or PVC pipes, at least 6 feet (180 centimeters) long

Description

Participants work in groups of three to six. Two people sit on the floor, with the sticks flat on the ground, and tap the ends of the sticks down to the ground twice. Then they lift the sticks about 4 inches (10 centimeters) off the ground and hit them together twice. Then they hit them on the ground about 1 1/2 feet (50 centimeters) apart. They should establish a rhythm (the original version is down, hit, hit; down, hit, hit; repeat). Another easy rhythm:

- One down, two down
- One hit, two hits
- Once the rhythm is established, the dancer may attempt to jump into the center while the sticks are in the down position.
- When the sticks are together, the dancer straddles the sticks.
- Participants change roles each minute.
- Older, more coordinated participants may change the rhythms of the sticks, and the dancer may create fun jumps, turns, and twists. You could also have multiple dancers.
- Music to use: Philippines music, Caribbean music, Jimmy Buffet's *Volcano*.

Setup

Look first; rearrange if necessary; put it back together.

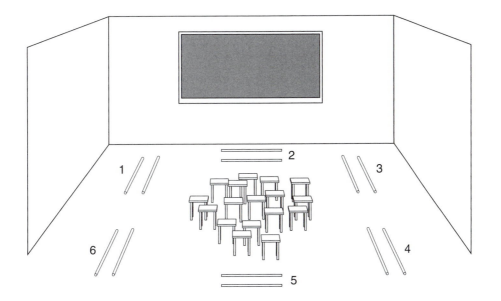

Break It Down in Detail

Lesson plans and in-depth information follow.

Objectives

- Students appreciate dances from other countries and cultures.
- Students manipulate objects to a rhythmic beat.
- Students create their own rhythms and movements.
- Students perform a basic tinikling step.

Warm-Up

Hand Jive

Cues and Concepts

Carry out the activities using the following cues:

- Stay in synch—try to move at the same time as your partners do.
- Timing—watch and count so that you time your jumps and hits.

Include the following concepts:

- Teach students to vary the speed of the rhythm. They should start slow and build from simple to more complex beats and movement.
- Students should design a rhythm and the dance steps to go with it. They can vary the number of taps and the timing, and create skillful ways of moving in and out of the sticks.

Assessment

Rubric

3 = Created as a team; skillfully moved to the rhythm; increased difficulty

2 = Created as a team; moved to the rhythm

1 = Lacked creativity as a team; tried to move to the rhythm

0 = Did not create as a team; did not move to the rhythm

Safety

Participants should not raise the sticks more than 6 inches (15 centimeters) off the ground. They should avoid banging the fingers when handling the sticks. If the jumper is still stuck in the middle, they must be careful not to bang the sticks into the jumpers' legs. Putting a carpet square or blocks under the sticks can help prevent any accidental bangs of the fingers. If you have bamboo sticks, check them for splinters.

Tips and Variations

- Some tinikling sticks available through PE and sports equipment catalogs have the sticks secured in a setting that prevents banging of the hands or the jumpers' legs. Jump bands are another option for learning the tinikling skill.
- For a project, older students can map out their steps on paper to describe the choreography of the steps that they will perform.
- Students can monitor their heart rate when they are dancing compared with when they are keeping the rhythm with the sticks.

Conclusion and Links to Real Life

"Tinikling is an activity that you might not have considered to be dancing. Different cultures play different sports, do different forms of dancing, listen to different styles of music, and live a little differently from the way that you do. It is great to learn and appreciate how people of different cultures interpret things a little bit differently from others."

Try at Home

"Find two sticks and try to create a rhythm or beat. Add dances to it. If your sticks are sturdy enough, jump and dance with them."

--- Have Arms, Will Dance ---

Rhythms—dancing, upper-body fitness

Skills	Activity Level	Intensity	Standards
Dancing, upper-body workout	Everyone is involved at once.	Medium to low	① ④ ⑤ ⑥

Invitation

"Just because we don't have a gym or dance studio doesn't mean that we can't dance. We will use our arms and lummi sticks to express ourselves through dance."

Equipment

- CD player and CD
- Songs with good beats—"Lollipop," "My Sharona" by the Knack, "We Will Rock You" by Queen
- Two lummi sticks per person

Description

Students participate as a group, following your directions, to do the following:
- Hand Jive (see directions in chapter 2)
- Macarena (see directions in chapter 2)
- Lummi stick dancing
    - Simply strike lummi sticks on the desks or floor to the rhythms or beats of songs.
    - Allow each student to come up with a quick part of a routine.
    - Have everyone start with a beat, like two hits down, two hits together.
    - Then, while the group keeps the beat, go around to each person and allow each a few seconds to showcase their creation.

Setup

Look first; rearrange if necessary; put it back together. No rearranging necessary for this activity.

Break It Down in Detail

Lesson plans and in-depth information follow.

Objectives

- Students move their upper bodies to perform dance movements.
- Students create a rhythm and copy rhythms designed by others.
- Students use their bodies as a means of expression.
- Students appreciate the benefits that dance provides as enjoyment and as a way to maintain upper-body fitness.

Warm-Up

Participants jog in place to the music (if the music is slow, they go slow; if the music is fast, they go fast). This lesson doesn't use the legs much, but the warm-up uses the big muscles of the legs to get the heart pumping blood throughout the whole body to prepare the body for some dance action.

Cues and Concepts

Carry out the activity using the following cues:

- Copying and following—watch and repeat the actions of others.
- Create a rhythm—come up with a pattern of beats.

Include the following concepts:

- Upper-body workout—the dances use the muscles of the upper body, including the **deltoids, trapezius, biceps, triceps,** and **latissimus dorsi.**
- Some dances use the **abdominals** and hip flexors, but minimally.
- Explain the use of arms as a way of communicating through dance.
- Explain that we can move using rhythms that we create or rhythms that we copy.

Assessment

Rubric

3 = Attempted all dances and rhythms and appreciated the experience

2 = Attempted all dances and rhythms but didn't try hard with all of them

1 = Attempted some dances and rhythms but not all of them

0 = Made minimal or no attempt at dances and rhythms

Safety

Participants should hold and use lummi sticks so that they do not poke or strike another person. Students should stay in their own personal space so that a lummi stick cannot reach into anyone else's space.

Tips and Variations

- Express your enjoyment and passion in an obvious manner. Your enthusiasm will be infectious. They will watch and mimic your moves. Perform without using your arms and notice how dancing is not as fun or as expressive as it could be if you used your arms. Have the students try it.
- Vary the speed of the hand jive. Speed up, if the students can keep up. Challenge them to go faster. For your students of middle school age, see how quickly they can go without missing the steps.
- Challenge students to do the push-up Macarena (see directions in Push-Up Dancing in chapter 3 on page 38).

Conclusion and Links to Real Life

"It was enjoyable to dance with you and watch you express yourself today. What area of the body did we work the most today? Can you name any of those muscles? Next time you are riding in the car, do some upper-body dancing. It's fun and good for your joints and muscles."

Try at Home

"Show everyone at home the dances and rhythms that you performed today. See if they can keep up with you and express themselves through dance. Try to dance to a song on the radio, TV, or a CD."

--- Rhythms Stations and Assessment ---

Rhythms—rhythmic movement

Skills	Activity Level	Intensity	Standards
Moving to a rhythm, timing, moving equipment to a rhythmic beat	Everyone is involved.	Medium	① ⑤ ⑥

Invitation

"Let's do various types of rhythmic activities and see what we know."

Equipment

- CD player and CD
- Four tinikling sticks or PVC pipes at least 6 feet (180 centimeters) long
- Two lummi sticks per person

Description

Participants work in stations, performing different rhythmic activities at each station. The fourth station, where students do creative dancing in groups, is an assessment station.

- Station 1—Tinikling. Participants start with two hits down, two hits together; they may change rhythms after they can do this one (see the tinikling lesson on page 110 for more information).
- Station 2—Lummi sticking. Participants build a rhythm with the others in the group; everyone's input should be used in the rhythm (see the activity on lummi sticks on page 113 for more ideas and information).
- Station 3—Dancing freestyle. Everyone dances, whether in a group or as individuals. Freestyle can be any school-appropriate style of dance.
- Station 4—Creative dancing in groups and assessment. In groups of at least three, students come up with dances and rhythmic movements to the music.

Setup

Look first; rearrange if necessary; put it back together.

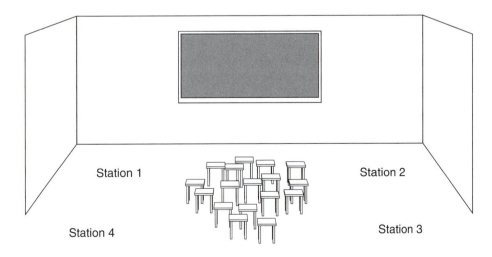

Station 1   Station 2

Station 4   Station 3

Assessment for Grades K-2

1. Draw your group dancing. Try to include the different steps.

From *No Gym? No Problem! Physical Activities for Tight Spaces* by Charmain Sutherland, 2006, Champaign, IL: Human Kinetics.

Assessment for Grades 3-8

1. Describe the dance.

   Steps:

   a. first

   b. second

   c. third

   d. fourth

2. Where did you get the idea?

   Feelings/emotions: What expressions or moves did you add to the dance?

3. Does your dance increase your heart rate?

4. Which muscle groups does your dance work?

From *No Gym? No Problem! Physical Activities for Tight Spaces* by Charmain Sutherland, 2006, Champaign, IL: Human Kinetics.

Break It Down in Detail

Lesson plans and in-depth information follow.

Objective

Students display their knowledge of dancing through a physical and a written assessment.

Warm-Up

Flexapalooza with the group at their first station before beginning the activity.

Cues and Concepts

Carry out the activities using the following cues:

- Express yourself—create dances that use expression.
- Feel the beat—move to the feeling or timing of the beat.
- Be unique—create something that is yours, something that you feel.
- Work as a team—each group should create a dance using each person's input.

Include the following concepts:

- Look for creative input in designing dances. Ask students why they are doing a certain move.
- Ask students about the effort and relationships within the dance.
- Dance is a great form of physical activity. Dance works both large and small muscles and, depending on the dance, can greatly increase the heart rate. Ask students to be aware of the fitness aspect of dancing.

Assessment

Rubric

3 = Completed the assessment; displayed enthusiasm in stations

2 = Completed assessment; participated in all stations

1 = Did not complete assessment; participated in all stations

0 = Did not complete assessment; did not participate in all stations

Option: Use the assessment as a grade to evaluate students, instead of just as an assessment to see how much students have learned.

Safety

Tinikling sticks must not be raised more than 6 inches (15 centimeters) off the ground. If the jumper is still stuck in the middle, participants must be careful not to bang the sticks into the jumpers' legs. Putting a carpet square or blocks under the sticks can help prevent accidental bangs of the fingers. If you have bamboo sticks, check them for splinters. Students should hit lummi sticks on the ground and hold them so that no one gets poked or struck by one. Students should stay in their own personal space so that a lummi stick cannot reach into anyone else's space.

Tips and Variations

- Walk around during the activity and try to get involved in a dance step or two that the students are working on. They like to know that you are interested. Your presence can help them create, and they will want to show you how clever they can be with rhythm.

- If you have not covered some of these skills, replace them with ones that you have covered.
- For K through 2 students, you may have to set a time limit for creating and assessing at station 4.

Conclusion and Links to Real Life

"I am looking forward to learning the dances and rhythms that you created for your assessment. Who designed a dance expressing happiness? How about sadness? How did your dance steps vary? Maybe your dance will be the next hot dance in our country, and we will be remembering your dance in decades to come."

Try at Home

"Ask your family to create a family dance. Everyone should have input! You can showcase your dance at family weddings, picnics, and celebrations."

Throwing and Catching

Throwing and catching provide the basic skills for many sports and activities. Participants can enjoy throwing at every level, from novice to expert. These activities provide the basics for basketball, softball, baseball, football, lacrosse, **netball,** and bowling. We can't forget that throwing is also important to sports like tennis, volleyball, and even soccer.

- - - Catch 500 - - -

Throwing and catching

Skills	Activity Level	Intensity	Standards
Catching, self-tossed, partner tossed; throwing	Everyone is involved.	Medium	① ② ⑥

Invitation

"Let's see if we can catch at least 500 times today. That's an awful lot of catching. Can you imagine how much better you will become at catching if you can accomplish that?"

Equipment

- One beanbag per person
- One balled-up piece of paper per person

Description

Participants pick up a beanbag, toss it upward to themselves, and catch it with

- palms facing upward, 50 times (older students, 50 times without a miss);
- the hand opposite the one they threw with, 50 times;
- the left hand and then a toss to the right hand, 50 times (younger students can pass it from left to right);
- both hands, clapping once between the toss and the catch.

Participants then toss a balled-up piece of paper upward to themselves and catch it with

- both hands, clapping twice between the toss and the catch; then clapping three times between the toss and the catch, and so on;
- both hands, turning around once before making the catch;
- both hands, clapping twice, turning around once, and slapping the knees before making the catch.

Participants then sit across from a partner and catch a beanbag thrown by the partner from a close distance. If they are successful for 25 throws (no drops), allow them to increase the distance apart. If they are not successful, they must stay where they are.

If space allows, students may stand and throw from a close distance. If they are successful for 50 throws (no drops), allow them to increase the distance apart.

Setup

Look first; rearrange if necessary; put it back together. Little to no rearranging necessary.

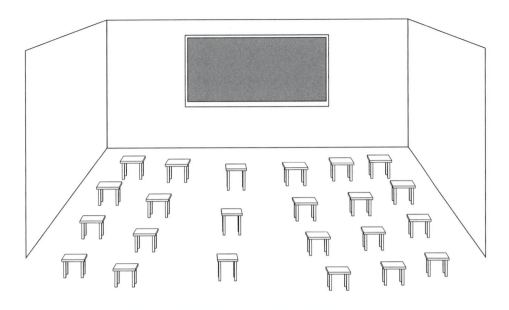

Break It Down in Detail

Lesson plans and in-depth information follow.

Objectives

- Students throw an object to themselves and catch it repeatedly.
- Students improve their hand–eye coordination, timing, and throwing by repeating the skill several times.
- Students challenge themselves and a partner to make good throws and catches.

Warm-Up

Fit Tic-Tac-Toe

Cues and Concepts

Carry out the activities using the following cues:

- Opposite foot forward—step with the foot opposite the one that you are throwing with.
- Don't move to catch—throw the object so that others don't have to move their feet to catch it.

Include the following concept:

- Through practice come improvement and mastery. Students will throw so many times that their hand–eye coordination and throwing and catching skills will improve. Five hundred repetitions is great practice.

Assessment

Rubric

3 = Attempted most tasks with best effort

2 = Attempted all tasks but didn't try hard with all of them

1 = Attempted some tasks but not all of them

0 = Did not attempt most tasks

Safety

All throwing should be controlled. Students should be in their own personal space and have enough room that they do not hit another pair when they stretch out their arms. Give students boundaries and fair warnings about the consequences of throwing something in a classroom. Stick to the consequences.

Tips and Variations

- Perform some throws and catches with students as you walk around. Explain how throwing and catching still helps you even though you've had many years of practice.
- Let students in grades 3 through 8 create a challenging task that will keep their interests yet maintain focus on repetition of the underhand and overhand throws. An example would be "How many times out of five throws can your throw hit your partner's shoe?"

Conclusion and Links to Real Life

"When you first learned to walk, you fell down. When you first learned to write, you couldn't write any letters. Now, after lots of repetition and practice in throwing and catching the beanbag and ball of paper, you improved. No matter what game or sport you are involved with, you will have improved after watching the objects and throwing and catching 500 or more times."

Try at Home

"How many throws can you make from the time you get out of school until you go to bed? See if you can match what we did today."

- - - Jacks - - -

Throwing and catching

Skills	Activity Level	Intensity	Standards
Catching a bounced ball, hand–eye coordination	Partners take turns.	Medium	① ④ ⑤

Invitation

"How quickly do you think you can pick up eight jacks? Jacks is an old game that is fun to play. You can play alone or with a group of people. At first, jacks seems easy, but when you drop the little ball and try to collect the jacks, suddenly it's not so easy. See how well your hand and eyes work together."

Equipment

- Set of eight jacks per pair, if possible; alternatively, eight small balls made from crumpled-up pieces of paper
- One small bouncy ball (1 inch, or 2.5 centimeter) per pair

Description

How quickly can you drop a ball and then collect a jack? That's the question. Participants work in groups of two.

- Partners sit on the floor with one small bouncy ball and eight jacks (real jacks or eight small balls formed by crumpled-up pieces of paper).

- The first partner drops the ball and tries to pick up one jack and catch the ball before the ball bounces a second time.
- If successful, the person goes again. He or she must pick up two jacks before the second bounce. The person progresses to picking up three, then four, and so on.
- After each turn, the other partner drops all eight jacks from his or her hand. In that way, both partners stay involved in the activity.
- The first person keeps going until he or she can collect eight jacks.
- At completing a turn, the person must do the number of jumping jacks equal to the number that he or she picked up.

Setup

Look first; rearrange; put it back together. No setup necessary.

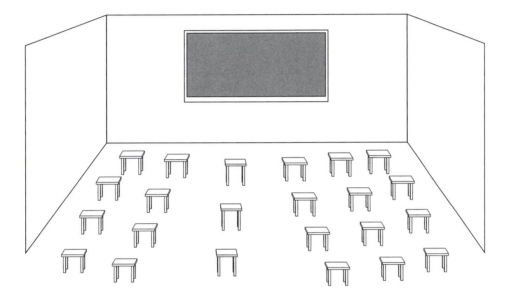

Break It Down in Detail

Lesson plans and in-depth information follow.

Objectives

- Students toss a small ball with a force that will keep the ball within the players' still vision.
- Students use their speed and tactile ability to catch the ball with the same hand that is picking up jacks.

Warm-Up

Find the Leader

Cues and Concepts

Carry out the activities using the following cues:

- Toss so that you can catch—toss the ball so that it will bounce right back into your hand.
- Keep the ball in sight—toss so that you don't have to move your head to see it.

Include the following concept:

- Explain how students can use their peripheral vision.

Assessment

Rubric

3 = Tossed the ball and caught it almost every time

2 = Tossed the ball and caught it most of the time

1 = Tossed the ball and caught it some of the time

0 = Tossed the ball poorly and rarely caught it

Safety

Students should bounce the balls no higher than the head. Do not allow students to throw balls toward other players.

Tips and Variations

- Toss and catch the ball as you are talking to the students. Doing this is like teasing a dog with a juicy steak. The students will want to play with that ball so badly that they will almost salivate over it.
- Allow younger or less skilled students to use two hands instead of one to catch and collect.

Conclusion and Links to Real Life

"Isn't it amazing how difficult it was at first to toss the ball and catch it successfully? Later, after training your eyes, brain, and hands, you improved your timing and eventually grabbed a jack."

Try at Home

"Make a set of jacks so that you can improve your skills at home. Play with them while you watch TV, during commercials, and especially while you are waiting for something."

- - - Throwing Every Which Way - - -

Throwing and catching

Skills	Activity Level	Intensity	Standards
Throwing at a target, aiming for a target, underhand and overhand throws, chest pass, hiking, pitching	Everyone is involved.	Medium	① ② ⑥

Invitation

"There are many ways to throw. Can you think of any games you play that involve throwing? How about basketball, horseshoes, softball, football, tennis, volleyball, lacrosse, water polo, netball, and even soccer. Let's try many of these throws."

Equipment

- 15 balled-up pieces of paper
- 3 scoops
- 15 beanbags
- 6 baseball-sized foam balls
- 3 basketball-sized foam balls
- 3 cones

Description

Participants visit each station and discover a throwing pattern or improve their throwing ability. Older participants can attempt to perform a designated number of good throws before moving on to the next station. Working in partners would be a good system.

1. Horseshoe station: Create a post (cone) that students can try to ring. Students toss the beanbag underhand, trying to get closest to the post (consider this ringing).
2. Tennis toss station: While standing, students toss a beanbag with the nondominant hand 12 inches (30 centimeters) above the head. The beanbag should drop 6 inches (15 centimeters) in front of nondominant foot.
3. Chest pass, basketball station: Partners are 6 feet (180 centimeters) apart and use a chest pass to pass a basketball-sized ball to one another.
4. Baseball (overhand) throw: Pretending that they are third basemen, students throw a foam ball overhand to the first baseman. The target is the partner's abdomen.
5. Lacrosse or **stxball** throw: Students use a scoop to throw a beanbag to a partner's abdomen. The partner catches the throw.
6. Softball (underhand) throw to a target, with an arc: Students pitch underhand to a partner, aiming at the partner's abdomen. Use a foam ball, beanbag, or balled-up piece of paper.
7. Football hike (backward, underhand throw): Participants straddle a foam ball as it sits on the ground. They look between their legs and push the ball back and upward toward the partner's abdomen.

Setup

Look first; rearrange if necessary; put it back together.

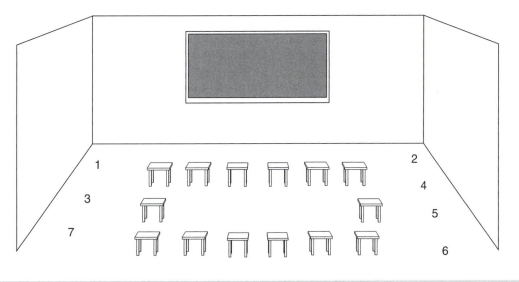

Break It Down in Detail

Lesson plans and in-depth information follow.

Objectives

- ☞ Students throw a ball to a target using a variety of throws.
- ☞ Students focus on their form and pattern as they throw.

Warm-Up

Show students how to loosen their shoulder muscles. Discuss the need for loosening the shoulder muscles **(deltoids)** as you do simple arm circles forward and backward slowly. Then increase from small circles to large.

Cues and Concepts

Carry out the activities using the following cue:

- Aim at target—point your hand toward the target in preparing to throw and in making the throw.

Include the following concepts:

- Discuss the various patterns for throwing:
  - To throw overhand, aim at the target, bring your arm back with the ball by your ear, step forward with the opposite foot, throw the ball, and follow through with your hand pointing at the target.
  - To throw underhand, aim at the target, bring your arm back behind your hips, step forward with the opposite foot, throw, and follow through with your hand pointing at the target.
  - To throw underhand with an arc, aim at the target, bring your arm back behind your hips, step forward with the opposite foot, throw the ball higher than the head of your target, and let the ball come down into the strike zone (this takes some practice). Follow through with your hand pointing above the target.
  - To throw sidearm, aim at the target, bring the ball back to the side of your shoulder, step forward with the opposite foot, throw the ball, and follow through with your hand pointing at the target.
  - To throw with an implement, aim at the target, give the beanbag a chance to scoot to the edge of the scoop, release with a slight jerking motion, and pull the scoop back on the release. The timing and release will take a little getting used to.
  - To fast-pitch underhand, aim at the target, bring your arm forward and then rotate your arm around to the back, step forward with the opposite foot, throw the ball, and follow through with your hand pointing at the target.

Assessment

Rubric

3 = Threw several different ways; hit target most of the time

2 = Threw several different ways; hit target some of the time

1 = Threw several different ways; rarely hit target

0 = Threw one way; rarely or never hit target

Safety

Students should control their throwing so that they do not have to chase the balls or beanbags. Explain the boundaries and limitations of safe throwing. No ball or beanbag should knock anything off a desk or wall.

Tips and Variations

- As you assess your students, notice those who are taking the time to aim, step, and follow through. Acknowledge and compliment their effort so that they will continue to concentrate. Instruct those who are throwing without thinking to slow down and concentrate.
- Use paper balls instead of beanbags when necessary.

Conclusion and Links to Real Life

"Can you imagine if basketball players threw the basketball as a football player hikes the ball? That method wouldn't be very effective or efficient. So we have to try many ways of throwing so that we will be prepared to throw in different sports."

Try at Home

"For fun, invite someone to throw with you and throw with a different pattern from what you would use to throw best. For example, hike the ball to the basket. Then switch to the proper way of throwing. See if the person you are throwing with notices the difference and then explain how to throw properly."

- - - March Madness - - -
Throwing and catching

Skills	Activity Level	Intensity	Standards
Throwing at a target, aiming for a target, throwing with an arc, shooting a ball into a goal, throwing underhand and overhand, rebounding	Everyone is involved.	Medium	① ② ⑤ ⑥

Invitation

"I've made it to the big dance. No, I'm not going to dance. I'm going to participate in the college basketball tournament called March Madness. Yes, my team was one of the best college teams in America, and we made it to the prestigious tournament. Get ready to become a college basketball player and experience the biggest dream a player can have."

Equipment

- 12 basketball-sized Nerf balls, foam balls, or gator balls
- 6 **polyspots** or cones for foul lines
- 5 boxes, buckets, or goals

Description

Participants work as a team competing against other teams as they attempt to throw, catch, and shoot at the hoop (goal). All teams will experience the feel of a tournament as they rotate from playing one team (give each team the name of a college team that is in the NCAA tournament) to another team. Each team of two competes by passing to one another at least once and then shooting the ball to score a basket. Offensive players may be on their knees or seated. The other team plays defense by sitting on their behinds and attempting to block shots for 1 minute. When a team scores a basket, the offense and defense switch roles as in the real game. The new offense takes the ball to the 6-foot (180-centimeter) line to begin their scoring drive. Each team plays a different team every minute.

For fun, list the colleges on the board and keep score using a tournament bracket.

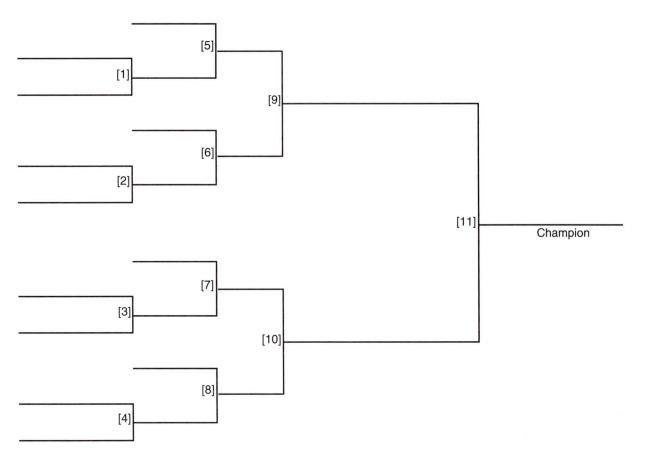

From *No Gym? No Problem! Physical Activities for Tight Spaces* by Charmain Sutherland, 2006, Champaign, IL: Human Kinetics.

Setup

Look first; rearrange if necessary; put it back together when finished.

- You will need six areas to serve as basketball courts.
- You will need about 6 feet (180 centimeters) of space from the wall for the players to shoot from.
- Four students play at each box, bucket, or goal.

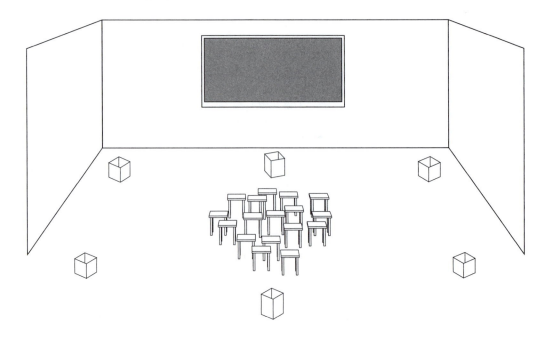

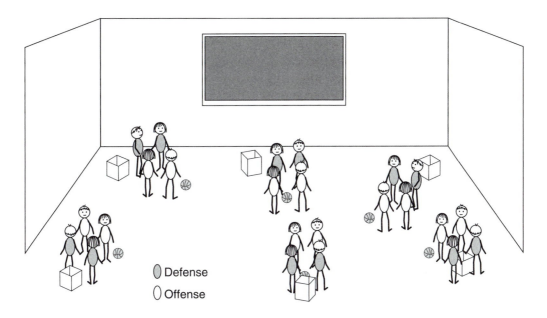

Break It Down in Detail

Lesson plans and in-depth information follow.

Objectives

- Students throw a ball to a target using an arc.
- Students focus on their form and pattern as they throw.
- Students identify with the March Madness basketball tournament.
- Students develop cooperation and sportsmanship skills as needed when playing, watching, or being involved in sports, athletics, and recreation..

Warm-Up

Shoot on the Floor and Scoot After Four. Have students do this warm-up until you have placed the baskets (goals, buckets, or boxes) in the room.

Cues and Concepts

Carry out the activities using the following cues:

- Body facing target—aim and shoot with your body facing the target.
- Follow through—pretend that your pushing arm is going through the target with the ball.

Include the following concepts:

- Explain shooting as a finesse throw toward a goal.
- Discuss and demonstrate the pattern:
  - The body faces the target.
  - Hold the ball in the nondominant hand, in front of the chin.
  - Use the dominant hand to push the ball upward and into the goal (allow K through 2 students to push with two hands).
  - Follow through with the dominant hand in line with the target after releasing the ball.

- ⬭ Teammates must pass to each other once before they shoot the ball.
    - Stress that it is important to pass to each other quickly because the object of the activity is also to end up with the most total points at the end of the tournament.
    - You may score each game as a win, but to keep the students guessing and never giving up, keep a running score.
    - To promote sportsmanship, award teams with sportsmanship points if you notice great sportsmanship taking place! This approach will help students practice fair play as they participate.
- ⬭ Rotate after each minute.
- ⬭ Take a brief time-out after each rotation to go over the bracket and the cues.

Links to other subjects:

- ⬭ Students realize where in the United States their schools are located (social studies, geography).
- ⬭ Students practice math by adding and subtracting scores.
- ⬭ Students in grades 3 through 8 gain some understanding of the concepts of odds and probability through the March Madness brackets

Assessment

Rubric

3 = Threw with an arc using proper technique and followed procedures

2 = Threw with an arc using proper technique most of the time and followed procedures

1 = Threw with an arc to the target using proper technique but did not follow procedures

0 = Did not throw with suggested arc or technique and did not follow procedures

Safety

Student must stay in their team area. Offense may kneel or sit. Defense may only sit on the **gluteus maximus.**

Tips and Variations

- ⬭ It's crazy . . . No, it's March Madness! Start the activity with music from the *Jock Jams* series, the *Like Mike* soundtrack, or the Harlem Globetrotters theme. Students enjoy seeing their college teams' names on posters. You can also have the names of each team on pieces of paper and have students carry their team names with them to post at the stations.
- ⬭ Adjust shooting techniques for younger students with smaller hands.
- ⬭ Explain brackets and probability to your fifth- through eighth-grade students. Your March Madness includes only 12 teams, but point out to your students that the NCAA March Madness involves 64 colleges in America. This event links well with math:
    - Odds of winning
    - **Seeding**
    - **Ranking**
    - Sweet Sixteen, Elite Eight, Final Four, Championship

Conclusion and Links to Real Life

"Find out which college is nearest to you. Follow them throughout the tournament. Imagine how much throwing, dribbling, catching, and running they do to be in the tournament. They started just as you did today."

Try at Home

"Follow the brackets at home. (Give students a bracket to follow). Fill in the college teams that you think will win each game. Look at the teams' ranks and records before making your choices."

- - - Memory Wheel - - -
Throwing and catching

Skills	Activity Level	Intensity	Standards
Catching a thrown or bounced ball	Everyone is involved in the group.	Low to medium	① ② ⑤

Invitation

"Can you juggle in a group? Can you juggle a big ball instead of the scarves? Juggling with a group is a lot more difficult than juggling by yourself, because you have to rely on other players to make good throws and catches."

Equipment

Three foam or lightweight balls per group

Description

Group players into teams of five or six. Each team forms its own circle, with the kids facing one another. The object is to make great throws so that teammates can catch the ball each time it comes to them. If a team is successful, they add more balls and maintain the pattern of throwing.

- Start with one ball. The beginning thrower, thrower 1, throws to someone, thrower 2, aiming for the chest so that thrower 2 can easily catch the ball.
- The team repeats throwing and catching until the ball has gone around the circle of players twice. If a player drops the ball, the team must start over. The pattern of who to throw to stays the same—thrower 1 to thrower 2, thrower 2 to thrower 3, and so on. If someone throws to the wrong person, the team must start over.
- After two successful rounds, the team adds another ball.
- Teams should see how many balls they can juggle during the activity.

Setup

Look first; rearrange; put it back together.

Break It Down in Detail

Lesson plans and in-depth information follow.

Objectives

- ⛶ Students throw with the intent to enable the receiver to catch with ease.
- ⛶ Students work with their teammates to reach a goal (to catch the ball each time it is thrown).
- ⛶ Students encourage each other to make good catches and throws and pay attention.

Warm-Up

Exerdice 100

Cues and Concepts

Carry out the activities using the following cues:

- ⛶ Throw at the chest—throw the ball by aiming at the chest.
- ⛶ Soft, catchable throws—throw softly so that your teammates won't drop the ball.
- ⛶ Follow the pattern—be sure to throw to the same person each time.

Include the following concepts:

- ⛶ Instruct students to decrease the force of the throw without losing accuracy so that teammates will be able to catch the ball easily.
- ⛶ Teach students to work as good team players and prepare their teammates by calling their names before throwing to them.

Assessment

Rubric

3 = Threw catchable throws and helped teammates succeed

2 = Threw catchable throws most of the time and helped teammates succeed

1 = Threw catchable throws some of the time and helped teammates succeed some of the time

0 = Rarely threw catchable throws and didn't help teammates succeed

Safety

The force of throws must be light and controlled. Do not permit uncontrolled throwing.

Tips and Variations

- Use the scenario of throwing an egg. Demonstrate throwing an imaginary egg with a group of three, in which if the egg were to fall, the group would have nothing left to throw. Use your acting skills to emphasize the urgency of not allowing the egg to drop.
- Have participants sit down for more control.
- Use paper balls.

Conclusion and Links to Real Life

"If your throws were good ones, then your team probably had several successful rounds of throws. Coaching and encouraging your teammates was important too."

Try at Home

"With people in your neighborhood, see how many rounds of successful throws around the circle you can do. Keep trying to improve the number of successful rounds that your neighborhood team can throw."

- - - Pitching Practice - - -

Throwing and catching

Skills	Activity Level	Intensity	Standards
Throwing at a target, aiming for a target, throwing underhand and overhand	Everyone is involved.	Medium	① ② ⑤ ⑥

Invitation

"Could you be a professional baseball player for the Yankees or the Florida Marlins? Do you think you could strike me out? Let's see how well you can pitch a ball, as if we were playing baseball or softball."

Equipment

- Five baseball- and softball-sized Nerf or foam balls
- Five polyspots or cones for the pitchers' mounds
- Five station markers, with explanations of throwing and pitching styles

Description

Participants go through a pitchers' training camp as they work on aiming and throwing at five different pitching stations. At the stations, participants play the following roles. Demonstrate each pitch and role.

a. Batter—stands with shoulder to a wall, facing the pitcher, in a batter's stance (no bat required, or advised).

b. Pitcher—stands on a spot in the middle of the room, facing the batter 10 feet (3 meters) away.

c. Umpire 1—watches the pitcher, checking for proper types of pitches.

    d. Umpire 2—watches the batter, calling a strike if the ball goes between the shoulders and knees, and a ball if it does not. The umpire should act out the call, saying, "Steeer-riiiike."

    e. Catcher—retrieves the ball and returns it to pitcher.

Each person gets two pitches and then rotates. Students can practice being pitchers in the following stations. Each time the pitcher throws a strike, everyone does two jumping jacks for joy, except the batter, who just got a strike.

1. Baseball pitcher—pitch two overhand throws to the batter.
2. Slow-pitch softball pitcher—pitch two underhand throws with an arc. The arc should be higher than 3 feet (1 meter) and lower than 10 feet (3 meters).
3. Fast-pitch softball pitcher—pitch two underhand throws with a windup.
4. Baseball pitcher throwing sidearm or throwing a knuckleball, screwball, slider, or other style of pitch that is different yet safe, and that you or a student can demonstrate—pitch two advanced pitches, using the overhand modified style of throwing.
5. Pitcher's choice—pitcher throws two pitches of his or her choice.

Try using points to make the activity competitive:

- ⬡ Pitcher delivers two pitches in a row in the strike zone = 1 point for the pitcher
- ⬡ Batter receives two balls (pitches out of strike zone) in a row = 1 point for the batter
- ⬡ Batter gets hit with the ball = 1 point for the batter
- ⬡ Batter gets hit with the ball = –1 point for the pitcher

Setup

Look first; rearrange if necessary; put it back together.

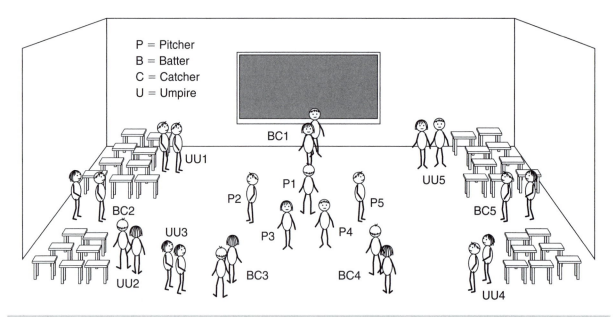

P = Pitcher
B = Batter
C = Catcher
U = Umpire

Break It Down in Detail

Lesson plans and in-depth information follow.

Objectives

- ⬡ Students throw a ball to a target using a variety of throws.
- ⬡ Students focus on form and pattern as they throw.

Warm-Up

Have students loosen up their shoulder muscles. Discuss the need for loosening the shoulder muscles (deltoids) as you do simple arm circles forward and backward slowly. Then increase from small circles to large.

Cues and Concepts

Carry out the activities using the following cues:

- Accuracy before force—make sure that you hit your target as a priority before you try to throw faster or harder.

- At each station, provide the cues, a picture, and the number of that particular station.

Include the following concepts:

- Explain that pitching is a style of throwing. Pitching could be overhand, underhand, sidearm, speedy, or slow.

- Discuss the various patterns for pitching:

  - To pitch overhand, aim at the target, bring your arm back with the ball by your ear, step forward with the opposite foot, throw the ball, and follow through with your hand pointing at the target.

  - To pitch underhand, aim at the target, bring your arm back behind your hips, step forward with the opposite foot, throw, and follow through with your hand pointing at the target.

  - To pitch underhand with an arc, aim at the target, bring your arm back behind your hips, step forward with the opposite foot, throw the ball higher than the head of your target, and let the ball come down into the strike zone (this takes some practice). Follow through with your hand pointing above the target.

  - To pitch sidearm, aim at the target, bring the ball back to the side of your shoulder, step forward with the opposite foot, throw the ball, and follow through with your hand pointing at the target.

  - To fast-pitch underhand, aim at the target, bring your arm forward and then rotate your arm around to the back, step forward with the opposite foot, throw the ball, and follow through with your hand pointing at the target.

  - Students can attempt to throw trick pitches, such as knuckleballs, curveballs, screwballs, and sliders. Do not emphasize or assess these pitches. Introduce trick pitches only to expand students' awareness and curiosity about throwing.

- As you place students into groups, try to group them according to ability.

- For fun and to relate the activity to real life, have each person in the group represent a team (Braves, Yankees, Cubs, Orioles, Twins, Angels, and so on).

Assessment

Rubric

3 = Followed tasks; umpired fairly; gave good feedback

2 = Followed tasks; umpired fairly; gave feedback

1 = Followed most tasks; did or didn't umpire fairly; did not give feedback

0 = Did not follow most tasks; did not umpire fairly; did not give feedback

Peer Assessment

- ☞ As students are umpiring, they check their classmates for
  - stepping with opposite foot,
  - attempting to perform proper pitch pattern, and
  - hitting the target.
- ☞ Umpires give the pitcher feedback immediately after pitch is executed.
- ☞ The batting umpire shouts the calls—"Ball" if the pitch is out of the strike zone and "Sttteeeriiike" if the pitch is in the strike zone.

Safety

Each student should be at his or her designated spot during the pitching activity. Make it clear that only the pitcher pitches and only the catcher retrieves the ball.

Tips and Variations

- ☞ Play ball. Have fun. Start the activity with the song "Take Me out to the Ballgame" and then play music that you hear when you are at a pro game, such as music from the *Jock Jam* series. Wear the cap of your favorite team. You could do this activity during the World Series to make the throwing focus and theme more embraceable.
- ☞ Challenge students to keep their own scores if they wish. Dispense with scoring for younger students.
- ☞ You could make this activity competitive by giving points. Award points as listed earlier.

Conclusion and Links to Real Life

"Pitching takes an awful lot of aiming, concentrating, and technique. Were you able to throw any strikes today? If so, you will get even better if you follow the technique and practice."

Try at Home

"Find out what your family's favorite baseball team is. Ask them what the World Series is. See if you can throw three strikes in a row to your parents."

- - - Target Time - - -

Throwing and catching

Skills	Activity Level	Intensity	Standards
Throwing, aiming, accuracy	Everyone is involved.	Medium	① ② ⑤ ⑥

Invitation

"Have you ever thought about all targets that you aim for every day—like when you aim for the trash can or the clothes hamper, or when you pour a drink? You have to aim and think about timing and accuracy. What would happen to your drink if you were not accurate? You'd have quite a mess. So let's aim for some targets today."

Equipment

- ☞ Two diving rings
- ☞ Target with bull's-eye; draw on a board or make a poster

- Hula hoop
- Jersey
- Classroom trash can
- One piece of paper, balled up
- Straw
- 32-ounce (1-liter) soda cup
- One penny
- Two small, light balls (golf-ball sized Wiffle balls)
- Piece of paper divided into quarters and balled up
- Brown paper lunch bag
- Foam ball

Description

Participants throw at several targets, focusing on aiming and accuracy. Students work in groups of two. One throws, and the other helps with the target. Then they switch. Students should throw from a distance of approximately 10 feet (3 meters) from the target. Adjust the distance according to the participants' ability; kindergarteners or first graders may start at 5 feet (1.5 meters).

Use the following stations:

- Throwing a piece of balled-up paper overhand into the wastebasket.
- Throwing a jersey, underhand, into the dirty clothes hamper or trash can.
- Throwing a ring, representing a life ring—the equipment used at a pool or beach to save someone who is struggling in the water—sidearm onto the partner's arm. Students could throw a Frisbee too.
- Throwing overhand to hit the bull's-eye of a target.
- Making a shot with a foam ball into the partner's arms (the partner forms a circle with his or her arms).
- Throwing a straw overhand into a cup.
- Tossing a penny onto the partner's shoe.
- Tossing a light object (Wiffle ball) through a small diving ring (6 inches, or 15 centimeters).
- Throwing through a large hoop
- Tossing small objects (such as small, balled-up pieces of paper) representing popcorn underhand into a bag.

Setup

Look first; rearrange if necessary; put it back together. Little to no rearranging necessary. Participants only need room to stand and throw or toss to their targets or partners. The throwing partner stands in the middle of the room, and the other stands against the wall.

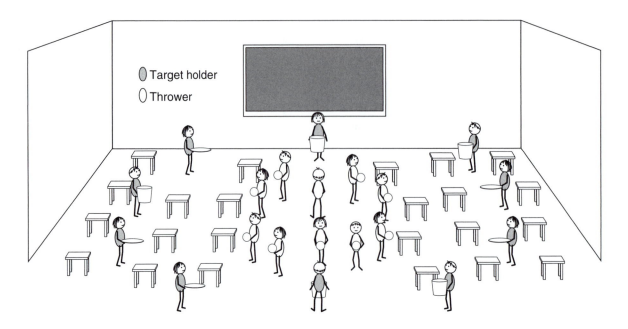

Break It Down in Detail

Lesson plans and in-depth information follow.

Objectives

- Students throw with mature form at targets.
- Students realize and practice safe throwing by throwing when others are not in their direct line of throwing.
- Students handle equipment and help with targets safely.
- Students enjoy becoming more skilled at throwing through effort and practice.

Warm-Up

Jacks and Jills Move Cube

Cues and Concepts

Carry out the activities using the following cues:

- Arm back—overhand throw starts with the arm back by the ear.
- Opposite foot—step forward with the opposite foot from your throwing arm (except for throws with the Frisbee or life ring).
- Follow through—end up pointing to the target.

Include the following concepts:

- Discuss mature throwing form and model it for each of the target tasks.
- Explain the difference with the Frisbee and life ring throws.
- Discuss the importance of targets:
  - We use targets to help us improve our throwing.
  - Targets give us a place to aim our throws.
  - We can measure and adjust the force and effort of our throws by using targets.
- Partners should be helpful with setting up targets safely.

Assessment

Rubric

3 = Aimed at and hit most targets with mature form

2 = Aimed at and hit some targets with good form

1 = Tried to aim at targets but didn't hit many targets and used poor form

0 = Didn't aim at or hit targets often

Safety

Students should throw only when the throwing path is clear. Students should say, "Excuse me," and wait for a safe opportunity before retrieving a strayed object.

Tips and Variations

- Kinesiological researchers say that we need to throw 3,000 times to improve our throwing. See for yourself if you can accumulate 3,000 throws by the end of teaching all your classes today. Nothing says that you can't improve and play too.
- Use targets that work best for your classes. When designing your stations, consider the needs of your students and the space in the classroom.

Conclusion and Links to Real Life

"Hitting targets is a perfect way for us to check our aiming and accuracy. The more we hit, ring, or go through a target, the more skilled we become at throwing. Researchers say that it takes 3,000 trials of throwing for us to become skilled in a certain type of throw. Did you get near 3,000?"

Try at Home

"Create several targets at home. Try to hit each one 10 times and then increase the difficulty of hitting that target. Tell me if you get near 3,000 trials."

- - - Throwing Stations and Assessment - - -

Throwing

Skills	Activity Level	Intensity	Standards
Throwing overhand and underhand, chest passing, tossing, hand–eye coordination, brain stimulation	Everyone is involved actively.	Medium	① ② ⑤ ⑥

Invitation

"Can anyone juggle flaming objects, like jugglers do at the circus? Probably not without burning something, right? Juggling takes concentration, hand–eye coordination, throwing, catching, and patience. Today, we will practice our throwing and catching and see what you really know about the skills."

Equipment

- 25 scarves (preferably three different colors)
- 12 beanbags

ⓢ 3 foam balls

ⓢ 3 containers for March Madness

ⓢ Polyspots to mark 10 feet (3 meters) for pitching and spots for standing and hitting at targets

ⓢ 3 paper balls

ⓢ 3 targets

Description

Participants visit several stations and perform assessments at each. Working in groups of five, students work at a station for 3 minutes and then fill out their assessment sheets.

1. Chest passing—pass to the chest. On the sheet, fill out the assessment.
2. Pitching—choose your favorite style of pitching and pitch to the batter. On the sheet, fill out the assessment.
3. March Madness—throw a foam ball with an arc into the bucket, basket, or target. On the sheet, fill out the assessment.
4. Target time—throw an object at a target. How many times can you hit that target? On the sheet, fill out the assessment.
5. Juggling—juggle two scarves for 2 seconds, then 4, then 6, and so one. See how long you can go before you drop one. Try to juggle three, four, or even five scarves. On the sheet, fill out the assessment.

Setup

Look first; rearrange if necessary; put it back together.

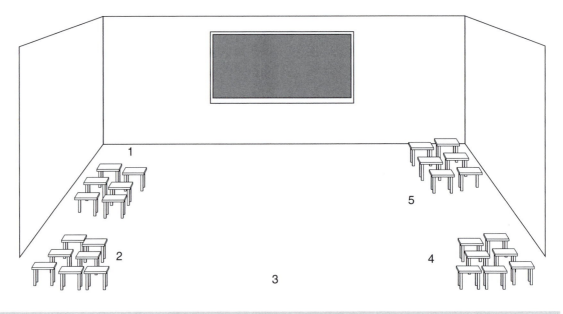

Break It Down in Detail

Lesson plans and in-depth information follow.

Objective

Students display their physical and cognitive skills in throwing.

Warm-Up

Exerdice 100

Throwing and Catching Assessment

1. Chest passing

   a. Where does the ball start in the chest pass?

   b. How many passes did you successfully make at the chest?

2. Pitching. Describe two styles of pitching.

   a.

   b.

3. March Madness.

   a. What is an arc? Why do you need it?

   b. Draw a picture of a ball arcing.

4. Target time. Describe the steps you take in throwing to hit your target.

   a.

   b.

   c.

   d.

5. Juggling. Circle the length of time you can juggle each:

a. two scarves:	5 seconds	10 seconds	15 seconds
b. three scarves:	5 seconds	10 seconds	15 seconds
c. four scarves:	5 seconds	10 seconds	15 seconds
d. five scarves:	5 seconds	10 seconds	15 seconds

From *No Gym? No Problem! Physical Activities for Tight Spaces* by Charmain Sutherland, 2006, Champaign, IL: Human Kinetics.

Cues and Concepts

Carry out the activities using the following cues:

- Arm back, aim, step, throw, follow through—in the overhand throw, start with your arm back, aim at the target, step with the opposite foot, release the ball, and point to your target.
- Push from your chest—start with your arms at your chest and push forward to your partner's chest.
- Eyes on—follow the object with your eyes as much as possible.

Include the following concept:

- Explain that throwing will help students in many sports. Knowing how to throw in different ways and knowing the steps will enable them to have more opportunities to play.

Assessment

Rubric

3 = Attempted most tasks with best effort

2 = Attempted all tasks but didn't try hard with all of them

1 = Attempted some tasks but not all of them

0 = Did not attempt most tasks

Safety

Students should look before they throw and stay out of the direct path of a thrower.

- Chest passing—students should pass with a force that is not too hard, making sure that no one is in the path of the throw.
- Pitching—students should pitch only when the path is clear.
- March Madness—players throw a foam ball with an arc, avoiding the ceiling and making sure that the throwing path is clear.
- Target time—students throw an object, making sure that no one is in their way.
- Juggling—participants make sure that they are not too close to another person so that their arms don't hit someone else.

Tips and Variations

- Ask students how they would practice throwing for a basketball, baseball, and football game. Ask them to describe the actions, as you perform them. This method will help them visualize what they are thinking, as you act out the technique.
- Add a throw that you might be working on (lacrosse, Frisbee, discus, shot put). Substitute a safe, classroom-friendly object instead of the real object (beanbags, foam ball, or paper balls).

Conclusion and Links to Real Life

"The one way to get better is to know how to do something and practice doing it. If you don't know the right way, you will get better at throwing incorrectly. So make sure that you know the correct technique and practice it."

Try at Home

"Visit a high school athletic event that involves throwing. Watch how the athletes practice. You can also watch professional games on TV and notice how they warm up."

Dribbling and Kicking

We can use our feet to kick and dribble. We can also dribble with our fingers and with sticks that we can manipulate. Basketball, field hockey, hockey, and soccer are sports that require dribbling to make the game complete. Light, soft tapping of the ball with the foot constitutes dribbling in soccer, and a hard, full-range-of-motion blast with the foot and leg constitutes a kick or a punt. Kicking and punting helps participants in soccer, speedball, and football and provides the opportunity to release a powerful action.

--- Dribble Like Beckham ---

Dribbling and kicking

Skills	Activity Level	Intensity	Standards
Dribbling with feet	Everyone moves and is involved.	Medium	① ⑤

Invitation

"What would Beckham, Pele, or Mia Hamm, three outstanding professional soccer players, do if they had to practice their soccer skills but didn't have any space? If we kick a soccer ball to score a goal in here, we would probably knock out a window. If we all were dribbling real soccer balls, we would be running into each other and knocking over furniture. So let's create a safe soccer ball out of three pieces of paper and kick around a bit."

Equipment

- ⚽ For each person, a ball made from three pieces of paper, taped to keep it together
- ⚽ Music or whistle

Description

Each person has a ball and dribbles around the room in a specified pattern. They can practice dribbling with the following games:

- ⚽ Team Humans Versus Team Desks: Set up a course that goes in and out of desks, with turns and challenges within the course. The object is to go in and out of the obstacles, dribbling with the inside and outside of the foot while not hitting others or the desks. Score 1 point for the desk team for each desk that gets hit. Score 1 point for the human team for each person that makes it through the course without hitting an obstacle.

- ⚽ Dribble Freeze. The next challenge is to go through the course dribbling and stopping on signal. Play music and stop it randomly after 10 to 20 seconds. Participants should be able to stop their balls and freeze on signal.

- ⚽ Dribble Freeze and Flee. The game is similar to Dribble Freeze, except that if a person does not stop on signal, he or she becomes a defender. The person sits in a desk, moving and reaching his or her legs out in an attempt to tap someone's ball. If a player's ball is tapped, he or she becomes a defensive player. Play until half the class is on defense. Then stop and allow everyone to get back into the game as an offensive player.

Setup

Look first; rearrange; put it back together. No setup necessary.

Break It Down in Detail

Lesson plans and in-depth information follow.

Objectives

- Students dribble a ball with their feet.
- Students dribble a ball while avoiding objects and opponents.
- Students vary the force of the kicks on the ground.
- Students use defensive and offensive strategies to steal and dribble a ball while it is on the ground.

Warm-Up

Over, On, and Beside or Watch the Shoes

Cues and Concepts

Carry out the activities using the following cues:

- Small taps—tap the ball softly, with the inside or outside or different parts of your shoe.
- Control the force—control the force so that the ball is never more than 2 feet (60 centimeters) away from your shoe.
- Be aware—keep your head up to see who is around you; look all around to see if any desks, chairs, or tables are in your pathway.

Include the following concepts:

- Explain that dribbling is kicking a ball by tapping it gently and keeping it nearby.
- If the ball is more than 4 feet (120 centimeters) from the person, he or she is kicking, not dribbling.
- A player is on offense when he or she has the ball.
- A player is on defense when he or she wants the ball but doesn't have it.

Assessment

Rubric

3 = Dribbled and kept the ball near at all times; rarely hit objects
2 = Dribbled and kept the ball close most of the time; rarely hit objects
1 = Dribbled but didn't keep the ball close most of the time; hit several objects
0 = Kicked but didn't dribble; hit many objects

Ask students to assess themselves with the criteria listed.

Safety

Students should be aware of clear pathways and try to avoid other people and objects.

Tips and Variations

- For fun, cheer for the desk team. This will encourage the students to focus on avoiding the desks. Keep score on the chalkboard.
- For students in grades 4 through 8, discuss offense and defense. Describe one strategy that each could do to achieve success.

⬤ Younger students should focus on the desks versus people, because they will probably kick the ball, intentionally, instead of dribbling, to prevent someone from stealing the ball.

Conclusion and Links to Real Life

"When we kick with soft taps, we are dribbling. If the desks scored more points than we did, we weren't concentrating on tapping the ball or avoiding others. Desks can't move on their own, so we should never let a desk beat us! If we focus and tap, we will be dribbling like Beckham."

Try at Home

"Use your paper soccer ball at home. You can dribble all around the house without knocking things over or making lots of noise. Challenge yourself by creating an obstacle course and timing yourself on each trial."

--- Globetrotters in Training ---

Dribbling

Skills	Activity Level	Intensity	Standards
Dribbling with hands, bouncing a ball, ball-handling skills, hand–eye coordination	Half the group moves for 1 to 2 minutes and then the other half moves.	Medium	① ⑤ ⑥

Invitation

"The Harlem Globetrotters are like magicians with a basketball. They dribble so naturally that they make it look effortless. They started just like you are, with practice, trial and error, and having fun."

Equipment

⬤ One bounceable ball per pair
⬤ CD player and CD

Description

Each person works with a partner, who analyzes dribbling technique. Partner 1 works with the ball first and then switches with partner 2 on signal. Participants follow along as you demonstrate the dribbling actions.

⬤ Sit, drop the ball, and catch it.
⬤ Sit and bounce the ball repeatedly, using the finger pads.
⬤ Sit and bounce the ball with the right hand.
⬤ Sit and bounce the ball with the left hand.
⬤ Kneel and repeat the previous action.
⬤ Stand and repeat the previous action.
⬤ Dribble with the right hand.
⬤ Dribble with the left hand.
⬤ Dribble with the right hand to the left hand.
⬤ Dribble very low.

- Dribble at the waist.
- Dribble from a seated position, to a kneeling position, to a standing position, and back to a seated position.
- Try some ball-handling skills.
- Pass the ball from the right hand to the left hand quickly.
- Roll the ball around the abdomen.
- Pass the ball around the abdomen, without the ball touching it.
- Pass the ball around one leg (younger students can roll it around).
- Pass the ball in a figure-eight pattern, between the legs (younger students may roll it on the floor or around the legs).
- While seated, try to spin the ball on your palm.
- While seated, try to spin the ball on your finger.

Create a cool pattern for the students to follow. Vary the degree of difficulty depending on the ability of your students. They should try to follow your pattern.

- Four right-hand dribbles.
- Four left-hand dribbles.
- Pass around the abdomen.
- Pass in the air, from the right hand to the left hand.
- Dribble from the right hand to the left hand.
- Dribble twice low and then twice at the waist.

Allow participants to create their own routines while you have the music on. Challenge them to create challenging patterns for their partners to attempt.

Setup

Look first; rearrange; put it back together. Create as much open space as possible.

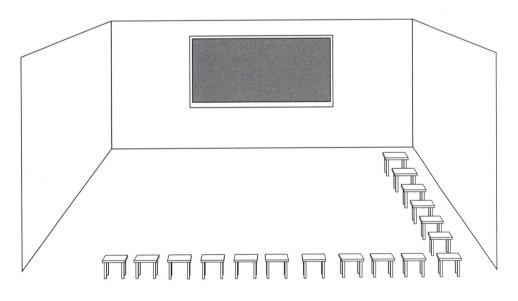

Break It Down in Detail

Lesson plans and in-depth information follow.

Objectives

- Students dribble a ball with their hands.
- Younger students bounce and catch a ball.
- Students are challenged and challenge each other to dribble and use ball-handling skills.
- Students in grades 3 through 8 create a routine involving dribbling and ball-handling skills.

Warm-Up

Flexapalooza

Cues and Concepts

Carry out the activities using the following cues:

- Finger pads—use the padded parts at the end of your fingers.
- No slapping—push the ball; don't slap it down.
- Knees bent—for more successful dribbles, bend at your knees.
- At your waist—dribble the ball at your waist for comfort and optimal repetitions.
- Eyes on the ball—keep looking at the ball to know exactly where it is.

Include the following concepts:

- Show students that to begin, they bounce and catch over and over. Suddenly this will lead to dribbling.
- Explain that critiquing is pleasantly explaining to others what you notice after observing a skill. Helping the partner to do better is the goal.
- Have students in grades 3 through 8 create a unique pattern of movement using dribbling or ball-handling skills or tricks. They can put it into a pattern with a rhythm.
- Students can imagine that they are one of the magical Harlem Globetrotters while creating their patterns and tricks.

Assessment

Rubric

3 = Attempted to dribble and handle the ball as demonstrated; used finger pads

2 = Attempted to dribble and handle the ball as demonstrated; succeeded some of the time; used finger pads most of the time

1 = Attempted to dribble and handle the ball, but not as demonstrated; used finger pads some of the time

0 = Did not attempt to dribble or follow the demonstrations; used other parts of the hand to dribble

After each trial, each student should critique his or her partner and give feedback.

Safety

Students should progress according to their previous successful skill. Trying skills that are too advanced will cause students to lose control of the ball, allowing it to escape and travel into someone else's space or knock into something.

Tips and Variations

- Pretend that you are one of the Globetrotters. Put on a short show to some cool music. Your routine will either wow the students or motivate them to do your routine as well as or better than you did (that would be the ultimate goal).
- Have older students create a routine as a graded project. Just like the rhythmic project, suggest criteria for the routines.

Conclusion and Links to Real Life

"Harlem Globetrotters, watch out! Here come the _____ Globetrotters (fill in your school name). I liked seeing you use your finger pads and handle the ball with each challenge. The more you practice, the better skilled you'll become at handling a ball and dribbling."

Try at Home

"Ask your family if they have heard about the Harlem Globetrotters. If they have, show them how you were training today. If they haven't, put on a show like the Globetrotters do and explain how practicing will help you improve your skills, just like the basketball magicians."

--- Hockey Pinball ---
Dribbling

Skills	Activity Level	Intensity	Standards
Dribbling with a long-handled implement	Everyone is involved at all times.	Medium to high	① ② ⑤

Invitation

"Pinball machines push a ball and bounce it off the sides of the playing area. As the ball travels down the slope, it ricochets, bumps, and bangs through the course, scoring points each time it hits a target. The game continues until the ball goes through the flippers. We are going to try human hockey pinball today."

Equipment

- 15 **polyspots**
- 15 beanbags
- 15 hockey sticks

Description

Half of the group become part of the game and act as targets, while the other half strike a beanbag through the course with a hockey stick, trying to score points as they move through the human pinball machine.

First, set up the polyspots in the shape of a U, with three spots in the center of the U. Half of the group stand on the spots. Then designate some players to be jumpers, some to be swingers, and two to be flippers. The rest of the players, the strikers, try to move the beanbag through the game. After 3 minutes of play, switch the groups so that the strikers become part of the machine and the targets become the new strikers.

- Jumpers: These players do jumping jacks. The beanbag must go through the jumpers' legs to continue.
- Swingers: These players swing one leg forward and one leg backward. As they do so, the right leg kicks the beanbag toward the flippers, and the left leg kicks it the other

way. The striking players attempt to hit the legs of these players. If they hit a leg, the strikers score a point.

- ⬤ Flippers: These two players pivot and save a beanbag if the striker pushes the beanbag through at just the right time. If the flippers time their action correctly, they will kick the beanbag back into the game. If not, the beanbag will fall through the flippers, which signals the end of the game for that striker.
- ⬤ Strikers: About half of the class are jumpers, swingers, and flippers, and the other half are strikers. Starting at the flippers, the strikers use hockey sticks to move the beanbag along through the pinball game, racking up points as they go.

Setup

Look first; rearrange; put it back together.

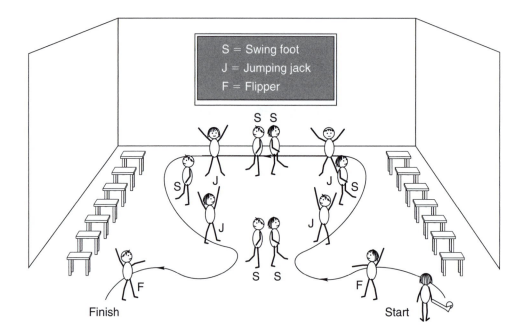

Break It Down in Detail

Lesson plans and in-depth information follow.

Objectives

- ⬤ Students strike an object with a long-handled implement toward a target.
- ⬤ Students attempt to aim at targets that are still, targets that are moving, and targets that will react after being hit.
- ⬤ Students appreciate the need for safety and controlled striking with long-handled implements.
- ⬤ Students interact and use their imagination, as if they were the mechanical moving parts of a game.

Warm-Up

Over, On, and Beside With Sticks

Cues and Concepts

Carry out the activities using the following cues:

- Eyes on the beanbag—keep watching the beanbag until the stick contacts it.
- Aim—look at your target and position your stick so that it is lined up with the target.
- Tap—when you don't want the beanbag to hit something accidentally, tap or hit it lightly.
- Follow through—after you strike the beanbag, bring the stick through the swing so that it is in line with the target.

Include the following concepts:

- Instruct students to keep the blade of the hockey stick on the floor.
- They should not raise the sticks off the floor, but instead should use a pushing motion.
- Like the mechanical parts of the game, students who are not striking must be continually moving or ready to do their part. This game can be intense and will really raise students' heart rates.
- Students must think about the angle that they must hit the beanbag in order to hit the target.
- Explain that students must consider the timing of the hit to make it through or to hit some of the targets.

Linking to other subjects:

- Math—geometry, angles, timing
- Science—timing, mechanical movements, force

Assessment

Rubric

3 = Struck safely and made it through the course successfully; exercised as part of the pinball game all the time

2 = Struck safely and made it through the course successfully; exercised most of the game

1 = Struck safely most of the time; exercised some of the game

0 = Did not strike safely; exercised some or none of the game

Safety

When striking with a long-handled implement, students must be especially cautious. To ensure that no one is hit with a stick, do not allow the blade to rise off the floor. All hits must be pushes.

Tips and Variations

- Imagine how fun it would be for games to come to life! Use the connection of the movie *Toy Story,* in which the toys come to life, to increase the excitability of your students.
- If the strikers cannot make it through your pinball game, reduce the level of obstruction created by the players who serve as game parts. Variations include the following:
  - Have the jumpers hold the jumping jack position for a count of 4 so that the legs stay apart longer.
  - Have the swingers swing their legs and then count to 10 before they swing again.
- If the floor is carpeted, use pucks or paper balls.
- This activity is recommended for students in grades 3 and up.

Conclusion and Links to Real Life

"Striking with a hockey stick involves safety, keeping your eyes on the beanbag, aiming, and following through. If you play hockey on the street, ice, or field, you will be prepared to dribble and will have developed more hand–eye coordination."

Try at Home

"If you haven't ever played pinball, ask your family or friends about the game. I bet they have never played human pinball before. Explain how you used striking to reenact the game, and then ask if you can play a real pinball game."

- - - Dribbling Stations and Assessment - - -

Dribbling

Skills	Activity Level	Intensity	Standards
Dribbling with long-handled implements, dribbling with feet, dribbling with hands	Everyone is active except during the assessment.	Medium	① ② ⑤ ⑥

Invitation

"Let's see what we know about dribbling while we do work at some stations and take an assessment at the end."

Equipment

- Six polyspots
- Six beanbags
- Six hockey sticks
- Six basketballs or bounceable balls
- Three paper balls, each made from three pieces of paper

Description

Create four stations for dribbling practice and one station for assessment. Allow enough time for everyone to be able to rotate to each station. Play upbeat music to start and stop.

1. Dribbling in and out of chairs, using hands and a bounceable ball
2. Dribbling in and out of chairs and defensive players, using feet and a paper ball
3. Dribbling in and out of chairs, using a hockey stick and beanbag
4. Dribbling with the feet and trying to avoid defensive players as they stand on polyspots and stick their legs out to stop the ball

For the assessment, students test their knowledge by taking a quick quiz.

1. What part of the hand would you use to dribble? (Have K through 2 students trace their hands and shade in the parts of the hand that touch the ball when dribbling.)
2. Describe the type of the force you use when dribbling with your feet.

3. How would you avoid an opponent while you are dribbling? (This question is for students in the upper grades.) Describe how you would do that in a sentence or two when you are

- dribbling with hands,
- dribbling with feet, and
- dribbling with a stick.

4. Draw yourself as an offensive player while dribbling and draw another person as a defensive player.

Setup

Look first; rearrange; put it back together.

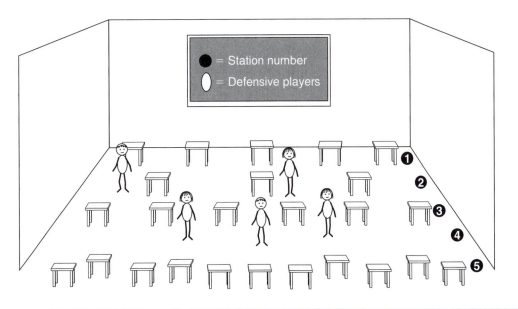

Break It Down in Detail

Lesson plans and in-depth information follow.

Objectives

- Students demonstrate their abilities to dribble with their hands, with their feet, and with a long-handled implement.
- Students demonstrate, on paper, their cognitive knowledge of dribbling.

Warm-Up

Watch the Shoes

Cues and Concepts

Carry out the activities using the following cues:

- Prompt students to show you what they know.
- At the beginning of the lesson remind students to
  - keep their eyes on the ball, puck, or beanbag;
  - use their finger pads when dribbling a basketball;
  - bend the knees;
  - dribble a basketball at waist level;

- keep the stick on the floor; and
- go for the object if they are defensive players.

Include the following concept:

- Dribbling is a moving skill. To be good at it, students must know how to keep their eyes on the object and know who and what is around them.

Assessment

Rubric

3 = Demonstrated age-appropriate dribbling; four out of four items correct on the assessment

2 = Demonstrated age-appropriate dribbling; two or three items correct on the assessment

1 = Dribbled but not at age-appropriate level; one item correct on the assessment

0 = Did not demonstrate the ability to dribble; no items correct on the assessment

Safety

Remind students about spatial awareness. All sticks must stay on the ground. Defensive players reach only for the object, not the person.

Tips and Variations

- Observe what your students can do. After you've prompted them, let them run the show. This is the time for you to see what you've taught your students.
- Take into account the grade level of your students when making assessments. Some of the assessment questions include options for different grade levels.

Conclusion and Links to Real Life

"You showed me how well you could dribble today, and what you knew about dribbling well. If you play any sport, especially soccer, basketball, or hockey, you will have the tools you need to succeed."

Try at Home

"Take your success to the court or the field. Join a sports team or club and put your skills to work. If you can't join a team, then try these skills in your neighborhood or at recess."

- - - Field Goal Super Bowl - - -

Kicking and punting

Skills	Activity Level	Intensity	Standards
Kicking, punting, aiming	Everyone is involved actively.	Medium	① ② ⑤ ⑥

Invitation

"The Super Bowl is one of the most popular and most watched sports events. We are about to host our very own Super Bowl right here. That's right—pick your favorite football team and prepare to kick and punt your way to winning your classroom Super Bowl."

Equipment

- One soft, very light foam ball per pair
- One paper ball per pair (up to three sheets for more weight)

Description

Participants need only a piece of paper or a very light Nerf or foam ball and kicking power.

- Each player picks a professional team to represent. You may have a tournament and post each player's team on the board with the player's points.
- Players perform the kickoff or the three-step approach for the punt.
- Players take turns on defense. They hold their arms up over their heads, as the officials do when a team scores a touchdown, to serve as goalposts for the kickers to kick through.
- The player on offense kicks to the goal (the upraised arms of the defensive player) from a distance of 10 feet (3 meters).
- If the offense scores, the offensive player does five jumping jacks for joy.
- Allow the offensive kicker or punter to kick or punt four times in a row.
- The two players then switch.
- The object is to score as many times as possible by kicking field goals.
- Switch players around so that they play someone different every few minutes.
- You may even determine a Super Bowl winner at the end by allowing the top two scoring teams play each other in the Super Bowl.

Setup

Look first; rearrange if necessary; put it back together.

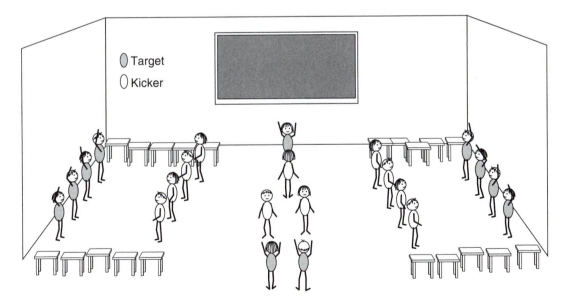

Break It Down in Detail

Lesson plans and in-depth information follow.

Objectives

- Students demonstrate a kick on the ground.
- Students in grades 3 through 8 kick using a three-step approach.
- Students in grades 3 through 8 punt using a three-step approach.

Warm-Up

Watch the Shoes

Cues and Concepts

Carry out the activities using the following cues:

- Step, step, step, kick—place the ball on the ground, take three steps toward the ball, and then kick the ball (start the step with the nondominant foot).
- Connect and follow—make contact with the ball and then let the kicking foot point to the target.
- 1, 2, 3, drop, punt—put the ball in your hands, take three steps, and then drop the ball and punt.

Include the following concepts:

- Explain that students should kick or punt using the dominant (strongest or most comfortable) leg.
- They should try to contact the ball with the shoelaces or top of the outside of the foot.
- Remind students to keep their eyes on the ball.
- When punting, students should drop the ball when the shoe is about 5 inches (12 centimeters) from the ball.

Assessment

Rubric

3 = Kicked and punted toward the target; positive defense; enthusiastic attitude

2 = Kicked and punted toward the target; positive defense; good attitude

1 = Kicked and punted toward the target; lack of effort on defense

0 = Did not attempt to kick or punt toward the target; lack of effort or made no effort on defense

Safety

Be sure that students realize not to cross into another person's area when retrieving a ball, unless they look first and say, "Excuse me." As an extra precaution, you could assign numbers to pairs of students and call them to kick or punt each second or so by saying, "Pair one, pair two," and so on.

Tips and Variations

- If you have a favorite pro team, let the students know how much you cheer for them and explain the huge following that football has in America. Then choose someone to be your rival. Compete against that student (four kicks or punts and four times on defense). Write your scores on the scoreboard. Your students will be dying to play after they witness this contest.

⬤ Younger students can attempt to punt, but you should not expect them to have great success or good form. Have these students simply drop the ball on their shoelaces.

Conclusion and Links to Real Life

"If you have never watched a professional football game, this can be your preview. Kicking is how the teams start the games and is one method of scoring. Practicing your kicking and punting will help your leg muscles get strong and will help in soccer and football."

Try at Home

"Kick all your dirty clothes into the dirty clothes hamper. You can help with the laundry, clean your room, and, of course, improve your kicking and aiming."

- - - Virtual Soccer - - -

Kicking

Skills	Activity Level	Intensity	Standards
Techniques of kicking, dribbling, heading, passing, making throw-ins	Everyone is actively involved.	Medium	① ② ⑤ ⑥

Invitation

"Does anyone here play soccer? Maybe you have, or maybe you haven't. Well, today we are going to follow the ball as we watch a video and perform the actions that the players do. If they kick the ball, then we will kick it. If they pass it, then we will pass it. Let's score a goooooaal!"

Equipment

⬤ TV, VCR, and video
⬤ One paper ball (three or four sheets balled up together) or beanbag per pair

Description

Videotape yourself or a team playing in a soccer game or use a video of professionals performing in a soccer game. Divide participants into pairs and place the pairs of students across from each other. Place the TV in the front center of the room. Each pair has a ball and follows the actions of the player on the video who has the ball.

⬤ If the player on the video is dribbling, the students dribble the ball up and down an imaginary line between them.
⬤ If the player on the video passes it, the student with the ball passes to his or her partner.
⬤ If the player on the video kicks toward a goal, the student with the ball kicks it toward his or her partner.
⬤ When a player on the video performs any action, the participant with the ball does the same thing.

Setup

Look first; rearrange; put it back together. Push the desks to the walls of the room.

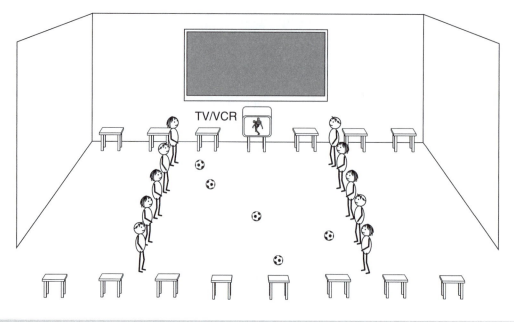

Break It Down in Detail

Lesson plans and in-depth information follow.

Objectives

- Students kick a stationary ball to a partner.
- Students trap and kick a moving ball.
- Students imitate mature kicking patterns.
- Students dribble the ball.
- Students maintain control of the ball while dribbling (control is the ability to keep the ball within 2 feet, or 60 centimeters, of the feet).
- Students aim for a target.
- Students respect others' space and attempt to stay within their own space, while helping others who have less control.

Warm-Up

Run and Scream or Watch the Shoes

Cues and Concepts

Carry out the activity using the following cues:

- Shoelaces—when you punt or kick, let the ball contact the shoelaces or outside top of your shoe.
- Little taps—when dribbling, tap the ball by lightly and gently pushing the ball with the inside, outside, heel, or toe of your shoe.
- Trap—stop the ball with the bottom of your shoe.
- Point to the target—aim your foot so that it points to the target on the follow-through.

Include the following concepts:

- Explain that controlling the ball means to keep the ball close to the feet, so that the person can maneuver it in a second's notice. For this activity, the ball should be no farther away than 2 feet (60 centimeters).

- Spatial awareness is important because students should stay in line with their partners. They must be aware of the players around them.
- By imitating and imagining the performance of you or players on videos, students have opportunities to enjoy themselves and to kick and dribble with good form and skill.

Assessment

Rubric

3 = Watched and imitated kicking and dribbling actions with best form for his or her ability

2 = Watched and imitated most of the time and used good form

1 = Kicked or dribbled some of the time without following directions and used poor form

0 = Sometimes or never kicked, dribbled, or followed directions; lacked control

Peer Assessment

- Did your partner get the ball to you most of the time?—good aiming.
- Did your partner dribble with light taps?—good controlled dribbling.
- Did your partner kick using the shoelaces?—gets behind or under ball.

Safety

Students must stay in line with their partners. Students should be cautious when retrieving the ball if it gets in other players' line of play. Students should say, "Excuse me," and wait for an invitation before moving into another group's line of play. If space is limited, have students work in shifts; they sit for 30 seconds and then switch and participate for 30 seconds.

Tips and Variations

- Line up the students so that all have a good view of the TV. For example, have your shortest students playing up front and your tallest playing at the back.
- If you don't have a video, use oral cues.

Conclusion and Links to Real Life

"When you were copying the actions of the people on the video or following my cues, you were kicking with your shoelaces, aiming at your targets, dribbling under control, and maintaining personal space. To close our lesson, your partner will describe what he or she noticed with your kicking and dribbling."

Try at Home

"Kick around a ball at home. Make the ball go with you everywhere you go for an hour. Try to maintain control as you kick a paper ball around."

- - - Kicking Stations and Assessment - - -

Kicking

Skills	Activity Level	Intensity	Standards
Techniques of kicking, dribbling, passing, punting	Everyone is involved except during the written assessment.	Medium	① ② ⑥

Invitation

"Let's see what you know and remember about kicking by kicking at some stations and then taking a quick quiz."

Equipment

- TV, VCR, and video
- Six paper balls (three pieces of paper balled up together) or beanbags
- Six deck rings or beanbags
- Pencils, quiz

Description

Divide participants into four groups, with an even number in each group. Rotate from station to station, making sure that everyone has enough time to get to each station. Use music as the stop and start signal.

- Station 1: Virtual Soccer. Participants watch a video and imagine that they are the athletes in the video kicking and performing other actions. See Virtual Soccer on page 157 for more information.
- Station 2: Field Goal Super Bowl. Students in pairs attempt to kick and punt a ball. See Field Goal Super Bowl on page 154.
- Station 3: Kicking and passing back and forth. Pairs pass back and forth, attempting not to require the other to move in order to trap the ring, ball, or beanbag.
- Station 4: Score a goal.
  - Pairs are 10 feet (3 meters) from each other and try to score a goal by aiming it between their partner's legs
  - If a participant scores, he or she does five jumping jacks for joy.
  - Partners switch positions after each goal attempt.
  - Challenge: If pairs or groups want to compete, they can keep score of how many goals they make.
- For the assessment (station 5), see what your participants know and recall.

Setup

Look first; rearrange; put it back together. Push the desks next to the walls of the room.

Dribbling and Kicking Assessment

1. Place an X on all parts of the foot that the ball hits when dribbling.

2. Place an X on the part of the foot that you should use when punting.

3. Describe how you would dribble:

    a. Tap, tap

    b. Bam, bam

    c. Smack, smack

4. When punting,

    a. drop the ball and run

    b. drop the ball on your shoelaces

    c. throw the ball into the air

5. Describe in a paragraph what it means to "have control" of the ball while dribbling. (3-8)

Draw a picture showing a person in control of the dribble.

Draw a picture showing a person who does not have control of the dribble.

From No Gym? No Problem! Physical Activities for Tight Spaces by Charmain Sutherland, 2006, Champaign, IL: Human Kinetics.

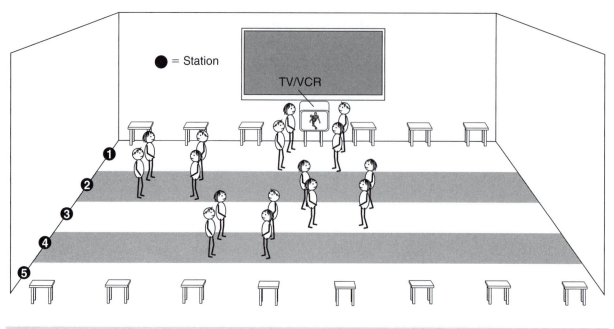

Break It Down in Detail

Lesson plans and in-depth information follow.

Objectives

- Students demonstrate their knowledge of kicking skills through a written assessment.
- Students demonstrate their dribbling, kicking, and punting ability at stations.

Warm-Up

Run and Scream or Watch the Shoes

Cues and Concepts

- Carry out the activity as described so that students can display their kicking, dribbling, and punting skills.
- Evaluate the students' kicking knowledge according to their written assessment.

Assessment

Rubric

3 = Exhibited skills in kicking, dribbling, and punting at all stations, following previous cues; scored five of five on the written assessment

2 = Exhibited skills in kicking, dribbling, and punting at all stations but neglected to follow some cues; scored three or four on the written assessment

1 = Did not display skills in kicking, dribbling, and punting at all stations; neglected to follow some cues; scored one or two on the written assessment

0 = Did not display skills in kicking, dribbling, and punting at any station; neglected to follow all cues; showed no knowledge base on the written assessment; scored zero on the written assessment

Safety

Remind students to respect others' space when they must track down their ball in another station.

Tips and Variations

- Explain to students that you are waiting for them to show you what they know about kicking, dribbling, and punting. Let them know that they are on stage and that it is time for the show and their assessment.
- Adjust the assessment according to the students' grade and skill level. Assess only what you have taught previously.

Conclusion and Links to Real Life

"You've kicked it into high gear today. I saw your kicking, dribbling, and punting skills, and I look forward to seeing what you know from looking at your written assessments."

Try at Home

"When you get your assessment back, take it home and test your family on their knowledge of kicking. You may have to teach them a few tricks about kicks."

Striking and Volleying

Hitting an object is attractive to both children and adults. Whacking a tennis ball with a 70-mile-per-hour (110-kilometer-per-hour) serve or smacking a baseball with all your might is certainly appealing. Striking involves hitting an object with the hand, body, or an implement such as a racket, stick, or bat. Volleying is striking in order to keep an object in the air, as players do in volleyball, tennis, badminton, and even soccer.

- - - Flapjacks and Frying Pan Shots - - -

Striking and volleying with short-handled implements

Skills	Activity Level	Intensity	Standards
Striking with short-handled implements	Everyone is involved.	Medium to low	① ② ⑥

Invitation

"Have you ever seen a chef, the person with the tall white hat, handle the frying pan in the morning and toss those fluffy pancakes into the air? How about becoming that chef and flipping a few flapjacks of your own, by using paddles and short rackets?"

Equipment

One beanbag and one paddle or racket per person

Description

Participants use a short-handled paddle as if it were a frying pan and the beanbag as if it were a pancake.

Direct students by leading the activity as if you were the lead chef; each person manipulates a paddle and beanbag.

- Grip the handle of your frying pan (paddle) tightly.
- Shuffle your pancake from the tip of the paddle face to the back of the paddle face; then shuffle the pancake from left to right.
- Now try to have the flapjack circle around the frying pan.
- Let's try walking around the kitchen with our frying pans and flapjacks. Keep your eyes on both your flapjack and the other cooks so that you don't bump into them.
- You must keep your grip tight and level to keep the flapjack from falling to the floor.
- Now let's try to advance from cook to chef by doing some fancy cooking, by tossing the flapjacks into the air and catching them in the paddle.
- Keep your feet still when you toss the flapjacks, because you don't want to make a mess in the kitchen with fallen flapjacks.
- Try tossing higher each time, little by little.
- Now become a tricky chef and strike the flapjack upward several times without dropping it.
- How many times in a row can you strike it without moving your feet? (Younger students with less control can start from a seated or kneeling position.)
- For even fancier flapjacking, try these tricks:
  - Add butter—touch the paddle to other hand while the beanbag is in the air before catching it.
  - Add syrup—touch your toes, knees, and head before catching the beanbag.
- For all the advanced chefs in the room, here's your challenge. Find someone in the kitchen to work with you and stand 3 feet (1 meter) apart.
  - Put one beanbag away and gently flip a flapjack to your partner so that it lands on his or her frying pan.
  - If you and your partner are expert chefs and have great hand–eye coordination, try striking the flapjack back and forth.
- Now try flipping your wrist as you toss your flapjack to yourself, and catch it on the other side. This is called backhand flapjack flipping.

⑤ Finally, let's add the frying pan shot to our list of skills. Place the frying pan in front of you, at eye level, so that the flat part is in front of your face. Toss the beanbag up with your other hand, just above your forehead, and tap it away from your body very lightly. The beanbag should fall just barely past your shoes.

Setup

Look first; rearrange if necessary; put it back together. Little to no rearranging necessary. Participants need room only to move their arms upward. They can strike to one another over the desks.

Break It Down in Detail

Lesson plans and in-depth information follow.

Objectives

⑤ Students strike with a short-handled paddle.

⑤ Students practice and realize the principle of progression while striking an object.

⑤ Students identify and practice techniques that make striking more successful.

⑤ Students use their imagination and creativity as they strike an object.

Warm-Up

Thumb Jack Wrestling

Cues and Concepts

Carry out the activities using the following cues:

⑤ Flat as a flapjack—strike the beanbag with the paddle or racket face flat.

⑤ Feet still—strike so that the beanbag comes right back to you; you should be able to keep your feet still.

⑤ Grip tight—hold the handle of the paddle or racket tightly; it should not be floppy.

Include the following concepts:

⑤ Introduce the grip as a handshake. Have everyone shake a partner's paddle or racket as if it were a hand. Participants should hold the paddle or racket firmly so that the partner cannot shake it out of their hands.

⑤ Students should keep the racket or paddle in the middle of the body. Holding it too high or too low will not produce successful hits.

⑤ Hand–eye coordination is important. Emphasize keeping the eyes on the beanbag.

⑤ Use the principle of progression. Start with contact of the object and an implement and gradually move to striking while the object is moving. Students eventually progress to working with another person.

⑤ Incorporate anatomy—**biceps, triceps, deltoids,** humerus.

Assessment

Rubric

3 = Handled paddle or racket safely; progressed to more complex tricks

2 = Handled paddle or racket safely; followed along with basic tricks

1 = Handled paddle or racket safely; had trouble following basic tricks

0 = Handled paddle or racket unsafely; did not follow basic tricks

Safety

Students should not perform a full swing of a racket or paddle in this lesson. If space is tight, have students work in shifts. They must not raise rackets or paddles above the chest.

Tips and Variations

- Play up the chef's role and talk about fallen flapjacks, the flattest flapjacks, or doing tricks by adding more than just syrup or butter. Add strawberries, whipped cream, chocolate chips, or sprinkles. If your flapjacks are beyond successful, start making pizza. Roll out the dough and flip the dough (beanbag) in the air. By touching their noses when the beanbag is in the air, students can add cheese. Have students come up with other tricks as they add sauce, pepperoni, and mushrooms.
- Put down a **polyspot** if a student cannot stay near his or her desk.
- If space is an issue, have only half the class work at one time.

Conclusion and Links to Real Life

"Like beginning cooks, you started by watching an object that was resting flat on the racket (pan). When you became more confident, you were able to do more with those flapjacks. When you had a tight grip and focused your eyes on the beanbag, you were able to strike upward and gradually increase the difficulty of striking. Finally, you became a chef, and you became a potential tennis, racquetball, squash, badminton, or table tennis player."

Try at Home

"You can do the same thing at home with a real frying pan, or if that's too heavy, use two arms or a spatula. Ball up some aluminum foil and make flapjacks at home."

- - - Paper Football - - -

Striking and volleying

Skills	Activity Level	Intensity	Standards
Striking, hand–eye coordination	Everyone is involved.	Medium to low	① ② ④ ⑥

Invitation

"Normally, we don't think of football as a striking skill, but paper football is all about striking with your hands."

Description

Each field is made of one or more desks or tables. Partners compete across the desk or table with a triangular-shaped paper football.

- Each pair of partners needs a paper football. Make the first fold going the long way on the paper, about 1 1/2 to 2 inches (4 to 5 centimeters) in from the edge. Crease, fold again, and repeat, until the paper is 1 1/2 to 2 inches (4 to 5 centimeters) wide. Then fold from the bottom left corner to form a triangle. Fold that triangle upward to form another triangle. Repeat making triangles until you come to the end of the paper. Tuck in the ends so that the paper stays in a firm triangle. Tape each football with a piece of tape for extra security. The students can write the two team names that they are representing on the sides.

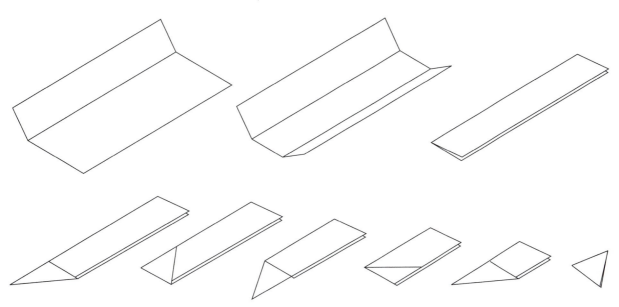

- Participants start play by having one of them toss the football in the air. Whoever's side lands face up chooses either to kick off or to receive.
- To kick off, the person flicks the football to the receiving team.
- The receiving team prepares to play by placing the wrist and the fingertips of one hand on the desk or table. The other hand must be under the desk or table.
- Players push and slide the football with their fingers in an attempt to cross the other team's goal line (end of the desk or table).
- Players cannot press their chests against the desk or table to stop the shot. They can only use that one hand.
- When a player crosses the goal line, he or she scores 6 points. The player then attempts an extra point.
  - Extra point, offense—the player holds the football at midfield by balancing one of the triangular points on the field and another on the tip of the finger. Using the dominant hand, the player aims and flicks the football between the goal posts, created by the hands of defensive player.
  - Extra point, defense—the player puts both fists on the desk or table, connects the index fingers, and extends the thumbs in the air.
  - Scoring—if the football goes above the index fingers, below the head of the player on defense, and between the thumbs, the try is successful, for 1 extra point.
- The game resumes with the scoring team kicking off to the receiving team.
- Students perform various actions after certain game events:
  - After a touchdown, they do 20 jumping jills, 3 push-ups, and 5 crunches.
  - After an out-of-bounds play, they do a 20-second stretch.
  - After a field goal, they run in place for 15 seconds.
  - A time-out occurs every 3 minutes. Students do jumping jacks for 15 seconds.

Setup

Look first; rearrange; put it back together. If the room has desks, reposition them so that each desk faces and adjoins another. If the room has tables, opponents sit at opposite ends of a table.

Break It Down in Detail

Lesson plans and in-depth information follow.

Objectives

- Students strike an object with fine motor skills.
- Students improve hand–eye coordination while striking with their hands.
- Students play fair while modifying a popular game and displaying good sportsmanship.
- Students play both offensive and defensive roles.

Warm-Up

Warm-Up Bingo

Cues and Concepts

Carry out the activities using the following cues:

- Look for openings—when you see an angle to score and your opponent is not covering, take a shot.
- Eyes on the ball—follow the ball with your eyes at all times.

Include the following concepts:

- Students will improve hand–eye coordination by watching the ball. The moment the eyes come off the ball, the opponent will score.
- Explain that the offense has the ball and tries to score. The defense doesn't have the ball, but wants it. The defense tries to prevent scoring.
- Explain strategies as plans to be successful.

Assessment

Rubric

3 = Used strategies; followed all rules; exercised at 100% effort

2 = Attempted to use strategies; followed rules; exercised at 100% effort

1 = Did or did not use strategies; followed some rules; did not exercise at 100% effort

0 = Did not use much, if any, strategy; did not follow most rules; exercised with minimal effort

Safety

Students must keep the ball below the neck. Any extra point attempt above the neck results in a penalty of a point for the other team.

Tips and Variations

- Play a couple of downs with a volunteer to set the tone of the game. Paper football is fast paced and fun. If you score, do a touchdown dance and a cheer for your team.
- Players can try using the nondominant hand to play. Compare the difference in scores. For more variety or for competition, have students play for 3 minutes and then switch teams so that players have the chance to play other teams. You may want to keep score and have a championship.

Conclusion and Links to Real Life

"We modified our football game to include striking, and we improved our hand–eye coordination, which helps us in every part of our lives. Some of you were strategic in your offensive and defensive moves today. I hope that you had a workout after scoring too!"

Try at Home

"Now you realize how simple it is to improve hand–eye coordination, exercise, and use strategies during games. Keep a piece of paper handy so that you can play paper football whenever you want to. It doesn't take up space or break anything!"

- - - Pencil Pool - - -

Striking

Skills	Activity Level	Intensity	Standards
Striking, strategy, aiming	Everyone is actively involved.	High to medium	① ④ ⑤

Invitation

"Do you have a table? Do you have a pencil? Good. Let's play pencil pool. Pool does not involve swimming. Instead, it includes striking with long-handled implements. Our table isn't as large as regulation table. It's only 8 inches (20 centimeters) wide. The pool balls aren't the size of tennis balls. They are the size of raisins or grapes. The skill and game are like the real thing, just downsized to fit on your desk."

Equipment

- One piece of paper per pair, at least 8 inches by 10 inches (20 centimeters by 25 centimeters)
- One pencil per pair
- Eight balled-up pieces of paper per person (one set of balls distinguished from the other by being colored or marked in some way by the participants)
- Optional—different balled-up piece of paper for each table to represent the eight ball

Description

Design a table on a chalkboard, overhead, or poster with six pockets and a triangle on one end for racking the balls. Students pair up and make their own table with a sheet of regular notebook paper. Each person makes eight balls out of paper, rolling them up tightly. One

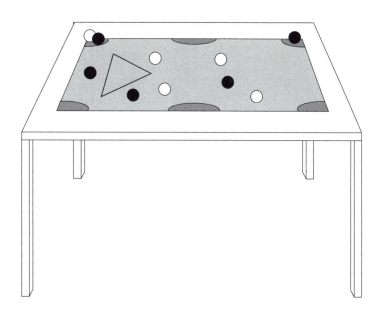

person must color his or her balls with a pen to distinguish them from the balls of the other. Don't worry about the cue ball; students will strike the balls directly, with the flat end of a pencil.

1. The object of the game is to be the first to get all the pool balls in the pockets. An option for fourth through eighth graders is to use an eight ball, marked with a big *8*. After hitting in all of his or her balls, the person must hit the eight ball in a pocket to win.

2. Each player takes one turn striking the ball with the pencil. If the ball goes in by sliding into the drawn pockets, the player goes again.

3. Each time a player takes a turn, he or she does two repetitions of a particular exercise; if the person makes it in the pocket, he or she does five repetitions of a particular exercise. Exercises could include push-ups, crunches, jumping jacks, arm circles, or heel raises. The exercise activity could also be dancing, jogging in place, or stretching for a certain number of seconds. Change the type of exercise every minute or two by writing the name of the exercise on the board or saying it aloud.

Setup

Look first; rearrange if necessary; put it back together.

Break It Down in Detail

Lesson plans and in-depth information follow.

Objective

Students strike an object with a pencil, representing a long-handled implement.

Warm-Up

Review the proper form of the exercises that you will be putting on the board.

Cues and Concepts

Carry out the activities using the following cue:

- Angle your shot—line up your shot so that the pencil strikes the ball at an angle that will cause it to go in the pocket.

Include the following concept:

- Variation of force is important in pool. Too much force will cause the ball to bounce out of the pocket, whereas too little force will require the player to hit the ball more often.

Assessment

Rubric

3 = Participated by concentrating on striking; exercised properly and did the appropriate exercise

2 = Attempted most turns at striking with concentration; exercised most of the time with the appropriate exercise

1 = Attempted striking but lacked concentration; did not always perform the appropriate exercise

0 = Did not attempt to strike with concentration; used improper form and inappropriate exercises

Safety

Students should be aware of their personal space while moving. They should be courteous when interrupting a game for some of the tasks by saying, "Excuse me" and "Thank you."

Tips and Variations

- Discuss the science and mathematical connection of pool and physical education. Include angles, force, action, reaction, Newton's law, and velocity.
- Set up a larger game on the floor. Using tape works well for making pockets. Use beanbags as balls and hockey sticks, bats, or clubs as pool sticks.

Conclusion and Links to Real Life

"If you were a pool player, you would strike with a larger stick, of course, but the concept of the miniature game is similar. Varying the force and angle of hits determined how successful you were at striking."

Try at Home

"You can create a portable game at home by using the top of a shoebox, cereal box, or other rectangular object. Try this at home when you are not able to go outside to play. Think of exercises or actions that will get your heart rate up for each hit you take."

- - - Putt-Putt - - -

Striking and volleying with long-handled implements

Skills	Activity Level	Intensity	Standards
Striking, putting in golf	Everyone is involved, actively.	Low to medium	① ② ⑤ ⑥

Invitation

"If you were Tiger Woods or Annika Sorenstam, two outstanding golf professionals, you would still need to go to the putt-putt range to sink the golf ball into the hole. So let's create our own course. We can invite Tiger or Annika to practice their putts—the smooth, close-to-the-hole shots."

Equipment

- Golf putters or any safe, long-handled implement
- One beanbag per person
- Tape for signs (A1 through A9, B1 through B9, C1 through C9)

Description

Each person has a putter or some safe long-handled implement—a hockey stick, pillo polo stick (a stick with a foam end that looks like a Q-tip), or broomstick—and tries to putt the beanbag from hole #1 to hole #9 in the fewest strokes or hits.

1. Divide the class into three groups of nine. Call one group the A group, one the B group, and one the C group. Each group creates a course with nine holes, using the desks and chairs as obstacles.

2. Each student in the group makes an obstacle (hole). Students number their holes and tape the numbers near the holes. For example, the A team's holes would be 1A,

2A, and so on. The B team's holes would be 1B, 2B, and so on. Ideas for holes include the following:

- Through the legs of the desk
- Certain spot on the wall
- Certain leg of the desk or chair
- Certain spot on the door
- Certain spot on the floor

3. After the groups make their courses, one representative from each group quickly walks through the group's course, displaying the holes.

4. The players start at hole #1 and count how many putts they need to make it all the way around one course.

5. Each time a player hits a hole, he or she jumps up and down 15 times.

6. Each time a player hits another player's beanbag, he or she must apologize and do 10 hops in place.

7. Players should see how many putts it takes to get to the end.

8. After completing a course, players move on to the next course and begin counting all over. They move from course A to B to C to A.

9. If players repeat a course, they should try to lower the number of putts they need to complete the course.

Setup

Look first; rearrange if necessary; put it back together. Students may arrange the desks, carefully, to create holes.

Break It Down in Detail

Lesson plans and in-depth information follow.

Objective

Students strike an object with soft force, using a long-handled implement that represents a golf putter.

Warm-Up

Find the Leader

Cues and Concepts

Carry out the activities using the following cues:

- Eyes on—keep your eyes on the beanbag until the putter hits the beanbag.
- Push—don't swing; push the club through the beanbag.
- Follow the putt—aim the putter at the hole; when finished, the putter should be lined up with the hole.

Include the following concepts:

- Explain that putting is a soft shot. Putting is striking, yet it is not done with a forceful swing. It is a combination of a sweep and a push.
- Instruct students to hold the handle with the nondominant hand at the butt of the putter (the top of the putter when lining up the putt) and the dominant hand gripping the handle so that the two hands are touching.
- Tell students to draw an imaginary line from the putter to the hole, in their heads. They should hit as if they were following that line, right to the hole.

Assessment

Rubric

> 3 = Performed safe putts; tried to putt with as few strokes as possible; followed the course
>
> 2 = Performed safe putts; putted softly throughout the course; followed the course
>
> 1 = Performed safe putts; putted often but without strategy; didn't follow the course
>
> 0 = Performed unsafe putts; putted often without aiming or strategy; didn't follow the course

Safety

Students must not lift the putter from the floor. Allow absolutely no swinging.

Tips and Variations

- If you have enough time, create a scorecard so that students have a written record of how well they did and how much they improved.
- If lack of equipment is an issue, have half the class act as a moving hole by doing jumping jacks or an exercise that keeps them involved and creates challenges for the others.

Conclusion and Links to Real Life

"Did you know that Tiger Woods, the famous golf pro, was on TV putting a golf ball when he was younger than 5 years old? He discovered the sport of golf, which involves striking and putting, and now he, like millions of other people, will probably play golf for the rest of his life."

Try at Home

"Create your own course at home. Use a broom, mop, or something with a long handle to work on your putting skills."

--- Tennis Camp ---

Striking and volleying

Skills	Activity Level	Intensity	Standards
Striking, volleying, hand–eye coordination	Everyone is involved.	Medium	① ② ③ ⑥

Invitation

"If Roger Federer or Andy Roddick came to show us a few tricks of the trade at a camp, what sports camp would it be? What if Venus and Serena Williams came too? That's right. Tennis is the name of the game. All you need to play is a racket and another person. Let's imagine that we are at tennis camp."

Equipment

Each person needs a balled-up piece of paper. They can write Wilson, Penn 1, Dunlop 3, or some other brand name on the ball.

Description

The camp starts with a warm-up. After that, the camp will be divided into five stations.

Stations at Tennis Camp

- ⬬ Station 1—Forehand. Participants use the inside of their hands and strike a balled-up piece of paper, mimicking the motion of a forehand stroke. They should strike the ball to a partner, who catches it and strikes it back with a forehand.

- ⬬ Station 2—Backhand. Participants use the back side of their hands and strike a balled-up piece of paper, mimicking the motion of a backhand stroke. They should strike the ball to a partner, who catches it and strikes it back with a forehand. Partners switch roles midway through so that everyone gets to backhand.

- ⬬ Station 3—Volley. Participants use the forehand or backhand strokes to volley the ball back and forth. Ask students to see how many successful volleys they can do without moving out of the station or dropping the ball.

- ⬬ Station 4—Smash. Participants work in pairs. One partner stands to the side and tosses the ball to the other, who does an overhead smash.

- ⬬ Station 5—Serve. Each person tosses the ball to himself or herself with the nondominant hand and performs a serve to a designated spot in the room.

Setup

Look first; rearrange; put it back together. Depending on what is easier, place the chairs and tables either all in the middle or all around the perimeter.

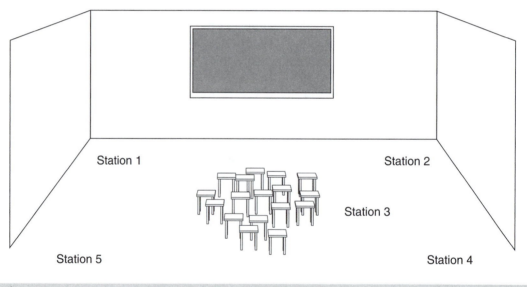

Station 1   Station 2

Station 3

Station 5   Station 4

Break It Down in Detail

Lesson plans and in-depth information follow.

Objectives

- ⬬ Students strike a ball, varying the force of their hits.
- ⬬ Students strike a ball using a forehand motion and a backhand motion.
- ⬬ Students improve hand–eye coordination by watching the ball hit their hands as they are striking.
- ⬬ Students cooperate with others to attain a goal in striking.

Warm-Up

Quick Feet

Cues and Concepts

Carry out the activities using the following cues:

- Quick feet—stay on the balls of your feet so that you can move quickly to position yourself for a good hit.
- Eyes on the ball—keep your eyes on the ball. If your eyes lose the ball, you will miss it too.
- Opposition—try to step with the opposite foot from the striking hand for a more balanced and smoother hit.

Include the following concepts:

- Instruct students to vary the forces of their hits. The smash is the strongest; volleying is the lightest.
- Students should aim at the target. As the students toss the ball to one another, they should attempt to strike the ball so that the tosser does not have to move his or her feet to reach the ball.
- Urge students to progress gradually. Striking should be slow and gentle, with students aiming at their targets. They can increase the force of their hits after they can hit the target consistently.

Assessment

Rubric

3 = Used appropriate force when striking; stuck to the task at each station; cooperated well as a partner

2 = Used appropriate force most of the time; stuck to the task at each station; cooperated well as a partner

1 = Used appropriate force some of the time; stuck to the task most of the time at each station; cooperated with partner

0 = Did not use appropriate force when striking; did not stick to tasks at most or any of the stations; lacked cooperation with partner

Safety

Students must stay in their stations. Use polyspots to avoid students' tendency to move in order to keep the volley going.

Tips and Variations

- As soon as you walk in, select a capable student to volley with you. The activity will intrigue students. Those in the upper grades will want to beat your volleying score, and younger students will want to volley just as you do. Bring in a tennis racket and demonstrate the motions of the smash, serve, forehand, and backhand. This demonstration gives a visual cue to students as they use their hands but imagine them as rackets.
- Younger students may not have the coordination or skill to perform a smash, serve, or volley, but they sure want to try. So let them. Reduce the number of balls at each station. Although using fewer balls reduces time on task physically, students then have the opportunity to watch others and analyze their movements. You will also reduce the number of balls that are loose in the room.

Conclusion and Links to Real Life

"At first Andy Roddick could barely hold a tennis racket. As he grew stronger with age and by practice, he was able to strike at his targets and hit them. Later he increased the force of his forehand and backhand. He developed so much force in his smash and serve that his opponents often could not return his hits. Today's lesson has started to work the same way for you. The great thing about tennis is that you need only one other person to play with and it involves all your muscles during play."

Try at Home

"You can volley paper, aluminum foil, socks, or foam balls almost anywhere and anytime. Ask friends or family to work with you. See how many volleys you can do without a miss. Tell me next time we meet."

--- Virtual Tennis, Hockey, or Golf ---
Striking and volleying

Skills	Activity Level	Intensity	Standards
Striking, striking forms, offensive and defensive tactics	Everyone is involved.	Medium to low	① ② ⑥

Invitation

"Have you ever imagined playing pro hockey or tennis? Maybe you are not quite sure how to play or how to use a stick, club, or racket. Well, today we are going to select a team or player to watch and become that player."

Equipment

TV, VCR, and video

Description

Videotape yourself playing a game or a team playing a game, or just use a video of professionals performing in a game involving striking.

Tennis

- Each participant chooses a player to follow. For example, if you play a video of Andy Roddick versus Roger Federer, the students each choose a player and move to the appropriate side. The Roddicks are on one side, and the Federers are on the opposite side, facing the Roddicks.
- Before you start the video, model the following skills so that you can prompt the participants to recognize and associate the words with the athlete's actions: serve, smash, forehand, backhand, volley.
- Each time their chosen player hits the ball, the participants perform the actions.
- With older children, explain tactics and scoring:
  - Love, 15, 30, 40, deuce
  - Game, set, match
  - Striking low and forcefully
  - Hitting where the opponent would least expect it

Hockey

- Use the Rangers versus the Capitals or supply other names of teams for them to pick from.
- Half the participants are the Rangers, and the other half are the Capitals. Students can choose a player on their team to follow, but if they choose the goalie they must switch midway through the class to get more full-range-of-movements shots.

- Model the skills that you would like them to learn and improve: shooting for goal, passing to teammates.
- As the participants watch, they should physically move their feet from side to side as if they were skating. They should mimic the actions that they see on the video—shooting the puck, blocking, and passing.

Golf

- Videotape a golf game.
- Each participant mimics every golfer, instead of following just one.
- Model the following skills so that the students can properly learn the techniques: driving, putting, making iron shots (as if they were using an iron club), making sand shots.
- Participants should learn scoring too. Each hit equals a stroke, and the lowest score wins.

Setup

Look first; rearrange; put it back together. Participants need only enough room to swing their arms and step from side to side. You can move the desks to the side if necessary; otherwise, leave them where they are as long as students can see the TV.

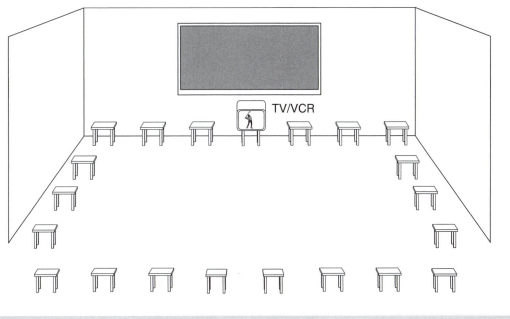

Break It Down in Detail

Lesson plans and in-depth information follow.

Objectives

- Students perform the striking actions of golf, hockey, and tennis.
- Students imitate mature forms of striking, as demonstrated by players on a video.

Warm-Up

Rock, Paper, Scissors—Action

Cues and Concepts

Carry out the activities using the following cues:

- Act as you watch—perform the actions that you see on the video.
- Full motion—swing, strike, and hit with the full range of motion.

Also include the following concepts:

- Explain that we can learn by watching. So watching and imitating will help students learn to strike with implements with more success, power, and accuracy.
- Explain that a player on offense has the ball and will attempt to score.
- A player on defense wants the ball and tries to stop opponents from scoring by blocking shots and causing opponents to have a more difficult time playing. Of course, golf doesn't include defense.

Assessment

Rubric

3 = Followed all actions on the video

2 = Attempted to follow all actions on the video

1 = Did not follow many actions on the video

0 = Did not attempt to follow the actions on the video

Safety

Students should stay in their personal space. Students should look before they perform vigorous swings and strikes.

Tips and Variations

- If you wanted to learn a certain dance move or sports skill, you would ask someone to show you. That is why this activity is so beneficial. Students can see the action and break down the skill. With video you can even slow down the movement to illustrate a particular aspect of a skill.
- If you don't have a video, perform the actions yourself. Ask a student to come to the front and have the others follow the model's actions.

Conclusion and Links to Real Life

"When we were babies we watched others and learned how to walk, talk, and run. At first we could not do it, but we watched and kept trying until we finally got it. That's how we learn. I'm sure you improved some part of the striking skills we imitated today. Sometimes we can improve even more without focusing on the object, because when we focus on the object we may forget how we should hit it."

Try at Home

"Watch someone play a sport that you want to know more about. See what you can learn from watching the player's form. You can watch TV, parents, or a sports team."

- - - What's Up? - - -

Striking and volleying

Skills	Activity Level	Intensity	Standards
Volleying, setting	Everyone is actively involved.	High to medium	① ② ④ ⑤

Invitation

"Do you think that I can keep this balloon from hitting the ground for the entire time that we have PE? If I volley well and use your help, I think we can keep it up."

Equipment

- One balloon for each player (at least two different colors; extra blown-up balloons in case some pop)
- One balloon with distinguishing marks

Description

Participants volley, catch, and strike a balloon in the air to themselves and others. Meanwhile, the whole group accepts the responsibility to keep one balloon up for the entire time. Make sure that the one balloon has marks that make it easy to be distinguished. Participants follow along with your guidance. As the difficulty increases, the exercise load increases too. Use the jacks and jills move cube (a large die with variations of jumping jacks on each side; see chapter 2) or pick an activity that varies the exercise after the successful completion of each level.

Each person gets a balloon. On your signal, they do the following (as you are talking, remember to keep the other balloon up):

- They toss the balloon in the air and catch it at eye level 10 times, while seated on the floor. (Increase skill level—20 repetitions of whatever they roll with the jacks and jills move cube.)
- They toss the balloon in the air and catch it at eye level 10 times, while standing. (Increase skill level—25 repetitions of whatever they roll with the jacks and jills move cube.)
- If successful, they set (push with the fingers of both hands) the balloon upward so that it comes back down at the forehead, and they keep setting it repeatedly, while seated. They continue for 2 minutes. (Increase skill level—30 repetitions of whatever they roll with the jacks and jills move cube.)
- If successful, they stand and set for 2 minutes. (Increase skill level—35 repetitions of whatever they roll with the jacks and jills move cube.)
- If successful, they get into pairs and sit on either side of a desk. They volley back and forth over the desk with each other for 3 minutes. They may count the number of consecutive successful volleys. (Increase skill level—40 repetitions of whatever they roll with the jacks and jills move cube.)
- If successful (if they can volley with their feet relatively still), players may stand and volley for 3 minutes. They may count the number of consecutive successful volleys. (Increase skill level—45 repetitions of whatever they roll with the jacks and jills move cube.)
- Split the class into two groups. One group sits in the chairs in one half of the room, and the other group sits in the chairs in the other half of the room. Give each group four balloons. Each group should have a different color. The task of the teams is to keep the balloons up. See which team will have a balloon, or the most balloons, up in the air at the end of a minute. (Extend the contest to 2 minutes for the next round.)

Setup

Look first; rearrange if necessary; put it back together. No setup needed.

Break It Down in Detail

Lesson plans and in-depth information follow.

Objectives

- Students volley a balloon upward.
- Students use volleying skills to keep a balloon in the air.

Warm-Up

Jacks and Jills Move Cube

Cues and Concepts

Carry out the activities using the following cues:

- Push—bend the elbows and push up to the ceiling.
- Eyes on—keep your eyes on the balloon.
- At your eyeballs—volley the ball so that it comes back down directly in line with your eyeballs.

Include the following concept:

- Explain that volleying is a method of striking repeatedly. Setting is pushing the ball upward with an angle that sends the ball where the setter wants it to go. When setting to themselves, students should try to make the object come down to their eyeballs. When setting to a partner, they push it up with the finger pads and angle it up and away so that it lands at their partner's eyeballs.

Assessment

Rubric

3 = Participated with best effort; volleyed balloons and kept them up longer than expected

2 = Attempted most exercises with best effort; volleyed balloons and kept them up most of the time, as expected

1 = Attempted all exercises but didn't try hard with all of them; volleyed balloons without trying to keep them up

0 = Attempted only some exercises; didn't follow directions for volleying

Safety

Students should hold balloons delicately in their hands. They must not squeeze, rub, or pull the balloons. Balloons will pop on occasion, but they should not pop often.

Tips and Variations

- Keep your designated balloon up at all times. When you need to help someone, say, "What's up?" and ask the students to keep your balloon up while you help. This venture brings the whole class together as a team and maintains focus.
- If you have time, introduce the dink (with the hand in a fist, gently tap the balloon with the back of the hand), the dig (with the hand in a fist, reach out for a balloon that is falling and prevent it from hitting the ground by punching it upward), the serve, and the smash.

Conclusion and Links to Real Life

"What's up? Are you still volleying our balloon? Volleying is fun and a challenge to do with another person. If we volley so that the balloon or ball comes back down near our eyes, then we will probably have long volleys. If we set the ball off to the sides of our eyes or our teammate's eyes, our volleying probably won't last too long."

Try at Home

"Challenge your friends and everyone in your family to a volley competition. They are all on your team. Volley with one person and count how many volleys you can do without a miss. Then volley with another person and see how many you two can do without a miss. Challenge each person to do better than the others as you work with each one as a team."

- - - Striking Stations and Assessment - - -

Striking

Skills	Activity Level	Intensity	Standards
Striking with short-handled implements, striking with long-handled implements, hand–eye coordination	Everyone is involved.	Low to medium	① ② ⑤ ⑥

Invitation

"Let's check out our striking skills in a variety of stations involving different types of implements, styles, and tasks."

Equipment

- Paper for three footballs
- Paper for one baseball
- Paper for three tennis balls
- Paper to mark the five holes in putt-putt
- Six beanbags
- Six paddles
- Pencils and test for each participant

Description

Using the striking skills from the previous lessons, choose a sample from each and use it as a station. Include quick test questions at each station to see what each person learned.

- Paper Football—Players choose teams to represent, make their triangular football, arrange their desks or tables to form a field, and play.
- Tennis Camp—Players start with a serve and then volley using their forehand and backhand. They use only a paper ball and no implements. They may use a chair as the net.
- Flapjack Kitchen—Using a short-handled paddle, players strike flapjacks (beanbags) into the air and catch them. They can flip them if they are in control (not having to chase the beanbag after they contact it).
- Putt-Putt—Create a five-hole course for players to go through. Players attempt to get the lowest score possible by putting a beanbag with a putter.

Setup

Look first; rearrange; put it back together.

- 🅢 Station 1—Paper Football. Place six desks in three groups of two desks each, one facing another.
- 🅢 Station 2—Tennis Camp. Place three desks 5 feet (1.5 meters) from one another to represent nets.
- 🅢 Station 3—Flapjack Kitchen. Players need only about 3 feet (1 meter) of room, so no rearranging is needed.
- 🅢 Station 4—Putt-Putt. Leave the desks in place and create a course by placing five markers (pieces of paper) on the holes, using the desks as obstacles and as actual holes to hit.

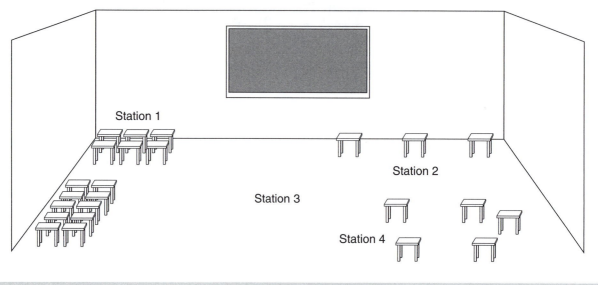

Break It Down in Detail

Lesson plans and in-depth information follow.

Objectives

- 🅢 Students demonstrate their physical as well as cognitive ability of striking.
- 🅢 Students safely use equipment to display their skills.

Assessment

Rubric

3 = Struck with an implement or hand safely and successfully most of the time; correctly answered seven items

2 = Struck safely and successfully most of the time; correctly answered six or more items

1 = Struck safely but not successfully some of the time; correctly answered fewer than five items

0 = Struck unsafely or unsuccessfully; did not try to answer the test items correctly

Students can take the assessment paper with them as they move to each station. You can use this as a graded assessment also.

Striking Assessment

Paper Football

1. What is it called when you push the football past the goal line?

serve   touchdown   hole in one

2. What did you aim for after you scored a touchdown?

extra point   quarterback   home run

Tennis Camp

1. When you hit the ball with the inside of your hand leading, what is it called?

backhand   forehand   strike

2. When you hit the ball with the outside of your hand leading, what is it called?

serve   forehand   backhand

3. To start the game of tennis, you use a

smash   serve   volley

Flapjack Kitchen

1. Keep your eyes on the _____ when striking with a paddle.

beanbag   floor   paddle

Putt-Putt

1. When putting, we _____ the beanbag with the golf club.

push   swing   clobber

From *No Gym? No Problem! Physical Activities for Tight Spaces* by Charmain Sutherland, 2006, Champaign, IL: Human Kinetics.

Safety

Before the assessment, remind students of all the rules that you have previously discussed. Reinforce classroom safety: avoiding desks, staying in personal space, and so on.

Tips and Variations

🖙 Demonstrate the forms before assessing the students. Your example will reinforce the forms that they should be executing and can give them the visuals they need to develop a more mature pattern of striking.

🖙 If younger students cannot read, allow them to answer assessments by raising their hands instead of reading. You may add more or different stations, depending on what you have covered.

Conclusion and Links to Real Life

"I wonder which of you might be the next slugger, or the next Tiger Woods, or who I may see playing some of these activities throughout their lives. I hope that you will choose one of these activities to do from now until you are 100. I can't wait to see how well you learned about striking on your assessment."

Try at Home

"When you go home, see if your family knows about striking. Do they continue to play any of these activities? If so, go out this week and play one activity with them."

Game Shows, Reality Shows, and Special Events Get Physical

Imagination, play, and pretending are wonderful ways to learn. Imagination is priceless. Play, imagination, pretending, and activity help children learn how to lead, follow, make decisions, and think before they act. Game shows, reality shows, and events on television are a great way to allow students to imagine that they are in a game, race, or show and trying to reach a goal.

- - - All Around the World Race - - -

Fitness

Skills	**Activity Level**	**Intensity**	**Standards**
Fitness, stretching, creativity, cooperating	Everyone is involved.	Medium	① ② ⑤ ⑥

Invitation

"The winners of the All Around the World Race will have followed all the clues and correctly and positively completed all the physical challenges. It will lead players all over the world in search of clues and adventure. If you can complete the race in under 15 minutes, then you have won."

Equipment

- Five basketballs
- Copy of the clues (Race 1 and Race 2) and a blank sheet of paper and pencil for each participant

Description

Divide the group into partners. One partner is the host, reads the clues, and judges and coaches the other as they try to complete the race. The performing partner needs a sheet of paper to write on. Partners switch roles after 15 minutes.

Race 1

1. Find your partner's desk and move from sitting on the floor to the chair 30 times. The **gluteus maximus** must hit the floor and chair each time.

2. Using the letters in your partner's first name, write something nice about your partner. For example, write the following for Paul:

   P = Pleasant
   A = Awesome dancer
   U = Understands math very well
   L = Loves to play baseball

3. Shake the hand of every host in the room.

4. Draw and design a new exercise that your partner can do to stretch his or her legs.

5. Go to California (front door) and dribble a basketball five times with the Los Angeles Lakers.

6. Crabwalk to Greece (back of the room) and draw the Olympic rings. If students don't get this pattern after 1 1/2 minutes, show them the correct pattern on page 189.

7. Go to Mexico (the board) and jump in place 50 times.

8. Catch the bus to Arizona and choose the end seat. You start at your own seat and then move forward to every seat in the room until you are back at your own seat. You must put your gluteus maximus down in every single seat.

9. Slide around the Grand Canyon (slide around the outside of all the desks).

10. Choose three more countries and five more states to visit. You must write down their names and do 20 jumping jacks after each country and state you visit (grades 3 through 8).

Race 2

1. Find the row or cluster of desks where you partner sits. Your partner names a state. Skip two laps around that state (the desks).

2. Take the letters from your partner's state and write positive words that describe your partner or your partner's state.

3. Catch the bus from your partner's state to Canada. Sit at the back of the bus. You start at your own seat and then move forward to every seat in the room until you are back at your own seat. Make sure that your gluteus maximus sits on every chair.

4. Watch out for the moose. Give 10 (two-hand slaps) to every host in the room.

5. Take a long journey by ship to England. Draw and describe new ways of stretching so that you don't get cramped. Practice the stretch for 15 seconds.

6. Wave to the queen with both arms for 1 minute.

7. Travel to Spain on your motorcycle. Hop around the desks and in and out of the rows on the same foot; come back on the opposite foot.

8. Crawl to Chicago (the front of the room) and then dribble a basketball five times with the Chicago Bulls.

9. Jump to Japan (the back of the room).

10. Climb Mount Everest (do 15 push-ups). Bicycle down the mountain (sit on your chair and pedal your legs around with your leg muscles). It is 80 miles (kilometers) down, so you must bike for 80 seconds.

From *No Gym? No Problem! Physical Activities for Tight Spaces* by Charmain Sutherland, 2006, Champaign, IL: Human Kinetics.

Setup

Look first; rearrange if necessary; put it back together.

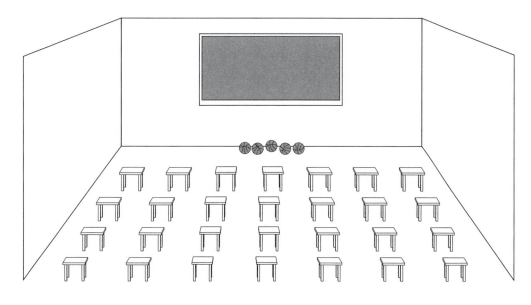

Break It Down in Detail

Lesson plans and in-depth information follow.

Objectives

- Students use several physical skills to accomplish a goal.
- Students interact with, show compassion to, and help others with their physical activity challenges.
- Students remain on task as they coach and help their teammates remain on task.

Warm-Up

Thumb Jack Wrestling

Cues and Concepts

Carry out the activities using the following cue:

- Listen and follow—listen to what the coach is saying and follow the directions.

Include the following concepts:

- Coaching is important in this activity. Students should encourage teammates to exercise and accomplish tasks.
- Include cues for skills that you have covered previously and reinforce them.

Assessment

Rubric

3 = Moved with vigor; followed all rules; listened to coaching; coached partner

2 = Moved with vigor; followed all rules; coached partner

1 = Attempted most challenges but didn't cooperate 100% with coach

0 = Did not perform some challenges; did not cooperate; did not follow all rules

Safety

Students must be courteous and polite as they race through the challenges. As students move, they should avoid collisions. Dock points or opportunities if they continue to move aggressively.

Tips and Variations

- Describe some other events that could occur in a world race:
  - Bungee jumping from a bridge over a waterfall
  - Trying to swim in clothes faster than all other contestants
  - Walking through a dark cave on an uneven surface
  - Catching a taxi, bus, train, boat, and plane to get to another country
- With younger students, coach half the class at one time for an event and then invite the other half to race. Alternate after each group has finished one race. Eliminate the writing portion and substitute an action.

Conclusion and Links to Real Life

"Some people feel as if they are in a race in their lives because they have to hurry to get somewhere, yet obstacles keep popping up. Have you ever had that happen? I hope that you coached others and yourself throughout the event."

Try at Home

"Next time your family goes somewhere, make it exciting by creating attainable time limits and obstacles to work through."

--- Say What You Know ---

Knowledge assessment and fitness

Skills	Activity Level	Intensity	Standards
Knowledge assessment, exercise	Everyone is involved.	Medium to low	② ④

Invitation

"I'll take Throwing for $100, please."

"The answer is: This person is the thrower in a football game."

"What is a quarterback?"

"That's correct for $100."

"Have you ever seen game shows that ask contestants questions for money? We are going to play a game right here. We'll call it Say What You Know."

Equipment

None, except chalk to write on the board

Description

Create five categories of items with which you would like to assess your students (for example, if you are working on throwing and catching, come up with throwing and catching questions). In each category, come up with five questions and **rank** them from easy to hard ($100 to $500). Vary your questions according to participants' age and knowledge level. Students play as a team and buzz in if they know the answer. Remember that they must phrase the answer in the form of a question. Keep score on the chalkboard. Penalize teams if they answer incorrectly but dock them only half the score of the question that they were attempting.

- Divide your class into four teams and give them names.
- Each team must come up with their own buzzer sound—clap, foot stomp, buzzzzzzz, whistle, and so on.
- You are the host and call on the group whose signal you hear first.

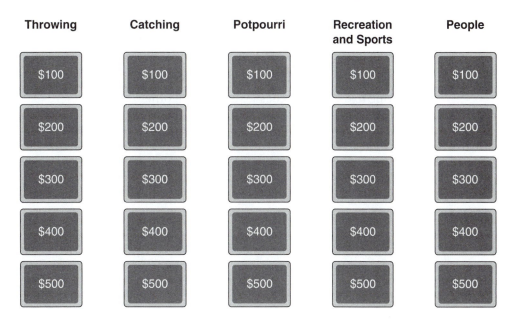

Throwing	Catching	Potpourri	Recreation and Sports	People
$100	$100	$100	$100	$100
$200	$200	$200	$200	$200
$300	$300	$300	$300	$300
$400	$400	$400	$400	$400
$500	$500	$500	$500	$500

- When the team answers the item correctly, team members must do an exercise for 20 repetitions. The exercises could be crunches, jumping jacks, arm circles, and so on.
- When a team answers incorrectly, they perform no activity.

Sample Categories and Answers

- Throwing
  - $100 = A type of throw that you use when you have the ball in your hand and the ball starts back by your ear (correct response: *overhand*).
  - $200 = A type of throw that you use when you begin your throw with your hand behind your hip (correct response: *underhand*).
  - $300 = Two types of throws using a basketball (correct response: *chest pass and bounce pass*).
  - $400 = The foot you would step with if your dominant hand was the right hand and you were throwing overhand (correct response: *left foot*).
  - $500 = What your hand should do after you release the ball (correct response: *follow through and point to your target*).

- Catching
  - $100 = Where your fingers point when the ball is thrown above your head (correct response: *fingers point to the sky*).
  - $200 = Where your fingers point when the ball is thrown below your waist (correct response: *fingers point to the ground*).
  - $300 = In baseball, the hand you would put your glove on if your dominant hand is your left hand (correct response: *right*).
  - $400 = When the ball is thrown hard, what you should do so that the ball doesn't bounce off you (correct response: *give* or *absorb the throw*).
  - $500 = A game in which you don't catch with your hands (correct response: *lacrosse* or **stxball**).

- Potpourri
  - $100 = A place where you can take your pulse (correct response: *neck* or *wrist*).
  - $200 = The muscle in your arm that flexes when you bend your elbow (correct response: **biceps**).
  - $300 = The muscles that help you do a curl-up or crunch (correct response: **abdominals**).
  - $400 = An exercise that works your cardiovascular system (correct response: *jumping rope, jogging,* or *aerobics*).
  - $500 = Three skills involved in basketball (correct response: *throwing, catching, dribbling*).

- Recreation and Sports
  - $100 = A sport involving throwing (correct response: *baseball* or *basketball* [other throwing sports accepted]).
  - $200 = Name of the teammate to whom a pitcher throws the ball when pitching (correct response: *catcher*).
  - $300 = The difference between pitching in softball and baseball (correct response: *underhand for softball, overhand or sidearm for baseball*).
  - $400 = A sport in which only one player can catch the ball (correct response: *soccer*).
  - $500 = Two sports in which you can throw the ball but never catch it (correct response: *tennis, volleyball*).

- People
  - $100 = The person who normally throws the ball in football (correct response: *quarterback*).
  - $200 = The name of a baseball team (correct response: *Baltimore Orioles, Los Angeles Dodgers, Minnesota Twins,* and so on).
  - $300 = The name of a professional sports team that throws a ball into a basket (correct response: *Utah Jazz, Miami Heat, Detroit Pistons,* and so on).
  - $400 = The name of the person who tells you if your pitches are good or bad (correct response: *umpire*).
  - $500 = Sisters who toss the ball and then hit it with an implement (correct response: *Venus and Serena Williams*).
- The Big Question (teams can risk all or part of their money). Use this question at the end of the game.
  - A sport that involves throwing, catching, and swimming (correct response: *water polo*).

Setup

Look first; rearrange if necessary; put it back together.

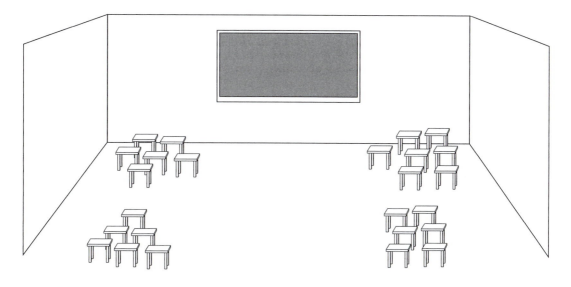

Break It Down in Detail

Lesson plans and in-depth information follow.

Objectives

- Students display their knowledge of physical education through a modified popular TV game show.
- Students reinforce correct answers with positive exercise reinforcement.

Warm-Up

Fruit Basket Upset

Cues and Concepts

Carry out the activities using the following cue:

- Give the answer and allow the students to give you the cues.

Include the following concept:

- Build on the material and concepts that you might put in your questions and answers. This activity would be a good enrichment.

Link to other subjects by throwing in physically related math, reading, social studies, or science questions like the following:

- Our football team is the Ravens. What city are they from? (correct response: *Baltimore*). What state is Baltimore in? (correct response: *Maryland*). What is the capital of Maryland? (correct response: *Annapolis*). Is Maryland north or south of Virginia? (correct response: *north*). Is Maryland east or west of California? (correct response: *east*).

- If we were ending the third inning, the New York Yankees were leading by 7 runs, and the Baltimore Orioles had scored once every inning, what would the game score be? (correct response: *10 to 3*).

Assessment

Rubric

3 = Attempted to answer and contributed to many correct answers

2 = Attempted to answer but didn't contribute to correct answers often

1 = Attempted to encourage group but didn't contribute to correct answers

0 = Didn't try to contribute or encourage group

Safety

When performing exercises, students should be mindful of desks and of others around them.

Tips and Variations

- Playing up the role as the game show host will make this activity more exciting for the students.
  - Use some of the mannerisms and phrases that a game show host uses.
  - Model a request: "I'd like People for $200 please."
  - Say, "Ooh, sorry—you did not answer in the form of a question."
- Vary the difficulty according to what you have taught in each grade level.
  - Kindergarten: What game do you play with a bat? (correct response: *baseball*).
  - Grade 8: Which sporting activity involves diamonds? (correct response: *baseball*).

Conclusion and Links to Real Life

"Although in real life you won't have to answer in the form of a question, knowing these answers and questions will help you become a better thrower and catcher. Of course, for our physical fitness, it was important to be active when we answered those questions correctly. Think about how many questions you got correct and then multiply that by 20; that's how much exercise you did today. We will revisit this game show set at the end of our next unit."

Try at Home

"Play along at home when game shows come on. Go ahead and exercise after each question you don't know. Come back next time and tell me why I had you exercise on the misses."

- - - Stay Alive and Thrive - - -

Cooperation, fitness

Skills	Activity Level	Intensity	Standards
Cooperation, fitness, balance, teamwork.	Everyone is involved.	Medium	① ② ⑤ ⑥

Invitation

"If you were on a deserted island, having to hunt for your food and live without a house or bathroom, could you make it? You are going to work in a tribe, which is like a team. Could your tribe make it through and stay alive? Could you play harder, think smarter, and last longer than other tribes and thrive? No one will be eliminated from our island. Instead, we'll celebrate our successes. Which tribe will stay alive and thrive?"

Equipment

- 10 pieces of paper (students can use their own crayons or markers)
- Torch (a citronella tiki torch, a tinikling stick with a cone on top, or similar object)
- 20 hula hoops
- Puzzle (already made, or one that you create by cutting up a picture)
- Trophy (make something that looks silly and gaudy to represent a trophy)

Description

Divide players into tribes of four or five. Each tribe tries to score more points than the other tribes as they compete to play harder, think smarter, and last longer on Physical Education Island. Each tribe participates in six challenges. They rotate to each station on signal.

Every person must contribute during each challenge.

- Team huddle: Each tribe sits together. Award each tribe a torch at the beginning of the game. If the torch is dropped at anytime or if no one is carrying it, the tribe loses 2 points (minus 2 points).
- Stay Alive and Thrive on Physical Education Island begins. Play the *Survivor* music or tribal music as the tribes walk to their first station. Stop and start the music for the challenges to begin and end. Each tribe is responsible for maintenance of the station before leaving. You may dock points from a tribe if they don't maintain the station.

Challenges

1. Each team cooperates to come up with a tribe name. They decorate a sign that displays their tribe name (2 points).
2. Who lasts longest? Tribe members each place one hand in the center so that they are touching each other's hands. They place the other hand on their heads (the person holding the torch holds the torch instead of his or her head). Tribe members take one foot off the ground so that the foot is at midcalf height. They attempt to hold this position for the duration of the station (2 points).

3. Think smarter. On a sheet of paper, tribe members list all the words they can think of that relate to physical education. They might use words like *physical, throw,* or *action.* The tribe that lists the most words earns the most points. You verify the suitability and number of words (5, 4, 3, 2, and 1 points, respectively).

4. Play harder. The entire tribe jogs in place for the duration of the station (this will vary, according to your time allotment for PE and the activity) (2 points).

5. Play harder. The tribe stands shoulder to shoulder, each holding one hand. The two end players have a free hand. The object is to cooperate, using teamwork, to see how many hula hoops they can send from the beginning of the line to the end, without letting go of the hands. After the first hoop has made it to the last person, they let it fall to the floor. As soon as it hits the floor, but not any sooner, the person at the beginning of the line may start another hoop traveling down the line (20 hoops = 5 points, 15 to 19 = 4 points, 10 to 14 = 3 points, 5 to 9 = 2 points, 2 to 4 = 1 point). Remember, the tribes cannot drop the torch.

6. Think smarter. Each tribe puts together a puzzle (number of pieces put together = number of points).

Team Huddle

- After each group has visited each station once, have all tribes come together, like a huddle.

- You may wish to award points to a tribe for outstanding sportsmanship or outstanding cooperation.

- Review the points earned by each tribe, discuss the valiant team effort that the tribes displayed, and finally announce the winner. Present a goofy, gaudy trophy as an award that the winners can touch but not keep. Use this trophy each time you play Stay Alive and Thrive; it will become prestigious, especially if you make it as gaudy as possible. If you'd like to award players with a certificate, copy the one in the figure or modify it to fit your needs.

I Thrived on PE Island

Play harder, think smarter, last longer

Setup

Look first; rearrange if necessary; put it back together.

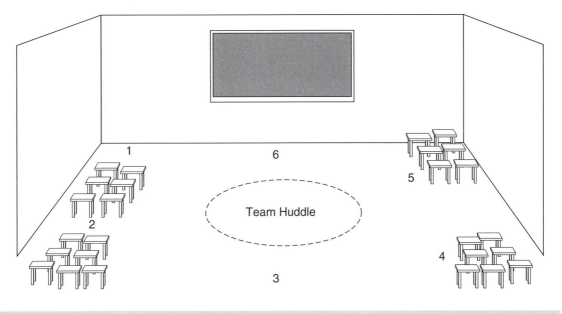

Break It Down in Detail

Lesson plans and in-depth information follow.

Objective

Students imagine that they are on an island and use their understanding and skills of physical education to stay alive and thrive in a game.

Warm-Up

Stay Alive and Thrive preparation:

- Students are in their own personal spaces.
- To warm up their bodies to stay alive and thrive, students physically act out the following story. They should act out the words in italics.

Play soft tribal music as the background.

You are *strong* and *brave*. You have entered a *tough* competition! Stay Alive and Thrive. You start out *slow, preparing your muscles* for an agonizing event. You *sit and stretch*, as you *sail* in a *rocking* boat. The boat *rocks forward, backward, sideways, up, and down*. The waves make you *sway from side to side*. You are forced to *jump* overboard and *swim, swim faster, swim faster, swim* away from sharks toward the island. You *reach, reach, reach* for the land. You finally *reach* land and then *sprint* from the ocean, through thick sand. You *sprint even faster*, because the sand is *boiling hot* on your feet. Now you are *tired* so you *jog* to your camp. You are *exhausted* and begin *walking*. Aaah, you made it. You *relax, stretch* out, and get ready for your challenge.

Cues and Concepts

Carry out the activities using the following cues:

- Work as a tribe—consider your tribe your family; help them and let them help you accomplish goals.
- Play harder—play and work harder than the other tribes.
- Think smarter—think more than the other tribes are thinking.
- Thrive—doing great.

Include the following concepts:

- Cooperation is working together with others for a purpose.
- Fitness is what skills in physical education you would need to stay alive on a deserted island:
  - **Muscular endurance**—how long can you last?
  - **Muscular strength**—are your muscles strong enough?
  - Agility—are you able to move freely and quickly forward and backward?
  - Balance is the ability to keep a static, steady position without falling over.
- Ask students what they have learned in PE that can help them stay alive and thrive.

Assessment

Rubric

3 = Completed challenges; cooperated and helped others; followed rules

2 = Attempted all challenges; cooperated with others; followed rules

1 = Attempted most challenges but didn't cooperate 100%; followed all rules

0 = Could not or did not perform challenges; did not cooperate; did not follow rules

Safety

Each student should be aware of the torches and the limitations of the room. Torches should always stay upright, never pointed at anyone.

Tips and Variations

- Pretend that you are the host of a reality show on TV.
- Act as if these tribes will really win $1 million, as contestants on reality TV shows sometimes do.
- As you are describing the activities and the warm-up, use an enthusiastic tone to make the theme come to life.
- Increase or decrease the difficulty of the activities depending on age level.
- Use this theme several times with different activities throughout the year. If you are doing a throwing and catching unit, create tasks using throwing and catching, such as having teams keep a ball in the air as long as they can. Students love this activity. If you'd like to make it more competitive, keep the same teams each time you play.

Conclusion and Links to Real Life

"Do you think that your family could stay alive and thrive on PE Island? What skills would they need to do to have been successful today?"

Try at Home

"Try a Stay Alive and Thrive challenge at your house. Be sure not to eliminate anyone. Instead, celebrate when someone thrives and stays alive."

--- Circle of Fitness Challenges ---

Fitness

Skills	**Activity Level**	**Intensity**	**Standards**
Fitness, stretching, cooperating	Everyone is involved but moves once every 30 seconds.	Medium to low	② ④

Invitation

"Is there an *S?* As the host turns over the *S,* our minds are scrambling to think of what word this letter might help to spell. Our brains might be racing to see which letter we should ask for next. Let's do an active version of a game show where you have a word puzzle that you must solve. Our puzzles have to do with fitness and activity."

Equipment

- The circle on the board or a poster
- A beanbag or paper ball

Description

You will be the host as you create words or phrases that correspond to something that you are working on. As you ask the players to spin the circle, you turn the letters over (write them on the board) when contestants answer correctly.

- Participants work in three teams. Each team takes a turn to spin the circle (adaptation: Throw a beanbag or paper ball at one of the numbers on the circle; the space you hit is how much the team wins).
- Team members work together and choose a letter that they think will be in the puzzle. If they are correct, they do an exercise.
  - $100—20 ski jumps (jumping side to side with flexed knees)
  - $200—20 arm circles each way
  - $300—10 push-ups
  - $400—20 crunches
  - $500—20 curl-ups
  - $600—20 seconds of stretching
  - Trip (worth $1,000)—20 jumping jills or 20 jumping jacks, one lap around the room
- If the team is incorrect, they lose their turn.
- When the team thinks that they know the answer to the puzzle, they must wait until it is their turn to spin.
- Teams can keep track of their total amount of money. If they do not guess the phrase, they lose the money.

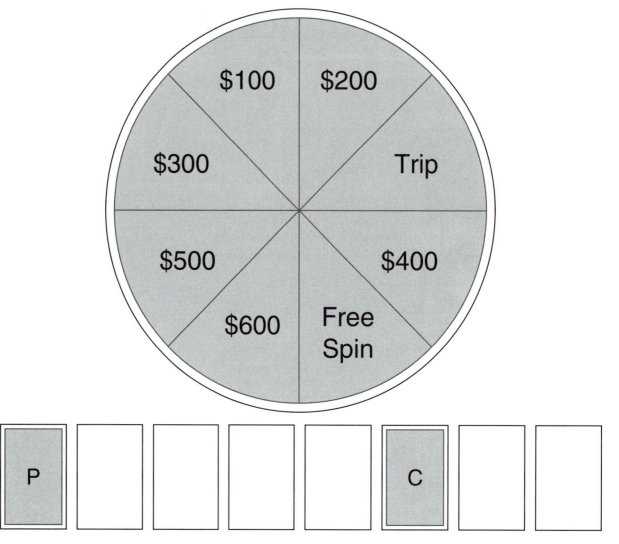

Phrase: **PHYSICAL**

Setup

Look first; rearrange if necessary; put it back together.

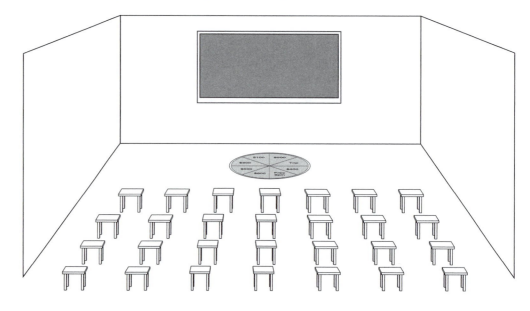

Break It Down in Detail

Lesson plans and in-depth information follow.

Objectives

- Students participate in an active version of a game show, like those on TV.
- Students perform exercises that work all the muscles and the cardiovascular system.

Warm-Up

Can You Guess, Judge? or Fruit Basket Upset

Cues and Concepts

Carry out the activities using the following cues:

- Think about subjects we have worked on (when students have difficulty guessing the answer to the puzzle).
- Aim for the trip—as in real life, aim for the greatest reward. Better health is worth the most!

Also include the following concept:

- Include ideas that will help the students complete the puzzle.

Link the words to language arts and spelling. Use words that the students have to learn in subjects like social studies or science.

Assessment

Rubric

3 = Actively involved in guessing, solving, and exercising

2 = Involved in strategic guessing and exercising

1 = Involved in guessing and exercising

0 = Not involved in guessing; did little or no exercising

Safety

Students should be aware of surroundings as they exercise, and they should stay in their personal spaces.

Tips and Variations

- Explain how lucky they are that they are able to exercise when they choose the correct letter. That way you use exercise as a positive instead of a punishment.
- Have students play Circle of Fitness Challenges individually. They will enjoy being able to test their own knowledge and will realize that a team can usually solve a puzzle easier.

Conclusion and Links to Real Life

"Although we are not walking away with a trip to Hawaii or loads of money, you are walking away with an even better prize. You were able to exercise for at least 30 minutes, which gives you health, flexibility, endurance, and strength. Without your health, nothing else matters. That's the greatest puzzle we can solve—how to keep active and stay healthy, and that is worth a fortune."

Try at Home

"When your friends need something to do, or when you have to wait somewhere with your family, try Circle of Fitness Challenges. Your parents or an adult can think of the puzzle, and you will exercise for every letter you get correct."

--- Activities From Around the World ---

Special events

Skills	Activity Level	Intensity	Standards
Cooperation, fitness, balance, teamwork	Everyone is involved.	Medium to low	① ② ③ ⑤

Invitation

"You know what fun activities you like to do in your country, but what do kids in other countries do for fun? Let's learn how to play some of the games that they play."

Equipment

- 2 deck rings for Spear the Ring
- 2 beanbags, golf-ball-sized balls, or paper balls for Spear the Ring
- 16 jacks (or balled-up pieces of paper) for Jacks
- 2 tiny bouncy balls for Jacks
- 40 pennies for Tiddlywinks
- 8 cups, bowls, or **polyspots** for Tiddlywinks and Chopstick Marbles
- 4 sets of chopsticks for Chopstick Marbles
- 20 marbles for Chopstick Marbles
- 2 tennis or bouncy balls for Palm Ball
- Paper or tape to make the two squares for Palm Ball

Description

Participants visit different countries (stations) and participate in an activity associated with that country. Place participants in groups of four to six.

- Japan (station 1): Slap Hands. Partners face each other with their hands out; one palm is up and one palm is down. The object is to slap the top of the hand of the opponent. At the same time, the players need to react quickly to avoid a slap. The first person to give 10 slaps on the hand wins.

- China (station 2): Chopstick Marbles. Partners each have a cup, bowl, or polyspot with five marbles each and a set of chopsticks. The object is for each partner to take the marbles from his or her cup, with chopsticks, and place them into the partner's cup. The player to have only one marble left in his or her cup is the winner. If time is an issue, the player with the fewest number of marbles in his or her cup when time runs out wins.

- America (station 3): Jacks.
  - This activity requires eight jacks (small balled-up pieces of paper if jacks are not available) and a small rubber ball.
  - The player drops the ball, picks up one jack, and then catches the ball on one bounce. If successful, the player goes for two jacks.
  - When the player misses the ball or drops the jacks, he or she must start over. The player wins when he or she can collect all eight jacks and still catch the ball on one bounce.

- England (station 4): Tiddlywinks.
  - Place two cups, bowls, or polyspots between two players. Each player has 10 pennies and a cup to aim for.

- The object is to flip the pennies, from the top of the thumb, into the cup. The first player to get 10 pennies in a cup wins.
- Italy (station 5): Palm Ball
  - Palm ball is like tennis, but without the racket. Make a court from two 2-foot (60-centimeter) squares, with an obvious line in the middle.
  - Partners try to hit the tennis or small bouncy ball with the palm of the hand across the midline to the opponent's court.
  - If a player misses the ball or hits it out, the other player gets a point. Players must hit the ball within one bounce.
  - The first player to reach 21 points wins.
- Native Americans (station 6): Spear the Ring
  - One player rolls a deck ring from the right hand to the left, approximately 5 feet (1.5 meters). This player rolls 10 times.
  - The other player takes a small ball, small beanbag, or balled-up piece of paper and tries to spear, or go through, the ring.
  - Players switch positions after 10 tries. The player with the most successful spears wins.

Setup

Look first; rearrange if necessary; put it back together.

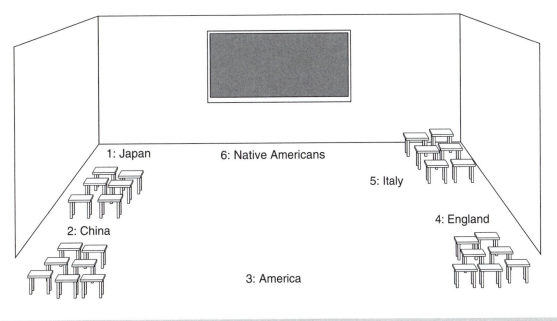

Break It Down in Detail

Lesson plans and in-depth information follow.

Objective

Students appreciate activities from other countries.

Warm-Up

Simon Says, "Action"

Cues and Concepts

Carry out the activities using the following cue:

- Appreciate others—play the games and appreciate the rules and culture of kids' games from other countries.

Include the following concepts:

- Review throwing and catching skills.
- Review striking skills.
- Discuss reaction time. Ask students how quickly they can think and move.

Assessment

Rubric

3 = Appreciated and followed all rules

2 = Followed all rules and played the games

1 = Struggled to appreciate and follow the rules of the games

0 = Lacked appreciation of the games; did not follow rules of the games

Safety

Slaps on the hand should be light and not hurt the opponent. While striking the ball, students should control the force so that the balls don't hit other students.

Tips and Variations

- If you can preface the games of each country with a little history, you could link history into the lesson and give students a clearer understanding of where these other kids are coming from.
- Ask the students in your class what they think is a typical game that kids play in your country or state. Ask students if they are from another country or state. Invite them to try out their games. Add them to the stations.

Conclusion and Links to Real Life

"Why do Americans not often play with chopsticks? Probably because most Americans don't have chopsticks readily available in their homes. We can appreciate kids' games and activities from other countries by understanding that they play different games not only because they have different interests, pastimes, and favorite sports but also because they play with what is available to them."

Try at Home

"Imagine that you had no TV, no video games, and no major sports equipment and that you were bored with all the games that you know. Create a new game that is fun and exciting."

--- Create a Movie ---

Special activities

Skills	Activity Level	Intensity	Standards
Perception, imagination	Everyone is involved.	Medium	② ③ ⑤

Invitation

"Imagine that a director for a movie has cast you as the lead actor in an adventure film. Adventure films are those with thrills and action, like *Spider-Man, Harry Potter, Lord of the*

Rings, Star Wars, and *Tomb Raider.* When you see the scenery, act out the action that you would do in that scene. You might see someone doing something, but you don't have to do what that person does. Make up your own movie."

Equipment

- ⚙ TV, VCR
- ⚙ Video camera

Description

Take out your video camera and be adventurous. Film scenes that will give your participants the inspiration to move and jump into action. Participants should be able to move vigorously and get their heart rates up.

Ideas

- ⚙ Film a large office building, starting at the base of the building and panning upward to the top.
- ⚙ Film while in a car on a highway.
- ⚙ Film while in a car on a narrow, winding road.
- ⚙ Film a stoplight and a green light.
- ⚙ Film while walking through a forest or park.
- ⚙ Film from the trunk of a tree to the top.
- ⚙ Film an anthill.
- ⚙ Film bees or birds flying.
- ⚙ Film up and down at a skateboard ramp.
- ⚙ Film digging a hole at the beach.
- ⚙ Film waves at the beach.
- ⚙ Film someone swimming at a pool.
- ⚙ Film a person on a bike; focus on fast-moving pedals.
- ⚙ Film inline skating or skateboarding.
- ⚙ Film a gymnastics event.

Setup

Look first; rearrange if necessary; put it back together.

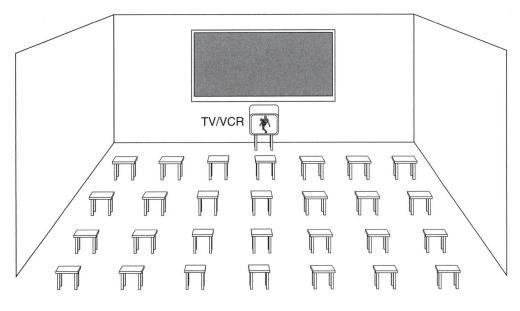

Break It Down in Detail

Lesson plans and in-depth information follow.

Objectives

- Students perform physical actions that correspond to the scenes they are viewing.
- Students increase their heart rate by moving according to their interpretations of what physical actions are occurring in the scenes.
- Students move as if they are in an action movie, performing **locomotor** movements and responding to specific visual and audio cues.

Warm-Up

Lucky Four Corners

Cues and Concepts

Carry out the activities using the following cues:

- You create the action—whichever action you choose to do is fine; your imagination and creativity are your own.
- Pulse check—find your pulse and count the beats using the **6-second pulse check.**

Include the following concept:

- Ask students to check their pulse throughout the activity. Let students know when they should be increasing their intensity.

Assessment

Rubric

3 = Performed actions independently and with appropriate intensity at appropriate times

2 = Performed actions independently; varied the intensity

1 = Performed actions by watching others; sometimes varied the intensity

0 = Did not use imagination or creativity; sometimes or never varied the intensity

Safety

Students should stay in their own spaces and perform actions safely.

Tips and Variations

- A little narration from you could help students who don't have an idea of what to do or can't imagine what they should do. Your voice could also stimulate changes in intensity. Imagine that you are promoting an action movie. Tell younger students what you are imagining as you watch the video. Guide them into action.
- As an extension, throw in a video clip of something that resembles a cool-down and will decrease the heart rate. See if your students can differentiate between the high-intensity and low-intensity activities.

Conclusion and Links to Real Life

"How was your movie? Are you the next action hero? Using your imagination today helped you exercise your heart by doing activities that you thought matched the scenes of the video. You could increase your heart rate by using your imagination."

Try at Home

"Play some music and imagine different places where you might be according to the speed and tone of the music. React by moving with the appropriate intensity and actions."

--- Sport Stacking ---

Special activities

Skills	**Activity Level**	**Intensity**	**Standards**
Dexterity, coordination, laterality	Everyone is involved.	Low to medium	⑥

Invitation

"Playing with cups is a real sport now! Yes, sport stacking is a recognized sport with local and national records in each state (check out www.speedstacks.com). We will practice simple sport stacking and then you can compete against others. If you like it, you may want to consider entering a tournament."

Equipment

Cups, as many as possible—the best cups to use are those made especially for sport stacking, because they are smooth and have holes drilled in the bottom of them. If you don't have tailor-made cups, use cups that are all similar in size and weight. Paper and plastic are fine, but glass, china, and ceramic are not.

Description

Sport stacking involves using the brain and coordination to build a set of cups from a stack to a pyramid formation. Participants can start with just 3 cups and then work up to 12. Later, they can time themselves and compete against others. They can even do sport-stacking relays.

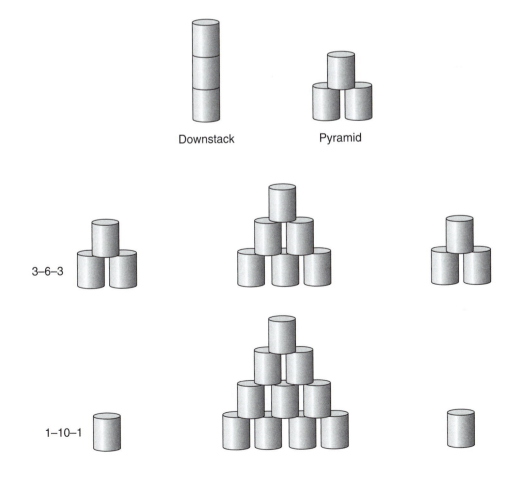

Downstack Pyramid

3–6–3

1–10–1

- Three cups
  - Start with three cups in a stack (column).
  - Place two on the bottom and one on top, building upward, or up stacking, to form a pyramid.
  - Then stack them down, or down stack, from a pyramid into a column.
- Six cups
  - Start with two columns of three.
  - Place two on the bottom and one on top from one column.
  - Then go to the other column and do the same.
  - Then stack one pyramid of three down to a column, and then the other.
- Three, six, three
  - Start with two columns of three and one column of six in the middle of the columns of three.
  - Make two pyramids of three and in the middle place three cups on the bottom, two in the middle, and one on top.
  - Then down stack the cups into two stacks of three and one stack of six.
- Relays
  - Teams of four have two columns of three cups, approximately 6 feet (2 meters) from the starting line and 6 feet (2 meters) from each other.
  - Each player runs up to the stack of cups, makes a pyramid with one stack, runs to the next stack of cups to make a pyramid, and then turns around and down stacks them into a column again.
  - The next person in the group tags hands and then repeats the process, until all four people on the team have gone.

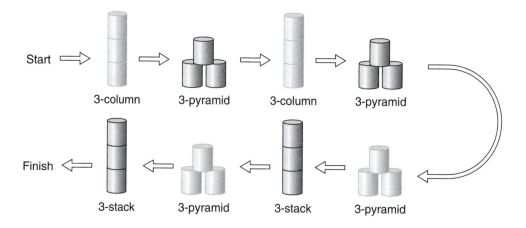

- Participants can work individually, with a group, or with partners. They can time each other. They can try to improve their own time or make this into a competition.
- There are more advanced methods for sport stacking, but this should get you started. Contact Speed Stacks Inc. for more information at www.speedstacks.com. The company often appears at AAHPERD conventions.

Setup

Look first; rearrange if necessary; put it back together. No need to set up anything, unless you are doing relays. If so, set up the relays between the rows of desks.

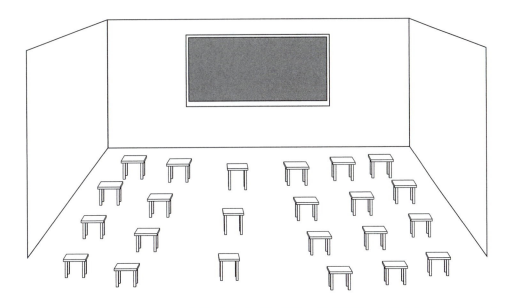

Break It Down in Detail

Lesson plans and in-depth information follow.

Objectives

- Students experience a unique, new activity and see it as a challenge.
- Students improve coordination, hand–eye coordination, dexterity, speed, and reaction time.
- Students continue to participate when not successful on the first try.

Warm-Up

Warm-Up Bingo

Cues and Concepts

Carry out the activities using the following cues:

- Slide the cups—feel the motion of sliding the cup instead of pushing and grabbing.
- Up stack—stack the cups in a pyramid.
- Down stack—stack the cups in a column.

Include the following concepts:

- Students should try to up stack and then fix mistakes to improve.
- Explain the importance of spacing and balancing. You can link this to science and math. This activity stimulates students to think using both the right and left hemispheres of the brain.

Assessment

Rubric

3 = Attempted sport stacking and practiced skills; showed much improvement

2 = Attempted sport stacking and practiced skills; showed improvement

1 = Attempted some sport stacking; did not show improvement

0 = Did not attempt most sport-stacking tasks as demonstrated; did not show improvement

Safety

Be sure that furniture is clear from movement paths for sport-stacking relays.

Tips and Variations

- Doing is believing. Until students try sport stacking, they may think that it will be boring and purposeless. As soon as they try it, however, they'll be hooked. They will immediately want to try to improve and become more efficient.
- Older, more advanced students can try the 1–10–1 combination and the cycle 3–6–3, 6–6, 1–10–1.
- Show the sport-stacking training video available from www.speedstacks.com.

Conclusion and Links to Real Life

"Sport stacking is much newer than soccer, but it is growing, has value, and is now considered a sport. You will need new skills for this activity and will have to practice to improve."

Try at Home

"Take out some paper cups and invite your family to a sport-stacking challenge. Ask your friends if they would like to be in a sport-stacking tournament."

- - - PE Olympics - - -

Cooperation, fitness, gymnastics

Skills	Activity Level	Intensity	Standards
Cooperation, fitness, balance, teamwork	Everyone is involved.	Medium to high	① ② ③ ④ ⑤ ⑥

Invitation

"The most awesome sporting event in the world comes around every 4 years in the summer and every 4 years in the winter. The best athletes in the world compete against each other. The very best athletes win gold medals, the second best win silver medals, and the third best take home bronze medals. Today we'll imagine that we are playing for a certain country in the Olympics, the greatest sporting event of all. We'll try to do our very best in our Olympic competition."

Equipment

- Five **pedometers**
- One balled-up piece of paper
- Two polyspots 20 feet (6 meters) apart (or a distance that is safe in the classroom) or taped lines on the floor for the multiple jump
- Paper and markers or crayons for the flags
- Three hurdles or cones
- Five carpet squares or mats
- Medals (cut them out from the figure)
- CD player and CD

Description

Divide students into teams to represent six or seven countries (four people per country). Participants can choose their country. Because most students will want the country that you live in, exclude that option. They move as a team to different event stations. Some stations are individual events, and some are team events. You can award medals for individual events when the station time ends.

Event 1 (Station 1): 50-Meter Dash

- Have participants put on pedometers. Time a run in place for 50 seconds.
- The person who records the most steps in 50 seconds wins gold, the second highest gets silver, and the third highest gets bronze.

Event 2 (Station 2): Country Allegiance

- Participants work together to come up with a flag and a motto. See the figure for an example.
- The team must work together. They can use markers or crayons to design the flag.
- All must sign the motto.
- At the end, the countries vote on which countries deserve the gold, silver, and bronze for their flags and mottos.

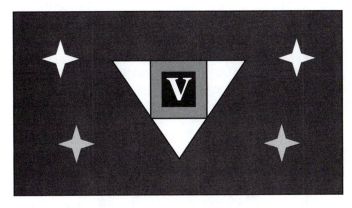

Rising to the top, one victory at a time.

Event 3 (Station 3): Olympic Rings

- Draw the five Olympic rings (yellow, black, green, red, blue) on the board.
- Each athlete throws a piece of balled-up paper at the yellow ring, using a shot put throw. The athlete continues until he or she hits the ring. Then the next person in line attempts the throw. Adjust the distance to make it challenging. Vary the distance for students of different ages. Use 10 feet (3 meters) for sixth graders and 5 feet (1.5 meters) for kindergarteners.
- After everyone has hit the inside of the yellow ring, the team moves to the black ring. They continue until time runs out.
- Record the color of the ring that every member of the team hit successfully.
- At the end of the class, award gold, silver, and bronze medals to the teams that got the furthest.

Event 4 (Station 4): Swimming (Muscular Endurance and Balance)

- Athletes place their bellies on mats or carpet squares, lift their arms out in front of them, lift their legs up, and do a flutter kick.
- The gold medal will be awarded to the person who can stay balanced and kick the longest.
- If a person's feet or hands hit the floor, he or she is finished.
- Award the medals at the end of the station.

Event 5 (Station 5): Hand Hurdles

🌀 Time the teams on how quickly they can race through the hurdles on their hands.

🌀 One person holds the ankles of a teammate who has his or her hands on the ground, in the wheelbarrow position. The person walking on his or her hands is in control and hurdles over cones, or small hurdles, and then returns to let the next person in line go.

🌀 Start the clock or watch when the team begins and stop it after all team members have had a turn to hurdle. Record the score on the board. Award medals to the teams with the fastest times at the end of the class.

Event 6 (Station 6): Multiple Jump

🌀 Teams attempt to use the fewest jumps possible to make it to a designated line or spot and back.

🌀 Each person travels to the line or spot and back by making as long and as few jumps as possible. Count each jump. When one person finishes, the next goes, until everyone has completed one turn.

🌀 Record the total number of jumps for that country. Award medals at the end of the class.

At the end of the class, tally up each team's points and award medals (paper cutouts of circles). You can also award medals to the most spirited team and the team that displayed the best sportsmanship or any other good behavior that you want to recognize. Have a ceremony and a display of the flags at the end of your Olympics. A nice finishing touch would be to play the anthem of each country and then the Olympic theme song.

Setup

Look first; rearrange if necessary; put it back together.

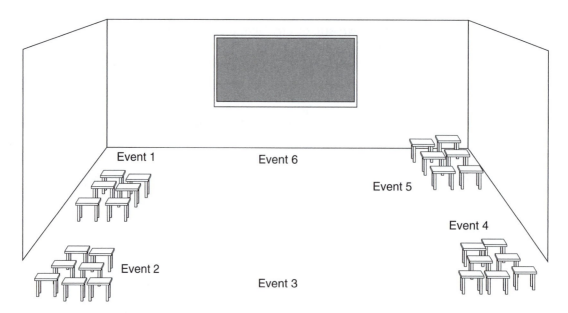

Break It Down in Detail

Lesson plans and in-depth information follow.

Objectives

- Students participate in activities that resemble Olympic events.
- Students perform skills needed to participate in Olympic events.
- Students work as one team as they collaborate and create a unique flag.

Warm-Up

Have students walk around in a circle as the Olympic athletes do when they enter the Olympic stadium at the Opening Ceremonies. Play the Olympic theme or strong classical music. Have them walk for about 1 minute.

Cues and Concepts

Carry out the activities using the following cues:

- Push from your neck—place the shot put at your neck and push it.
- Collaborate—work together and share ideas with each other.

Link the lesson with social studies and history. Talk about the history of the Olympics, which started in Greece and returned there in 2004. Discuss events, mythology, and training principles.

Assessment

Rubric

3 = Embraced the Olympic experience; tried to earn medals

2 = Participated in the Olympic stations; tried to earn medals

1 = Participated in the Olympic stations; didn't show effort at all stations

0 = Participated in some Olympic stations; didn't show effort

Safety

For the multiple jump station, make sure that nothing is in the way. For the hand hurdles station, the person on the floor leads the way. The person holding the ankles should not push the person on the floor.

Tips and Variations

- Setting the tone about the greatness of the Olympic games is vital. Props such as a real medal, an olive wreath, or any Olympic paraphernalia will create the scene and set the tone for the lesson.
- You can have great fun even if you don't award paper medals. You could discuss the medal distribution, but you don't have to give students anything to have a great lesson.

Conclusion and Links to Real Life

"The Olympics are held every two years, alternating between the Summer Games and the Winter Games. Maybe you will be involved someday. The Olympics is the greatest showcase of athleticism in the world. Be sure to watch and start training now if you want to be in them. Physical education prepares you for the events that you will see in the Olympics or be involved in if you want to train and compete."

Try at Home

"Look up the Olympics on the Internet or in an encyclopedia. Find your favorite sport. Find where the most recent Olympic Games were held, who did well, and how your country performed."

--- Read and React Stories ---

Special activities

Skills	Activity Level	Intensity	Standards
Creativity, exercise, imaging	Everyone is involved.	Medium to low	① ⑥

Invitation

"Have you ever seen one of those movies that get you so involved that you feel as if you are actually in the movie yourself? I'm going to read a story, and I want you to act it out. Be creative and get ready."

Equipment

We're Going on a Bear Hunt, Michael Rosen and Helen Oxenbury, illustrator; publisher: Margaret K. McElderry, 1989

Description

Create an adventure for your participants. Imagine that you are taking the adventure with them and act out the scene with them. A wonderful book to do this with is *We're Going on a Bear Hunt,* which teaches going over, under, through, and around. But you can tailor your adventure to fit your age group and what you want to teach. The key is to keep it active and have the participants repeat the action phrases that you say. Here is an example:

The Snorkeling Adventure

🄢 I *wriggled into my bathing suit.* (Students repeat the italicized words.)
- Wriggle and twist. (Students wriggle about and twist their bodies.)

🄢 I *jumped onto the boat.*
- Jump up and down.

🄢 The waves were really choppy. I *swayed from side to side.*
- Sway, balance, and rock from side to side.

🄢 I swam in the great big ocean, *as fast as I could swim.*
- Arms do the crawl or breaststroke.

🄢 I thought I saw a dolphin, *jumping through the waves.*
- Jump and pretend to dive through waves.

🄢 Instead, it was a shark. I'd better *swim away.*
- Swim.

🄢 He's swimming right behind me. I'd better *swim faster.*
- Swim fast.

🄢 He's gone the other way. I can *slow down.*
- Swim slowly.

🄢 Look, there is a sea turtle, *crawling on the bottom.*
- Crawl slowly.

🄢 The waves just flipped him over. He's *swimming on his back.*
- Lie on back with legs and arms kicking in the air.

🄢 Oh, look at the jellyfish. Its legs and arms *move in and out.*
- Lie on back and slowly move legs and arms in and out.

- Look how gracefully the stingray *flies through the water.*
  - Walk slowly, with arms moving slowly in and out.
- Yikes, watch out for the stingray's tail. Hurry, *better swim away quickly.*
  - Swim around the room briskly.
- Let's swim back to the boat. *Climb up the high ladder.*
  - Reach up with arms and legs as if climbing a tall ladder.
- *Sit down* and enjoy the ride.
  - Sit down in a seat.

Setup

Look first; rearrange if necessary; put it back together.

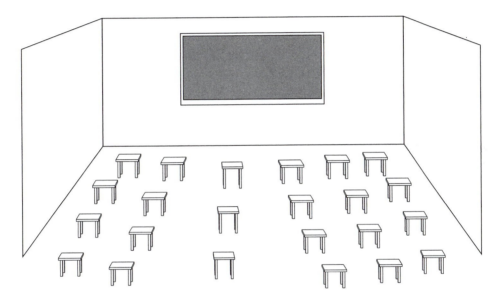

Break It Down in Detail

Lesson plans and in-depth information follow.

Objectives

- Students interpret movement cues and respond with action.
- Students demonstrate variations in effort as they travel.
- Students express feelings and emotions through movement.
- Students use the body and movement to communicate ideas and feelings.

Warm-Up

Run and Scream or Physical Musical Chairs

Cues and Concepts

Carry out the activities using the following cue:

- Move as you feel—move your body according to how the story makes you feel.

Include the following concept:

- Effort is as individual as one's own thoughts. Be unique and do your own thing. Follow your imagination to discover the correct way for you to move.

Assessment

Rubric

> 3 = Moved with enthusiasm; varied effort on an individual basis
>
> 2 = Moved with enthusiasm; varied effort
>
> 1 = Moved and reacted with some varying effort; lacked individuality
>
> 0 = Moved without any or much enthusiasm; lacked variation in effort; lacked individuality

Safety

Warn students of areas in the room that are off limits. Although parts of the room such as underneath the teacher's desk may seem like fun places to explore, warn students what they are not allowed to get near or touch before their imagination takes over.

Tips and Variations

- With lively enthusiasm, tell a brief story and use action and sound effects as you tell it. Then ask students to do the same after you are ready to tell your big story. Your enthusiasm should inspire students to communicate their feelings through movement.

- Ask students to create their own stories with a group or partners.

- Ask middle school students to write a story, underlining all verbs and adverbs.

Conclusion and Links to Real Life

"When we feel a certain way, our bodies react in response. The story may have made you respond slowly or with the speed of a cheetah. By using the energy and emotions inside us, we can communicate better."

Try at Home

"Ask a friend or family member to read or tell you a story, as we did today. See if you can find one with lots of action."

Board Games Aren't Boring!

Sitting almost motionless around a table for hours playing a board game might give our arms or hands something to do by moving our game piece from one spot to the next. But that's not much action to look forward to. Typical board games can be boring if you like physical action. So, let's take the board games that we enjoy and increase the activity level by inserting action wherever we can. Suddenly, you'll be sitting less and in motion most of the time.

- - - Sink the Boat - - -

Fitness

Skills	Activity Level	Intensity	Standards
Exercise	Everyone is involved.	Medium to high	② ④

Invitation

"Hit, sunk. . . . Hey, you sunk my boat. You know the game—you hide your boats in the ocean, and the other person calls out letters and numbers and tries to find and sink your ships. Well we don't have the laptop game boards, so we are going to make our own. But instead of just sitting there, you'll get to exercise for every hit and every miss."

Equipment

- Two grids per person
- One pencil per person

Description

Partners work against one another to guess where the other has hidden his or her boats. They take turns calling grid letters and numbers in search of the boats.

Each player hides five ships:

- A five-space boat
- Another five-space boat
- A four-space boat
- A three-space boat
- A two-space boat

Players use one grid to look for and mark where the partner's boats are and the other grid to mark where they have hidden their own boats. Participants fill in squares in one grid to represent the length of their boats (five boats total: 5, 5, 4, 3, 2).

- Players should hide the hidden boat grid from the opponent.

	1	2	3	4	5	6	7	8	9	10	11
A									▓	▓	▓
B		▓	▓	▓	▓						
C											▓
D					▓						▓
E		▓			▓						▓
F		▓			▓						▓
G											▓
H											

- Players take turns calling the letter first and then the number. For example, the guesser might ask, "A-4?" If the partner has no boat at that space, he or she would answer, "Miss." If the partner has a boat at that space, he or she would answer, "Hit."

☞ The guesser marks the appropriate square of his or her grid with an *M* for a miss or an *H* for a hit. When all the squares of an entire boat are hit, the owner of the boat announces that the boat has been sunk. The guesser then circles that boat on his or her grid.

	1	2	3	4	5	6	7	8	9	10	11
A								M	H	H	
B											
C					M						
D	M				H						
E					H						
F				M	H			M			
G					H						
H											

☞ Players exercise when they attack. If they score a hit, they do two jumping jacks. If they miss, they do two push-ups or curl-ups.

☞ When a person has lost all his or her boats, the game is over.

Setup

Look first; rearrange if necessary; put it back together. No need to move furniture, but partners should be near each other.

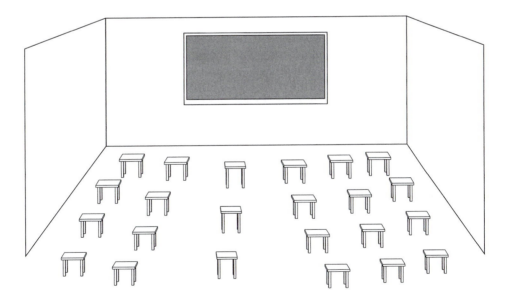

Break It Down in Detail

Lesson plans and in-depth information follow.

Objectives

- Students bring a sedentary game to life.
- Students work on their upper-body strength and abdominal strength, as well as total-body exercises.
- Students realize certain physiological effects that occur with exercise.
- Students stay active and think strategically for an entire 30-minute period.

Warm-Up

Demo Show

Cues and Concepts

Carry out the activities using the following cue:

- Think strategically—think about a plan for discovering your partner's patterns and where he or she hid the boats.

Include the following concepts:

- Ask students what muscles they are working. They are working **abdominals, pectorals, biceps, triceps, deltoids, trapezius, latissimus dorsi, gastrocnemius, quadriceps,** and **hamstrings.** Positively reinforce responses as you walk throughout the classroom.
- Ask what made them more tired—hits (jumping jacks) or misses (push-ups or curl-ups). Have students explain what physiological effects of exercise they feel.

Assessment

Rubric

3 = Exercised with good form; actively participated

2 = Exercised with good form most of the time; actively participated

1 = Lacked good form while exercising; actively participated

0 = Exercised with poor form; inactively participated

Safety

Students should stay in their own personal spaces during exercises.

Tips and Variations

- A good visual would be the actual game boards. Bring one in, show students how you would normally sit around a table and play, as opposed to what you have redesigned.
- Decrease the grid size or increase the number of boats to allow students to achieve more hits.

Conclusion and Links to Real Life

"Taking control of your life is not a matter of hits or misses. Staying active will keep you stronger and healthier. If you choose to stay inactive and sit around a lot, you will have lots of misses. You'll miss the chance to have fun, get stronger, live longer, and look better. Your health will start to sink. Don't get sunk. Stay afloat by hitting the fields, the courts, the stage, the water, the ice, or any arena that floats your boat."

Try at Home

"If you are riding in a car or waiting at the doctor's office, make your own grid and play. Adjust your exercise to fit the environment. No jumping jacks in the car—try arm circles or stretches."

--- PE Bingo ---

Fitness

Skills	Activity Level	Intensity	Standards
Exercise	Everyone is involved actively.	High to medium	② ④

Invitation

"If you can spell out the word *bingo,* you can win this game. You'll have to move a lot to win this bingo. It sounds simple, but you have to look at a graph, plot your points, and then see if you have all five letters and numbers in a row."

Equipment

- PE Bingo card for each person
- 25 paper spots per person (size of a penny)
- Cut out B1 through B10, I1 through I10, and so on, and put in a bowl or cup

Description

Participants have a PE Bingo card and try to fill up their cards as you call pairs of letters and numbers. You can use the preprinted cards on these pages, or you can have participants choose numbers 1 through 10 and the letters *B, I, N, G,* and *O* and write them on blank PE Bingo cards (copy the blank card).

1. You draw a number–letter combination from a cup or hat, or just call out a letter and number. Participants put a marker on the letter and number that you call. The object is to get five spots called in a row (across, diagonal, or down) to achieve PE Bingo.

2. With each match, participants perform an exercise from the exercise bank:

   B = Push-ups

   I = Jumping jacks

   N = Jumping jills

   G = Twists (knees bent)

   O = Arm circles

3. So, if you call B6, they do the B exercise, which is push-ups, and they do six repetitions.

4. If the number is not on the card, students do three get-ups (they stand up beside their seats and sit down in their seats three times).

5. When someone gets PE Bingo, he or she skips three victory laps around the room.

PE Bingo

B	I	N	G	O
1	2	3	4	5
10	9	8	7	6
2	3	4	5	10
6	7	10	1	2
5	4	7	6	3

PE Bingo

B	I	N	G	O
2	4	6	8	10
1	3	5	7	9
10	9	8	1	2
5	6	7	4	3
7	1	2	3	4

From *No Gym? No Problem! Physical Activities for Tight Spaces* by Charmain Sutherland, 2006, Champaign, IL: Human Kinetics.

PE Bingo

B	I	N	G	O
3	6	9	10	7
10	7	4	1	4
7	4	1	3	6
5	1	3	6	3
2	8	5	7	10

PE Bingo

B	I	N	G	O
5	10	1	2	4
7	9	10	8	6
8	6	5	4	3
6	8	9	1	2
1	2	3	5	7

From No Gym? No Problem! Physical Activities for Tight Spaces by Charmain Sutherland, 2006, Champaign, IL: Human Kinetics.

PE Bingo

B	I	N	G	O

From *No Gym? No Problem! Physical Activities for Tight Spaces* by Charmain Sutherland, 2006, Champaign, IL: Human Kinetics.

Setup

Look first; rearrange if necessary; put it back together. No setup required.

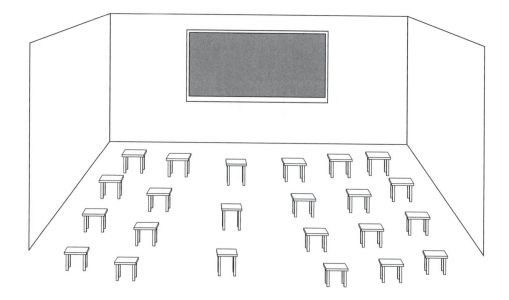

Break It Down in Detail

Lesson plans and in-depth information follow.

Objectives

- Students exercise various muscle groups and increase their heart rates by participating in a simple game.
- Students realize the difference that they can make in their activity level by slightly changing the procedures of a game.

Warm-Up

Find the Leader

Cues and Concepts

Carry out the activities using the following cue:

- **6-second pulse check**—check your pulse for 6 seconds and add a 0 to that number to find your heart rate.

Include the following concept:

- Exercise increases the heart rate. Have students compare the intensity of their heart rate to the type of exercise they just completed. They should perform pulse checks every few minutes.

Assessment

Rubric

3 = Followed the procedures; exercised with 100% effort

2 = Followed the procedures; exercised with effort most of the time

1 = Followed the procedures; exercised with effort some of the time

0 = Didn't follow all procedures; didn't exercise with much effort

Safety

Students should exercise in their own personal space.

Tips and Variations

- Explain how popular the game of bingo is with some adults who play it consistently as a form of recreation. Show a real bingo card and a dabber. Explain the difference between the sedentary version of the game and the physical version.
- Allow a student who wins to call the numbers.

Conclusion and Links to Real Life

"You played a popular game that normally has no physical action at all and turned it around so that you exercised your entire body and increased your heart rate. You can do that with all kinds of games and situations."

Try at Home

"If you know any family member who plays bingo, ask how he or she plays bingo. Ask them how much their heart rate increases."

--- Nutriland ---

Fitness, health-related concepts

Skills	Activity Level	Intensity	Standards
Fitness, health-related fitness and concepts, nutrition, wellness	Everyone is actively involved.	High to medium	① ② ④ ⑤

Invitation

"Have you ever played the game Candyland? Well, this is the PE version of that board game. We'll see how well you do in the world of fitness and nutrition."

Equipment

- 13 pieces of paper of one color, the size of a penny, and 13 pieces of paper of another color (each player has one color as a spot marker)
- CD player and CD
- Copied board game for each pair; one penny per pair

Description

Using a game designed like Candyland, students play against another person and attempt to reach the finish line before the opponent does. The cool thing about Nutriland is that it involves action as well as luck, whereas Candyland involves pure luck and is played while sitting still.

- Players start at the square marked "Start."
- The person closer to the teacher flips a penny. If the penny lands on heads, the person moves one spot. If the penny lands on tails, the person moves two spots.
- The person reads the task in the box and performs it in order to move forward.
- If the player does not satisfactorily perform the task, as judged by the other player, he or she does not earn that square and must move back to the spot where he or she started.
- If the player lands on a go-back square, he or she must perform the action on the square that he or she is directed to move to.
- The next player takes a turn. Players repeat this procedure until there is a winner.

Setup

Look first; rearrange if necessary; put it back together. Players may turn desks to face one another.

Break It Down in Detail

Lesson plans and in-depth information follow.

Objective

Students work out their bodies with various fitness-related exercises while following rules as they play a game.

Warm-Up

- Review the proper form of the exercises that appear on the boards so that students have a current visual of correct techniques.

Start	**Do 20 jumping jacks** Cardiovascular	**Do 6 push-ups** Arm strength	**High-five 6 people near you** Cooperation	*Ooh, sorry, but too much sugar has slowed you down. Go back 2 spots.*
				Tell your teacher the name of 3 food groups Nutrition
Twist from left to right 20 times Flexibility	**Jump up and down 30 times** Cardiovascular	**Give a compliment to your partner** Social awareness	**Stretch your hamstrings, legs for 10 seconds each** Flexibility	**Run in place quickly for 15 seconds** Speed, cardiovascular
Oh, no, not enough exercising has made you weak. Go back 2 spots.				
Shake hands with all the girls in the class Cooperation	**Do 25 crunches** Abdominal strength	**Balance on toes, with one hand on head, one on nose for 20 seconds** Balance, gymnastics	**Dance, moving arms and legs, for 10 seconds** Dance	**Smile, showing your teeth, 15 times to your partner** Social awareness
				You skipped your breakfast and have no energy. Go back 3 spots.
Finish!	**Shake hands with all the boys in the class** Cooperation	*You didn't take your vitamins and now you're tired. Skip a turn, and take a nap.*	**Sit on floor with arms crossed, and get up and down 10 times** Leg strength, balance	**Thumb wrestle; if you win, you stay; if you don't, move back 2 spots** Reaction time

From *No Gym? No Problem! Physical Activities for Tight Spaces* by Charmain Sutherland, 2006, Champaign, IL: Human Kinetics.

Start				Ooh, sorry, but too much sugar has slowed you down. Go back 2 spots.
Oh, no, not enough exercising has made you weak. Go back 2 spots.				
				You skipped your breakfast and have no energy. Go back 3 spots.
Finish!		You didn't take your vitamins and now you're tired. Skip a turn, and take a nap.		

● Thumb wrestle: Players face a partner with the insides of their hands facing each other. They curl their fingers and grip the opponent's four fingers. They place their thumbs side by side. On the "Go" signal, each player attempts to place his or her thumb on top of the thumb of the other person.

Cues and Concepts

Carry out the activities using the following cue:

● Effort counts—always perform your exercise to the best of your ability. If you do not perform the exercise well, you cannot receive credit for it and must move back to your starting space.

Include the following concept:

● Explain that students are their own judges and referees. Go over the proper form of the exercises in the exercise bank so that the students have fresh, vivid pictures in their minds of what is considered satisfactory. Have them do a pulse check every 5 minutes. Then ask them a question about health-related fitness that they can answer by looking at the board. Any person who answers correctly can move forward one space.

Assessment

Rubric

3 = Participated with 100% effort

2 = Attempted most tasks with 100% effort

1 = Attempted all tasks, but didn't try hard with all of them

0 = Attempted some tasks but not all of them

Safety

Students should be aware of their personal space while moving. They should be courteous when interrupting a game for some of the tasks by saying, "Excuse me" and "Thank you."

Tips and Variations

● Bring in the real game Candyland to show students what Nutriland relates to in real life.

● Older students can use the board with the blank spaces and fill in their own challenging tasks.

● Younger students may need pictures to go along with their tasks.

Conclusion and Links to Real Life

"You brought an old game to life with action today. For a game night, play Nutriland with your family or friends. Remember that your health is not about luck, like Candyland. It is about making good choices to keep moving forward, not backward—just like what we witnessed today."

Try at Home

"Play Candyland or Monopoly and designate exercises for spaces on the board."

--- Art in Motion ---

Fitness

Skills	Activity Level	Intensity	Standards
Fitness, stretching, creativity, cooperating	Everyone is involved.	Medium	② ④

Invitation

"Do you know the game in which you draw something and people guess what you are trying to draw? The game that we will play today is similar except that we will be using sports objects and activities as our drawing objects."

Equipment

- Several pieces of paper for each group
- One pencil per group

Description

Divide participants into groups of three. In each group, one person is the drawer and picks an object from a bowl to draw for the group. Group members take turns guessing until someone guesses correctly or until 3 minutes pass.

- After each guess, the guessers in the group must do a designated exercise. You can designate the exercise by placing the name of the exercise on the board. Change the exercise often.
- Each additional guess increases the number of repetitions of the exercise that the guessers do. For example, the group does one push-up after the first guess, two push-ups after the second guess, and so on.
- The guessers must do these exercises immediately after guessing and before they can guess again. This provision will slow down the guessers and help them focus.
- The object is to be the first group to guess what the drawing is.
- After the group guesses correctly, they stand up and do jumping jacks for joy. They get to keep jumping until every other group gets it or until time runs out.
- Then another member draws for the group.

Subjects to Draw

- Objects: bat, tennis racket, glove, basketball, lacrosse stick, hockey stick, cleats, puck, skates, football, softball, tennis ball, tennis court, infield, outfield, pitcher, jump rope, scooter, volleyball, Frisbee, bike, cricket bat, soccer ball, javelin, Olympic rings
- Activities: throwing, catching, volleying, batting, running, jumping, hopping, serving, smashing, swimming, surfing, lifting weights, tinikling, dancing, skating, sailing, hiking, diving

Setup

Look first; rearrange if necessary; put it back together.

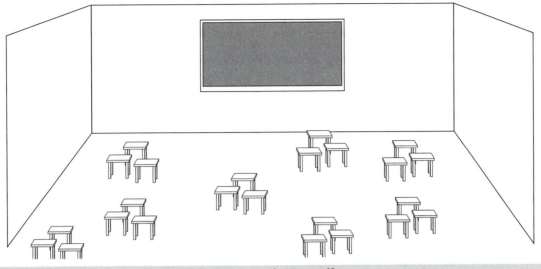

Break It Down in Detail

Lesson plans and in-depth information follow.

Objectives

- Students think about objects that remind them of physical activity.
- Students celebrate each guess with exercise.

Warm-Up

Rock, Paper, Scissors—Action

Cues and Concepts

Carry out the activities using the following cue:

- Think as you exercise—exercise circulates the blood and oxygen, so you will be able to think while you do your exercise.

Include the following concepts:

- Exercise has been proven to help our brains function better. Exercise helps us think clearly and reduces the stress levels in our bodies.
- When we are excited, we feel it in our bodies. Exercise and movement are natural ways that we show excitement.

Link art with physical education. Students use creativity and artistic expression to communicate.

Assessment

Rubric

3 = Exercised after each guess; concentrated on physical activity while drawing and guessing

2 = Exercised after most guesses; concentrated most of the time on physical activity while drawing or guessing

1 = Did not exercise after each guess; lacked concentration on physical activity while drawing or guessing

0 = Did not exercise after each guess; did not concentrate on physical activity while drawing or guessing

Safety

Students should exercise in their own space.

Tips and Variations

- Play two rounds with your students, as a group, to get them excited and pumped up for their own team challenge. You'll be the drawer.
- Use dry erase boards, clay, or Play-Doh to communicate. Play-Doh, which you can buy at KMart, Target, Wal-Mart, and other stores, is available in small containers that keep it fresh and contained. Play-Doh promotes creativity and works the fine motor muscles of the hands as participants sculpt the objects instead of drawing them.

Conclusion and Links to Real Life

"You communicated your vision of physical activity through drawing today. I hope that you were concentrating on what the activity means to you as you guessed and drew. Exercising helped you celebrate and think today."

Try at Home

"You can use any subject to draw at home. Try to use exercise as a reward and an opportunity to guess again. You can even draw on the sidewalk or driveway with chalk or in the dirt with a stick."

- - - Sports Hang-Ups - - -

Fitness

Skills	Activity Level	Intensity	Standards
Fitness, stretching, creativity, cooperating	Everyone is involved.	Medium	② ④

Invitation

"You've played the game hangman, right? It's the game in which you try to guess what the secret word is, one letter at a time. If you don't answer correctly, something is put on the hanger. This time, you guess about things relating to physical activity and perform a **locomotor** pattern around the room when you guess a letter correctly. If you guess a letter incorrectly, then you have to place an item on the hanger."

Equipment

- Several pieces of paper for each group
- One pencil per group

Description

Divide the class into groups of three students each. One person in each group comes up and gets the word from you, goes back to the group, and draws the hang-ups. The other two students take turns guessing. Note that this is a tamer version of the original game and uses hangers instead of a noose.

- Each miss causes the guessers to have a piece of sports equipment placed on the hanger as follows:
  - 1st guess: baseball
  - 2nd guess: bat
  - 3rd guess: football

- 4th guess: shoe
- 5th guess: tennis racket
- 6th guess: hockey stick
- 7th guess: soccer ball
- 8th guess: jump rope
- 9th guess: golf ball
- 10th guess: surfboard

☙ When the guessers are correct, they perform a locomotor pattern around the room. Change the locomotor pattern every minute or two.

☙ If the team hangs their surfboard, they are out of the running and the game is over. After the team is out, they must stretch their muscles until the other groups come up with the answer or are also out.

☙ To start a new game, designate a new person to draw the hang-ups and come up to you to get the next word.

Words or Phrases to Guess

☙ Objects: bat, tennis racket, glove, basketball, lacrosse stick, hockey stick, cleats, puck, skates, football, softball, tennis ball, tennis court, infield, outfield, pitcher, jump rope, scooter, volleyball, Frisbee, bike, cricket bat, soccer ball, javelin, Olympic rings

☙ Activities: throwing, catching, volleying, batting, running, jumping, hopping, serving, smashing, swimming, surfing, lifting weights, tinikling, dancing, skating, sailing, hiking, diving

Setup

Look first; rearrange if necessary; put it back together.

Break It Down in Detail

Lesson plans and in-depth information follow.

Objective

Students revise an old, inactive game and turn it into an opportunity to be active.

Warm-Up

Simon Says, "Action"

Cues and Concepts

Carry out the activities using the following cue:

- ☾ Whisper and hide—don't let anyone hear or see your responses.

Include the following concept:

- ☾ Moving is good. Activity is a reward, and we should do it whenever we can put it into our lives!

Link this activity to spelling and phonics. Ask the language arts teacher to supply some spelling words to work on.

Assessment

Rubric

3 = Actively involved in guessing and moving

2 = Actively involved in guessing or moving, but not both

1 = Involved but not actively

0 = Passively involved or not involved

Safety

Students should stay clear of desks and people as they do their laps.

Tips and Variations

- ☾ Describe useful strategies from a spelling perspective. Discuss the need for vowels and silent letters.
- ☾ Pick more difficult words for older students and easier ones for younger students.
  - Easier: run, ball, bat, jump, ran, hit
  - More difficult: home run, pop fly, grand slam, hole in one, triple play, hat trick, double play, sequence, parallel bars, slap shot, receiver, layup, World Series, World Cup, line dance

Conclusion and Links to Real Life

"Did you get hung up today, or did you exercise your way to figuring out the words? The traditional way to play hangman would have made you stiff and inactive. Today you used your brain and your brawn."

Try at Home

"Play Sports Hang-Ups anytime and anywhere that you need to entertain yourself but have no equipment or space. Explain this version of hangman to your family."

- - - Show Off Your Physical Knowledge - - -

All skills

Skills	Activity Level	Intensity	Standards
Assessing knowledge of skills, throwing	Everyone is involved.	Medium to low	② ④

Invitation

"For a long time, board games were played using luck and strategy but didn't really tap into our brains. Then, several came out that forced us to think in order to win. Let's see how we would do if we played this type of game but changed the questions and categories to relate to activities. And, instead of sitting after a successful turn, we break out some action."

Equipment

- Four game pieces (colored pieces of paper or anything that is distinguishable)
- One die per group
- Frisbee
- Two beanbags
- Target on the board or on a poster board

Description

Create questions for the game that will challenge participants to think about what you are teaching in physical education or covering at your establishment. Divide the class into four teams. Teams attempt to earn the most points and the three trophies (blue, red, yellow) as they move around the board.

Designate any starting point on the board for each team. A team representative rolls a die and moves the appropriate number to a colored spot. The goal is to move toward the trophy spots, which are worth the most points. The players move in any direction on the board while attempting to get all three trophy spaces (they may go to each spot only once). Once on a spot, the team tries to answer a question. They will probably want to go for certain categories more than others; the categories are listed later. When the team answers the question correctly, all team members get an opportunity to perform a designated throw at a target; the specific types of throws are listed later. If a player hits the target, add the points according to the area that the player hit (5, 3, 2, or none). Each member of the team gets a chance to throw once for each correct answer. Add all the team's points together and keep a running total.

Trophies are worth 100 points. At the end of the allotted time, the team with the most points wins.

The team must answer a question related to these categories:

- Red = Skills
- Blue = Sports
- Yellow = Fitness

Color and Skill Bank

- Red = Throw overhand to the target; total the number of points the team scored as they threw.
- Blue = Throw underhand to the target; total the number of points the team scored as they threw.
- Yellow = Throw a Frisbee to a target; total the number of points the team scored as they threw.

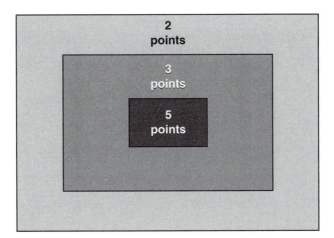

blue	yellow	red	red	yellow	red
red		red	red		blue
yellow		Blue **Trophy**			yellow
blue					red
red					blue
yellow	red	red	blue	blue	yellow
blue	red	red	blue	blue	red
red					blue
blue	yellow	yellow	blue	blue	yellow
red	yellow	yellow	blue	blue	red
yellow					blue
Red **Trophy**				Yellow **Trophy**	

Question Bank

● Red, Skills

- Show the part of the foot that you dribble with.
- Show the part of the hand that you dribble with.
- Explain the proper overhand throw.
- At what level is it best to dribble a basketball?
- Show the difference between static and dynamic balance.
- Explain opposition.

● Blue, Sports

- Name three sports involving throwing and catching.
- How do you start the game of volleyball?
- In which sports would you flee an opponent?
- In which sport would you find March Madness?
- Where would you see a triple play?
- In which sport might you see a hat trick?
- Name four sports in which you would use striking.

● Yellow, Fitness

- Do 40 jumping jacks.
- Do 20 crunches.
- Do 20 get-ups (start by sitting with legs and arms crossed; get up and sit down).
- Do 10 good push-ups.
- Jump up and down for 15 seconds.
- Skip for 15 seconds.
- Stretch your hamstrings for 15 seconds.
- Stretch your quadriceps for 15 seconds.

Setup

Look first; rearrange if necessary; put it back together.

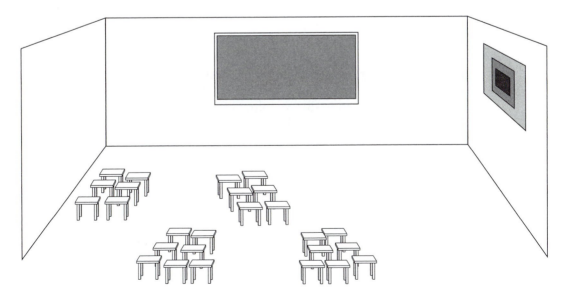

Break It Down in Detail

Lesson plans and in-depth information follow.

Objectives

- Students display their knowledge of physical skills and activity.
- Students perform exercises as a way to progress in a game.
- Students aim as they throw so that they can hit a target.

Warm-Up

Fit Tic-Tac-Toe

Cues and Concepts

Carry out the activities using the following cues:

- Aim before you throw—place your body in position to hit your target.
- No slacking—only properly executed exercises count toward earning points.

Include the following concepts:

- Students will use various types of throws—overhand, underhand, and Frisbee.
- Students should take their time and make good throws. Remind them to aim, release, and follow through.

Assessment

Rubric

3 = Thought and performed well with 100% effort

2 = Thought and performed well with good effort

1 = Thought and performed well enough to finish the game

0 = Didn't concentrate or perform well enough to play the game

Safety

Students must exercise in their own space. When throwing at the target, players must wait until the throwing pathway is clear. All desks and chairs should be clear from the throwing pathway.

Tips and Variations

- Explain the incredible difficulty of the first types of trivia board games that came out where the questions were so difficult, and then describe what it was like to sit and wait to get a question that you could finally answer. If activity had been part of the original games, players might have lasted longer, stayed active, and had more fun.
- Change the throwing part to a skill that you are working on. Include various throws, such as a hike or throwing with an implement.

Conclusion and Links to Real Life

"The original questioning games are designed to find out what you know. Show Off Your Physical Knowledge tested your skill and knowledge. The way we improve at both games is by learning more and staying active in our quest to do better. I hope that you will always try to improve your skills and knowledge in your pursuit of a healthy life."

Try at Home

"When you play any of the many kinds of brain games available, add a bit of energy and activity by exercising or performing a skill after each correct answer."

Cool-Downs

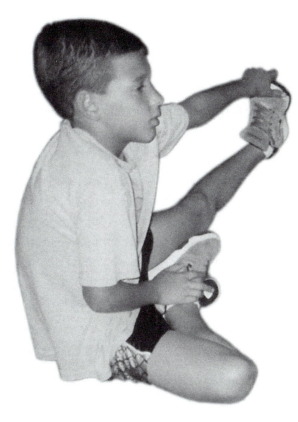

After a high-energy activity or lesson we can't expect our participants' heart rates and excitement to subside instantly. That is why the cool-down is important. Cool-downs will help ease the body back to the calm state, lowering the heart rate and preparing the body to relax. The excitement level of the activity determines whether a cool-down activity is necessary. Although not every activity in this book will need a cool-down, you will have these activities ready in case you do need to calm down the participants after they have been very active.

--- Current Events Cool-Down ---

Activity Level	Intensity	Standards	Skills
All participants are stretching.	Low	② ④ ⑥	Cool-down, flexibility

Equipment

None

Organization

While participants stretch after an activity, check their knowledge and awareness of current events. This is a great opportunity for you to review and tie in your subject matter with real-life events.

Examples

Ask general questions like these:

- What is the name of the high school sports team in our area?
- What is the name of the nearest pro football team?
- What is the name of the nearest pro basketball team? Women's pro team?
- What is the name of the nearest pro hockey team?
- What is the name of the nearest college team?
- What are some events in track and field?
- What are the differences among badminton, tennis, table tennis, and racquetball?

During an Olympic year, ask questions like these:

- How many medals did your country earn?
- Who are some of the medal winners in the events?
- Can you name some of the events in the Olympics?

In fall, ask questions like these:

- Can you name some pro football teams?
- Which teams are still alive in pro baseball?
- Who is playing in the U.S. Open?
- Who is in the World Series?
- Who is the local high school playing in the homecoming game?

In winter, ask questions like these:

- What is the Iditarod?
- What kind of training and exercise will you do when you are on winter break?
- Which teams are in the Super Bowl?
- What are your New Year's resolutions?

In March, ask questions like these:

- What is March Madness?
- What is the Sweet Sixteen?
- What is the Final Four?
- What does it mean when you go to the big dance?

Setup

None

--- Heads Down, Seven Around ---

Activity Level	**Intensity**	**Standards**	**Skills**
Seven people walk slowly, and the others are still.	Low	①	Cool-down

Equipment

None

Organization

- Choose seven people to walk around the room while the other participants calmly fold their arms on their desks, put their heads down, hide their eyes, and keep one thumb up.
- Each of the seven walkers secretly taps someone's thumb.
- After 1 minute, the seven tappers move to the front and face the others.
- The people who were tapped each have one attempt to guess who tapped them. Guessers should pay attention to the noises and clues around them as their heads are down and to the others' guesses.
- If a person guesses correctly, he or she becomes a tapper and the tapper takes a seat.

Setup

None

The kids in this variation of Heads Down, Seven Around are tapped on their shoulders, not their thumbs.

--- Make Me Laugh ---

Activity Level	Intensity	Standards	Skills
Four people are still, and the others move at 15-second intervals.	Low	① ⑤	Cool-down

Equipment

None

Organization

- Divide the class into four groups.
- Each group selects a person to sit and watch a fellow teammate do school-appropriate actions to make the selected person laugh.
- After 15 seconds, someone else in the group tries to make the selected person laugh.
- The activity continues in 15-second segments until 2 minutes is up or until the person laughs.
- The person being entertained must have eye contact with the person trying to make him or her laugh.
- Once the person laughs or after 2 minutes is up, another person moves into position to be entertained.

Setup

None

--- Physical Education Charades ---

Activity Level	Intensity	Standards	Skills
Participants move for 30 seconds and then sit for 90 seconds.	Low	①	Cool-down, various skill actions

Equipment

None

Organization

- Divide the class into five groups.
- One person in every group is the actor; the others are guessers. The group should face only their actor.
- The actors come to you and receive an action, sport, or skill, which they must act out so that the group can guess what it is.
- The group that guesses correctly stands and stretches, so that everyone knows that they got it.
- After one group guesses correctly, that round is over. If you want to keep score, you can keep track of which group gets the answers first and keep a running total.
- Change actors every round.

- Bank of skills, actions, and sports: soccer, hockey, basketball, baseball, coaching, Olympics, throwing, catching, volleying, batting, running, jumping, hopping, serve, smash, swimming, surfing, lifting weights, tinikling, dance, skate, sailing, hiking, diving

Setup

None

Glossary

abdominals—The muscles in the abdominal area of the body between the chest and the pelvic area.

biceps—The muscle on the front side of the upper arm that contracts to bend the arm at the elbow.

cardiovascular endurance—The ability of the heart and body to continue to exercise over a long period.

deltoids—The muscles at the arm and shoulder that lift our arms.

Fitnessgram—A fitness assessment that helps people determine whether they are in a certain zone, the Healthy Fitness Zone. See www.cooperinst.org.

gastrocnemius—The large muscle on the back of the lower leg.

gluteus maximus—The muscles of the buttocks; also called glutes.

hamstrings—The muscles on the upper back of the leg that bend the leg backward and the lower leg upward.

Healthy Fitness Zone—A range of scores on the Fitnessgram fitness test that indicates that a person is healthy.

isometric holds and balances—Holding muscles in a still position for a long time to strengthen them without lifting weights or moving weight.

latissimus dorsi—The muscle in the upper back; also called lats.

locomotor—Methods of moving and movements used to move from one place to another.

muscular endurance—The ability to contract or shorten muscles many times without tiring or the ability to hold a position for a long time.

muscular strength—The maximum amount of force that the muscles can put out.

National Standards for Physical Education—NASPE (National Association for Sport and Physical Education) recommends that people be active for at least 60 minutes each day. NASPE has developed six national standards that physical educators should follow in providing worthwhile physical education and activity:

- Standard 1. Demonstrates competency in motor skills and movement patterns needed to perform a variety of physical activities.

- Standard 2. Demonstrates understanding of movement concepts, principles, strategies, and tactics as they apply to the learning and performance of physical activities.

- Standard 3. Participates regularly in physical activity.

- Standard 4. Achieves and maintains a health-enhancing level of physical fitness.

- Standard 5. Exhibits responsible personal and social behavior that respects self and others in physical activity settings.

- Standard 6. Values physical activity for health, enjoyment, challenge, self-expression, and social interaction.

netball—A sport similar to basketball; popular in England.

No Child Left Behind Law (Public Law 107-110)—Law designed to close the achievement gap with accountability, flexibility, and choice so that no child is left behind.

obliques—The stomach muscles on the sides of the abdominals.

pace—Maintaining a steady rate of movement to reach a goal.

Pacer Test—A Fitnessgram test designed to improve and test cardiovascular endurance.

pectorals—The muscles located at the chest that pull the arms.

pedometer—A technological instrument used to measure the number of steps taken.

Physical Best—A health-related fitness program to promote independence as students take charge of their own fitness and health through regular, enjoyable physical activity. See www.aahperd.org/NASPE/physicalbest/.

polyspots—Rubber spots that are flat like a pancake and used to mark places on the floor.

President's Challenge—A fitness assessment that bases its scores on national scores of people of various age groups. Participants try to reach the National Level (50th percentile) or the Presidential Level (85th percentile). Awards, including certificates and patches, are available for children as well as adults. See www.fitness.gov.

quadriceps—The muscle that contracts to straighten the leg at the knee.

rank—To put in order according to a category or system.

seeding—Dstributing teams or players in a tournament so that those with the greatest skill are not matched against one another in the early rounds.

6-second pulse check—A quick and simple method of checking heart rate. Students find the carotid (neck) artery or the radial (wrist) artery and feel the beats by lightly touching two fingers to the surface. The teacher counts for 6 seconds as students count how many beats they feel. Adding a 0 to that number approximates the number of beats that the heart is pumping in 1 minute. For example, 7 beats in 6 seconds is equal to 70 beats per minute

static stretching—Stretching slowly and holding a position that is farther than normal without bouncing.

stxball—A noncontact form of lacrosse.

trapezius—The triangular muscle located on the upper back and neck used to reach backward and move the head.

triceps—The muscle in the back of the upper arm that contracts to straighten the arm.

Related Organizations

American Alliance for Health, Physical Education, Recreation and Dance (AAHPERD)—www.aahperd.org

Fitnessgram—www.cooperinst.org

National Association for Sports and Physical Education–www.aahperd.org/naspe/

PE Central—www.pecentral.org

PE Links 4u—www.pelinks4u.com

President's Council on Physical Fitness and Sports—www.fitness.gov

Bibliography

Champion, W.T. 1990. *Fundamentals of Sports Law.* Deerfield, IL, New York, and Rochester, NY: Clark Boardman Callaghan.

Cooper Institute. 2004. *Fitnessgram.* Champaign, IL: Human Kinetics.

Corbin, C.B., and R. Lindsey. 1997. *Fitness for Life.* 4th ed. Champaign, IL: Human Kinetics.

Ennis, C.D. 2004. *Be Active Kids Project.* University of Maryland.

Graham, G., S. Holt-Hale, and M. Parker. 2004. *Children Moving: A Reflective Approach to Teaching Physical Education.* 6th ed. New York: McGraw-Hill.

Great Activities. A Newspaper for Elementary and Middle School Physical Education Teachers. Durham, NC: Great Activities Publishing.

Journal of Physical Education, Recreation and Dance (JOPERD). American Alliance for Health, Physical Education, Recreation and Dance.

Mohnsen, B. 2003. *Concepts and Principles of Physical Education: What Every Student Needs to Know.* 2nd ed. Oxon Hill, MD: AAPHERD.

National Association for Sport and Physical Education. 2004. *Moving Into the Future: National Standards for Physical Education.* 2nd ed. Reston, VA: McGraw-Hill.

Pangrazi, R.P., and C.B. Corbin. 2004. *Guidelines for Appropriate Physical Activity for Elementary School Children.* A Position Statement. AAHPERD Convention. New Orleans, LA.

The President's Challenge: Physical Activity and Fitness Awards Program. 2004. Bloomington, IN.

Rink, J.E. 1997. *Teaching Physical Education for Learning.* 3rd ed. Boston: McGraw-Hill.

Teaching Elementary Physical Education. The Independent Voice of Elementary and Middle School Physical Educators. Champaign, IL: Human Kinetics.

U.S. Department of Health and Human Services. 1996. *Physical Activity and Health: A Report of the Surgeon General.* Atlanta: U.S. Department of Health and Human Services, Centers for Disease Control and Prevention, and National Center for Chronic Disease Prevention and Health Promotion.

About the Author

Charmain Sutherland is a physical education specialist at Severn Elementary School in Severn, Maryland, which is part of the Anne Arundel County Public School System. She has taught physical education in both private and public schools for more than 14 years—6 years of those without a gym. Sutherland has taught every type of student—at risk, disadvantaged, and privileged—and has coached a variety of sports. She was part of the curriculum writing team for a $1 million grant project with the University of Maryland, National Institutes of Health (NIH), and Prince George County Public Schools. In 2001, Sutherland received a national teaching award presented by Coca-Cola and HealthSouth for developing a dynamic physical education program that exceeded the expectations of her city, state, and school. A member of the American Alliance for Health, Physical Education, Recreation and Dance (AAHPERD) and MAHPERD, Sutherland is a popular speaker at state conventions and countywide in-services. She is also a member of the Association for Active Lifestyles and Fitness (AALF) and National Association for Sport and Physical Education (NASPE). Sutherland earned a master's degree in physical education, administration, and supervision from Old Dominion University. She previously coordinated activities as a recreation specialist for Norfolk Naval Station and Virginia Beach Parks and Recreation in Virginia. Currently, she owns and runs a physical activity camp, Physical Activity Central, for children in grades K to 5.